Modern Dharma

MODERN DHARMA

Seeking Family Well-Being
in Middle-Class Nepal

Paola Tiné

PENN

UNIVERSITY OF PENNSYLVANIA PRESS

PHILADELPHIA

Published by
University of Pennsylvania Press
Philadelphia, Pennsylvania 19104-4112
www.pennpress.org

Printed in the United States of America on acid-free paper
10 9 8 7 6 5 4 3 2 1

A Cataloging-in-Publication record is
available from the Library of Congress.

Paperback ISBN 978-1-5128-2732-3
Hardback ISBN 978-1-5128-2733-0
eBook ISBN 978-1-5128-2734-7

To Josh

CONTENTS

LIST OF FIGURES

ANKS: Akhil Nepal Kisān Sangathan (All Nepal Peasant Organization)
BDP: Bhaktapur Development Project
CBS: Central Bureau of Statistics
GDP: gross domestic product
IOM: International Organization for Migration
IT: information technology
NPR: Nepali rupees
NWPP: Nepal Workers' and Peasants' Party
UNO: United Nations Organization
USD: United States dollar
WB: World Bank
WHO: World Health Organization

Figure 1. View of Bhaktapur expansion area from the forest of Suryabinayak.

NOTE ON TERMINOLOGY AND TRANSLITERATION

Newar people in Bhaktapur speak predominantly Nepali with the interjection of a variety of Newari words, often including Neplish terms (a combination of Nepali and English). In general, only older people speak the Newari language (also known as Nepal Bhasa). The romanized form of the Nepali words used in this book is taken from *A Comparative and Etymological Dictionary of the Nepali Language* by Ralph Lilley Turner (2022). This involves the use of diacritics (e.g., *chinā*, to indicate double vowels). I followed the same as a guide for the transliteration of Newari terms. I added [n] following a vowel to indicate the nasalization of the sound in Newari words, for example *che[n]*. Caste names have been capitalized, but not in the cases in which they refer to a profession (e.g., *Jyāpu* for caste name and *jyāpu* for farmer). I pluralized Nepali and Newari terms by adding an "s." The most recurrent words are included in the glossary at the end of the book. Within informants' quotes, I sometimes added my comments and clarifications (based on my own knowledge or follow-up enquiries) in square brackets. The reader can assume that local terms used are in the Nepali language (whether or not these coincide with Newari expressions). When a term was exclusively Newari, I indicated this as "New." and used "Nep." on the same occasions to indicate a Nepali term. Words are directly introduced in the idiom used by local people (Nepali, Newari, or Neplish), and accompanied by English or Nepali/Newari translations in brackets where needed. Throughout the text, I use the term "Newari" solely for indicating the language, while for all other purposes (e.g., to indicate the people and adjectives) I use the term "Newar" instead. When words are spelled in a different way in cited sources, I have maintained their spelling. When the term "society" is used as a human-like entity as discussed by informants, I have used quotation marks. All names of participants used in the following pages are pseudonyms while the caste background has been maintained.

PROLOGUE

Once upon a time, a rich merchant lived with his seven sons, providing them with all of the luxuries that they could ever want. One day, he asked them how they intended to live their lives in the future. While six of the sons replied that they wanted to live with him following his fate (karma), the youngest son replied that he wanted to follow his own destiny. Having been banned by his father from his house, the young man went in search of his own fate. On his way walking across the fields, he saw a fig tree that was half green and half dried up. The tree asked him where he was going, to which he replied that he was looking for his karma. The tree requested his help to determine its own karma too by understanding why it had become half shriveled. The young man promised to help the tree and continued on his path. He soon came across a Brāhman man whose whole body was shaking in pain, and who asked him to help him find out why he had to live in sufferance.

After having promised to help the Brāhman and proceeding on his journey, the son of the merchant came across a house in the middle of a vast land. Here an old lady lived with her daughter, whom the young man immediately liked very much. The old lady asked him to help them to solve the mystery of why their land was producing sterile crops. After making his promise, he went back on his journey until he finally met a hermit and explained to him his quest. The hermit was struck by the young man's courage to go about alone in search of his own karma, and he also admired his determination in wanting to help others. Therefore, he began to explain the circumstances of his encounters: "There is a vessel of jewels buried under the tree that has dried up half of its roots. And the Brāhman is selfish and does not share his knowledge with others, which is why he suffers. The old lady does not want to allow her daughter to get married because she wants her to be her caretaker in the years to come." Hearing these explanations, the young man returned to the house of the old lady and conveyed the hermit's words to her. She then let her daughter marry him, and her crops immediately became full of grain.

The happy couple went to meet the Brāhman, who imparted all of his knowledge to the brave young man, and as a consequence he quickly recovered his health. They then went to dig up the treasure at the feet of the fig tree, and the yellow leaves soon became green. As the tale goes, not only did the young man find "his karma, but he also helped others release themselves from their problems, obtaining mutual benefit" (Sakya and Griffith 1980, p. 104).

This folk story, which was recounted to me by local people and which I adapted here from a written version found in the *Tales of Kathmandu* (Sakya and Griffith 1980), reveals first of all a tension between individual will and submission to social hierarchies, showing how it is from the interconnectedness of wills and benefits that dharma (as the moral way of life) should be pursued in order to improve one's fate. Also, this story suggests that one should not only find one's own karma by following individual desires and instincts rather than passively accepting the destiny established by the weight of one's ancestors' sins, but also by collaborating, adjusting, and communicating with others. Here mutual help and the ensuing benefits become a moral way of attaining improvement of one's life. Of course, folk stories do not always support ethics that are in line with public opinion, but they do very often demonstrate concrete social tensions. The themes traced in the story, such as that of the father suppressing his son's independence and of the mother controlling her daughter, are real themes animating the lives of Nepali people. As I shall demonstrate in this book, the will to control one's own future emerges and becomes an established mantra of new generations of Nepali people who embrace and shape their own ideas of modernity (*bikās*) as a period in which better well-being can be sought and achieved. This in turn creates tensions and dilemmas on how to do so in a moral way. In Bhaktapur, while the moral worlds of people are being revised under the influence of new ideas and material conditions of life, novel strategies need to be found to establish an intersubjective ground in which individuals can conduct their lives as moral persons and achieve better well-being. This book accounts for how these negotiations occur in the domestic sphere.

CHAPTER 1

Moralities in Transition

During fifteen months of ethnographic research among Hindu Newar middle-class families in Bhaktapur in 2018–2019, I recurrently came across personal narratives of conflict occurring in the domestic sphere in the quest for improved well-being. This book builds on such narratives to investigate the making of a modern domestic dharma through the negotiation of social roles and relationships in the pursuit of an idealized well-being.

By adopting the theoretical lens of intersubjectivity by Husserl (1970a) and the notion of conversation by Schutz and his associates (e.g., Schutz and Luckmann 1973), I demonstrate that through interpersonal conversations, social actors actively coordinate with one another to attune their existential dimensions. Throughout the chapters of this book, I trace different relationships and examine a range of topics, including parental attempts to provide moral guidance to their children; child-peer solidarity in pursuing emotional happiness; marriages that challenge domestic hierarchies; house structures that reveal transitioning ideas of family and self; ongoing moralities of friendships and financial support; and finally how older adults rethink their roles in relation to their children's and their own well-being. Ultimately, I advance the interpretation that well-being is conceptualized and experienced in Bhaktapur as a moral and relational matter, as a psycho-physic state of balance in which individual goals are achieved and harmony with others is maintained. I show that dimensions of struggle and well-being are deeply intertwined with the making of moral consciousness through the negotiation of domestic relationships.

By putting the family at the center of analysis, this study provides a new perspective on the making of moral modernities in Nepal as a self-reflexive as well as dialogical process. I believe with Zigon (2014, p. 21) that speculation

on moral reasoning need not necessarily be framed "in terms of judging, eval-
uating, and enacting the good or right, but instead to be about the making,
remaking, and maintenance of relationships." Following from these considerations, the main questions guiding this research are: How are new pressures
and aspirations of life betterment negotiated with local moralities and cosmologies? How are moral selves shaped in this process? How do these negotiations
contribute to social change?

I engage primarily with the work of two anthropologists of Nepal: Mark
Liechty (2008) and Steven Parish (1994). The former has provided crucial
contributions to the study of the interrelated emic concepts of modernity
and middle-classness in Kathmandu, and the latter has explored in depth the
moral consciousness of Newar people in Bhaktapur with a focus on the interconnections between moral self-making and the reproduction of sociocultural structures. The present study contributes new empirical knowledge to
this scholarship through an exploration of domestic transformations among
middle-class families in Bhaktapur. By approaching the domestic as a locus
of moral reasoning and looking at conflict occurring across various relational
levels in the domestic sphere, I demonstrate that conflicts are in productive tension with adjustments, ultimately leading to a redefinition of moral
selfhood. In this book, I take the "self" as one's sense of personal identity.
A Newar ethos (even if in constant change) is what makes a process of relational moral self-making peculiar to the Newars of Bhaktapur in this particular time in history. As it will become clear in the chapters, an ethos of union
and of domestic hierarchy are being contested.

In this introductory chapter, I situate this work in the context of previous
studies of Newar society, and I lay the methodological and theoretical foundations for exploring well-being as a moral and relational experience in the
context of domestic transformations in Bhaktapur. In Chapter 2, I provide a
historical background that traces the material, social, and ideological basis
of the emergence of a Newar middle class in Bhaktapur, a large portion of
which developed from the Jyāpu caste of farmers influenced by the work of
local intellectuals and inspired by upper-class practices. This chapter establishes the historical background to the notion of well-being as experienced
through a domestic perspective. In the remaining chapters, I move on to
explore changing domestic relations in the context of larger societal transformations. With a focus on the role of parent–child relatedness in the process
of moral reasoning, Chapter 3 unveils the intimate dynamics through which
parents and children choose whether or not to confront each other regarding

their own perspectives and desires to achieve better well-being. It looks at how parents aim to teach their children the notion of "moral measure" while also demonstrating how colliding ideals of well-being between parents and children lead to conflict and avoidance. I then turn to the perspective of the youth and to the tension between the moral emotion of shame and the new Neplish notion of "advanceness," and I outline how younger people establish alternative venues of moral creativity with their peers, suggesting that parent–child avoidance continues until later years, when adult children come to negotiate their needs and desires with their parents on the occasion of marriage. In Chapter 4, I explore how new emerging ideals of companionate marriage and individual well-being among younger generations challenge social expectations and are mediated at the family level, particularly in conversation between parents and their adult children, and between spouses.

By focusing on the increasing phenomenon of household fission, in Chapter 5 I argue that transitions in domestic structures not only represent the consequence of improved economic possibilities, but also communicate dramatic social transformations and a redefinition of hierarchies of value and power between family members, which emerge alongside new ideas of family and self. Chapter 6 explores the moralities of friendship, particularly the concept of "heartfelt help" in the context of the new institution of the "friendship *guthi*" (where the term *guthi* stands for a particular kind of Newar social and ritual association). I discovered that these are formed with the function of providing either or both funerary and economic support to their members in the form of rotating credit associations. This chapter argues that while building on preexisting practices of socialization, the new institution of the friendship *guthi* plays a crucial role in the networking between middle-class households in a climate of social, economic, and ideological change. Chapter 7 offers a local perspective on aging from the point of view of the elderly. It demonstrates that a dynamic of reciprocity that was once entailed in domestic transactions is being reshaped on new moral premises. In unpacking the phenomenon of generational breakdown, in which adult children often choose to take care of their own nuclear families over their elderly parents, this chapter suggests that the effort to empathize with one's children's hardship makes up another, less explored, dimension of social change in Nepal, becoming an important point of observation for understanding kinship transitions. In the concluding chapter, I draw the findings together, highlighting emerging key themes and further discussing them through the notion of "hierarchies of values" (Robbins 2007). As a whole, the stories discussed demonstrate that in

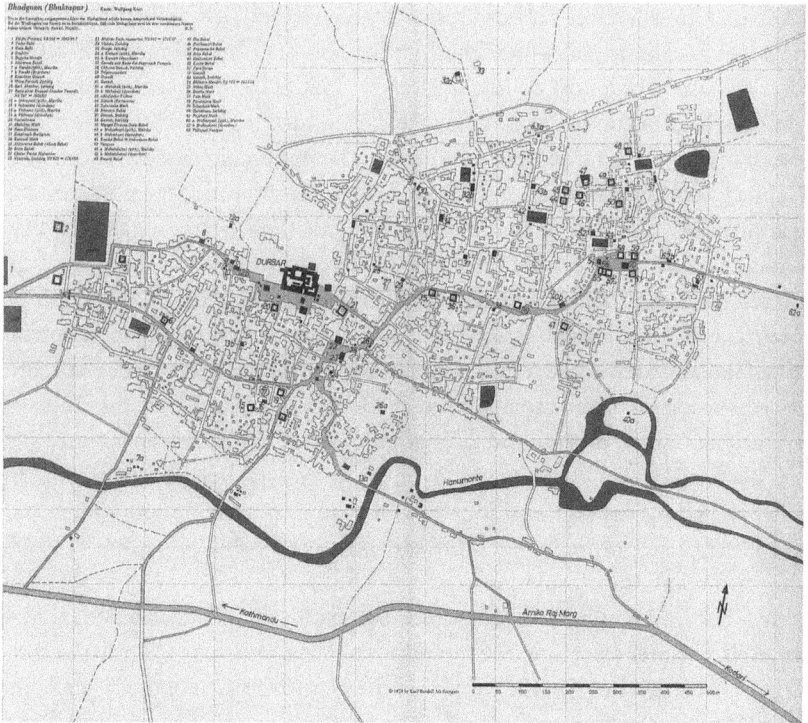

Figure 2. Map of Bhaktapur by Wolfgang Korn (1998).

Bhaktapur well-being coincides with a balance between the achievement of one's goals and the maintenance of domestic harmony through the negotiation of needs and desires.

The Research Context

The Newars are the earliest inhabitants of the Kathmandu Valley, a basin fifteen miles long consisting of extremely fertile lands surrounded by mountains. Their ethnic origin is still uncertain, but it is generally accepted that the ancestors of the Newar people arrived in the Kathmandu Valley sometime during the prehistoric era, roughly two millennia ago (Gutschow and Michaels 2005, p. 15; Fürer-Haimendorf 1956). Bringing their own caste system, they remained culturally distinct from the other ethnic groups, who were divided by a different caste system (Slusser 1982; Gellner 1986). In general, their language, a distinctive material culture (including architecture and artisanal activities), and their preference for urban settlements have distinguished the Newars from other ethnic groups over the centuries (Doherty 1978, p. 434). Following years of intra-ethnic marriages, they remain at present a distinct ethnic group with their own language, although this is now prevalently spoken only by elderly citizens, and in some cases as a second language by younger generations. In the past, Newar people made up to 80 percent of the valley's population, while these days their prevalence has decreased due to the immigration of other ethnic groups from rural and hills areas to the Kathmandu Valley. Today, out of the approximately 2.5 million people living in the Kathmandu Valley, there are 641,963 Newar people (Central Bureau of Statistics [CBS] 2012) who live primarily in major urban settings such as Kathmandu, Bhaktapur, and Patan, and in other smaller towns such as Panauti and Dhulikhel.

Founded in the twelfth century by Newar kings and located on the eastern side of the Kathmandu Valley, some 11 kilometers from Kathmandu, the town of Bhaktapur[1] extends over 119 square kilometers, counting a current population of 304,651, among which there are 64,775 Newar people (CBS 2012). Bhaktapur can be reached from Kathmandu through the smoky and dusty Arniko Highway, a long road that connects the major cities of the Kathmandu Valley. Traffic jams can cause hours of delay submerged within black clouds of pollution. When we moved there from Kathmandu to start my fieldwork in April 2018, it was immediately clear to me and my husband, Josh, why local people often refer to Bhaktapur as "heaven," a definition that is striking for its opposition to the epithets given to Kathmandu, for example "crazy Kathmandu" or "Dust-mandu." Bhaktapur's relative isolation from the business districts of Kathmandu has contributed to preserving many of its ancient rhythms in the old town and in most surrounding areas. Here days are peaceful, with slow vibes and the persistence of traditional activities, alongside which new jobs have emerged. Some people dry clay items in Pottery Square, sell vegetables in the local markets, carve wooden windows and furniture, or work in small grocery shops, in banks, schools, and hospitals. The central road, Dettatraya, connects the main gates north and south of the city, and it is here and in the temple squares that most of the commercial activities and festivals are conducted. Around the old town, the city is in constant expansion. People are increasingly selling their lands to fund their children's education abroad, and these lots are often used for construction purposes.

Bhaktapur has for centuries been a rare example of a "rural town" (Pieper 1975, pp. 64–69) whose social organization was based on the Newar caste system. Under the rule of the Malla (1200–1768), the Gorkha (1768–1846), and the Rana (1846–1951), conformance to the social order was grounded on the religious belief in the *samsāra*, meaning in Sanskrit "the ever-turning wheel of life," that is, the Hindu belief in metempsychosis, a continuous process of reincarnation toward a final release (*moksa*).

Social rules were determined by caste status, age, gender, male lineage (*phuki*), and clan (*thar*)[2] belonging and included the observance and management of certain behaviors between castes, the arrangement of proper same-caste wedding contracts and ceremonies, and the performance of caste-specific death pollution and life passage rituals.[3] Sanctions were imposed by the king and by the whole community on those who did not respect the prescribed social rules through exclusion from caste membership, loss of social status and dignity, as well as exclusion from the service of funerary practices (provided by *siguthī*). The regulation of social relations and religious practices in Bhaktapur was and still in large part is supervised by the *guthi* institution, a religious association whose presence dates back to the Licchavi era (fifth to ninth centuries), with various funerary and ritual functions, whose members by tradition cover various age groups and are composed of male *fukee* people. The *guthi* groups have important functions in the organization of feasts and in the maintenance of religious life, while also holding jurisdictional power. Among the various types of *guthi* groups, the funerary *guthi* (*siguthi*) is the most powerful, and membership in a *siguthi* is necessary for each household to ensure social status and funerary service. The *siguthi* had the power to control households' dynamics by surveilling the marriage choices of their members and by reserving the right to deny funeral services to those who did not comply with rituals and caste regulations.

One of the major scholars of Newar society, Robert Levy (1990), defined Bhaktapur as a "mesocosm," a middle ground made of rituals, social interactions, and festivals, lying between the microcosm of individualities and the macrocosm of the deities. Stressing the continuity and fixity of social roles in the city as based on religious beliefs, Levy (1990, p. 16) referred to Bhaktapur as an "archaic city," which, as opposed to modern cities, runs "in very much the old way, like a clockwork mechanism assembled long ago that no one had bothered to disassemble."

Levy stressed the importance of the household for the socialization of individuals to the social order. While these constrictions are still strong today, their contestation has become now very visible. Within the household, a hier-archical structure imposes expectations over individual actions that should be fulfilled through adherence to domestic dharma, which literally means the "moral way" or the "way of life" as a religion-based moral behavior. In prac-tice, dharma is that ensemble of ritual and social responsibilities and obliga-tions that each individual is expected to follow in order to preserve harmony in the family, to ensure the rebirth of the dead in a new state of existence, to please the gods in order to obtain rain and fertility, and to be reborn in a "better life," that is, on an upgraded level of the caste system, eventually being freed from the cycle of rebirth. Dharma duties involve the observance of daily rituals, appropriate social behavior according to caste, age group, and so on, and of life passage rituals (*samskāra*) that gradually shape a person's transi-tion through the stages (*āśrama*) of a householder's life.

As observed by Levy (1990, p. 110), "the household is the setting for inti-macy, for the education of the young, for preliminary (and usually effective) attempts at controlling deviant behaviour, and for much family religion." In fact, it is not only through caste observance that the order of the cosmos can be maintained, but also through the reproduction of asymmetry in relation to expectations of respect in the household (see Gray 2008, p. 52). As is the case for other Nepali ethnic groups (see, e.g., Gray 2008 and Bennett 1983), Newar traditional family structures follow the Hindu system of the patriar-chal family, with the elders holding decision-making power within the family and with women being generally submissive to the decisions of husbands and fathers-in-law (Levy 1990). Within a domestic hierarchy, individual roles are interconnected and ensure a family's location in the religious order. Together, local political and religious institutions and personalities, kinship lineages, and the local community have contributed for centuries to shaping what people call "society" (*samaj*). "Society" is conceived of as a human-like entity that oversees people's behaviors and prevents wrongdoing.

The study of Bhaktapur's religious background conducted by Levy was necessary to unpack for the first time how religion underpins all social dimen-sions within the city, and how this was strictly interwoven with political struc-tures in the past. Yet, Levy's research revealed little information on the reality of domestic relations and on the incumbent social change. In fact, his descrip-tion of Bhaktapur's society as animated by religious and group ideology, where the individual is subordinated and agentless and where the city is treated as a static social system, encountered some critiques (Gellner 1997; Mikesell 1993, p. 233). Another major scholar of Newar society, Todd Lewis (1994,

p. 55), praised Levy's research, while calling for a second volume that would focus on "the household, the status of women, life-cycle rites, and psychoanalytically informed individual biographies." This was in fact the intention of Levy himself, who was planning to write a second volume on the social life of the city, which unfortunately he never completed.

Fulfilling this task, Parish (1994) located the social lives of Bhaktapurian people in space and in time and within a net of relationships that linked individual selves to the local cultural system. Parish's work is an anthropological study intersecting with cultural psychology, examining how Bhaktapurian Newars produce themselves as moral persons through "a dialogue with culture" (Parish 1994, p. 1). Through this approach, Parish debunked Western dominant psychological theories that ignore the role of culture in the shaping of moral consciousness. Of course, the dialogue between the self and culture is much more than an abstract process, and, as Parish's analysis of ethnographic material also demonstrates, it involves the practical role of families in guiding individuals toward the formation of moral consciousness. While Parish recognizes the role of moral creativity, he places more emphasis on the cultural reproduction of the social order. A study of norm deviance and contestation is now urgent due to dramatic social changes that have been occurring in Nepal over the last decades and that have brought about significant material improvement in many people's lives and the emergence of a middle class animated by notions of the "good life." Influenced by both foreign development discourses and Hindu ideals of wellness, these new ideas challenge the social order discussed so far.

Following the end of the despotic Rana regime, in 1951 Nepal opened its borders to economic and cultural contact with Western countries after a century of isolationist politics. Largely due to the Land Reform Act in 1964 and the later economic liberalization in 1990–1994, an increasingly educated middle class inspired by ideas of life improvement started to challenge preexisting local ideologies in Bhaktapur (Hachhethu 2007, p. 77; Haaland 1982, p. 28). The following decades have featured dramatic transformations, including a massive influx of tourism, an increase in out-migration, the spread of education and media, the reduction of child and maternal mortality rates, and a gradual lessening of malnutrition. Through sociopolitical emancipation and a bloody civil war (1996–2006), local people have owned and shaped the transition to a democratic state in 2008. Ideas of well-being and of the good life as something that can be achieved in one's lifetime rather than through cycles of reincarnation started to become predominant. Concomitantly new imaginaries of wellness and socioeconomic individual and collective growth were established among an emerging middle class, following the spread of media from Western and non-Western countries. Western cultural worlds[4] and wealthier local social groups soon became an example of modern lifestyles (Liechty 2008) but also, as I unveil in this book, of substantially different modes of relationships.

The Middle Class

Before moving on, I will introduce how I am approaching the notion of "middle class." The Nepali middle class is generally discussed by economic and political scientists in discourses of development in terms of economic potential. For example, the World Bank's (WB) (2016) definition is based on criteria of financial security versus vulnerability, where the latter refers to a probability more significant than 10 percent of falling back into pov-erty.[5] Here the middle class is seen as a relatively secure group in contrast to the most insecure and poor strata. According to the same report by the WB (2016, p. 14), 22 percent of the current population fall in the middle-class category (which is a decisive improvement considering that in 1995–1996 this group stood at 7 percent), while 45 percent are classified as vulnerable and 31 percent as poor. However, according to a Gallup world survey (in WB 2016, p. 14), a self-perceived sense of security (meaning "a positive outlook about the next five years") is only experienced by less than 10 percent of the population, while 70 percent are struggling ("their well-being is moderate but inconsistent") and 20 percent are poor ("has poor outlook for the future"). The incongruences emerging between these reports suggest that there is an overlap between class status and perceived vulnerability, and shows how "middle class" is a slippery concept. This data also shows that people with diverse economic and social backgrounds can fall into this category and that the largest section of the population has potentially reached a middle-class status but also remains vulnerable to losing it. As such, their lifestyle, aspira-tions, and worries make them more similar to each other than to the more secure upper-class group.

Vulnerability in Nepal largely derives from a precarious job market and the rise of competition (WB 2016; Liechty 2008, p. 211; also Nepali 2015, p. 423).[6] According to a report by the WB (2016), the reason for this can be found in the "atypical structural transformation" of Nepal, a phenomenon by which, in economic discourse, a society jumps from agriculture to services, skipping the manufactory phase. In the case of Nepal, this could have been caused by specific historical evolutions such as the civil war (1996–2016) (WB 2016, p. 15). While in the preconflict phase the manufacturing share of industries rose to 23 percent, in 1996 it dropped dramatically to 16 percent. Following this trend of declining industry, half of Nepal's GDP is today produced by services that are insecure and depend on the oscillations of the market. The country's economic hardship also derives from patterns of development in which policy choices have not invested in agriculture and the manufacturing sector and have not pursued capital accumulation, building instead upon foreign aid–derived capital and remittance, and thus falling into a trap of low productivity growth (World Health Organization [WHO] 2017). While representing an important push to the economy and to the beginning of a money-based economy, the introduction of foreign aid in the Nepali economy also has a darker side that has been criticized by various parties including local anthropologists (e.g., Bista 2020) and by major Western bodies such as the World Health Organization (2017). Largely due to a lack of secure jobs, despite the large amounts of money entering the country, poverty remains a serious problem for the majority of Nepali people. This in turn has led many people to divert their efforts away from farming, often seeking better-paid working opportunities in foreign countries, with hundreds of thousands of Nepali people having moved to work abroad in various countries such as Qatar, Malaysia, Saudi Arabia, the United Arab Emirates, Kuwait, and India since 1990 (WB 2016, p. 6).[7]

Migration is another problematic aspect for Nepal's sustainable economic development. On the one hand, data reveal that remittance income is a driver of poverty reduction in Nepal (WB 2016, p. 6). This is because remittance has an immediate positive effect on the households of the people migrating, and because it impacts society at large, with agricultural wages growing due to the lessening of the labor supply. Furthermore, remittance-induced growth produces a new economy and new consumer behaviors, which in turn fuel the economy through a demand for goods and services. On the other hand, large-scale migration is a sign of profound social issues and chronic recession in which, while individual households are lifted from poverty, the economic growth of the country is conversely slowed. This is because large-scale migration prevents the competitiveness of businesses and markets and causes stagnation of prices, quality, and productivity of public services and infrastructure including public education and health care systems (WB 2017, p. 5). In turn, the appearance of an improving economy relieves pressure on policymakers regarding the needs of the country (WB 2017, p. 6).

Nepal's precarious economic situation was worsened by the 2015 earth-quake, which caused thousands of deaths and left millions of people without a home. Other geographical difficulties include frequent floods and unstable political and economic relations with India and China, whose borders are shared and a necessary passage for commerce with nearby countries. While things are slowly improving, with the poverty rate of the country having halved over the last nine years and with income inequality dramatically decreasing (WB 2016, p. 5), nevertheless, Nepal remains one of the poor-est and slowest-growing economies on the Asian continent (WHO 2017). As poignantly noted by Liechty (2008, p. 51), "living these contradictions breeds enormous anxiety: In the father who feels dragged into illicit ventures to support his family's growing consumer demands; in the housewife who dreads going to the markets where years of double-digit inflation have cut ever deeper into her fixed food budget; in the teenager forced to negotiate the demands of being a 'modern youth.'"

While caste and class are ephemeral notions and certainly fluid, in cer-tain contexts specific social logics are in play that involve caste thinking and class consciousness. Following from these considerations, in this book I take the notion of middle class as a broad group experiencing ambivalent existen-tial conditions of aspiration and uncertainty that is involved in a process of negotiation of moral selves from a relational perspective. I also believe with Liechty (2008, p. 15) that middle-class cultural practices in Nepal can best be conceptualized by their self-reflective nature, especially for how they nego-tiate and balance old pressures and new cultural influences. What interests me here is people's willingness and power to shape social change. If there is one aspect that brought all of my informants together, it was their active reflection on what direction they perceived change is taking and what direc-tion it should take for improved well-being to be attained. These reflections were carried out through commentaries on society and through a discus-sion on what everyone's role, responsibility, and potential could and should be. Based on these conversations, I suggest that local middle-class people conceive of well-being as a relational and moral experience encompassing a revision of dharma through a clash with preexisting norms and values. Theoretically, then, this book is an ethnographic contribution to an under-standing of well-being as a moral and relational process. As Sarah White (2010, p. 158) has poignantly noted, well-being "is something that happens in relationships—between individual and collective; between local and global; between people and state."[8] In the specific case of middle-class desires in Nepal, my approach resonates with Appadurai's (2004, p. 67) stance that "aspirations are never simply individual (as the language of wants and choices inclines us to think). They are always formed in interaction and in the thick [net] of social life."

Well-Being as a Moral and Relational Experience

Studies of ideas and practices of well-being across the globe have increased in recent years across several disciplines and have progressively appeared in governmental goal agendas. In the field of social sciences, well-being has generally been conceptualized in terms of happiness and human rights, and has broadly been encompassed in studies of development. With the notion of "development," scholars, governments, and nongovernmental bodies refer unanimously to an improvement in people's lives (Khokhar 2019). Nevertheless, the term remains elusive to define as well as what exactly makes a good and concomitantly better life.

Scholars exploring well-being in countries marked by strong social change have demonstrated that ideals of the "good life" are profoundly shaped by the media imaginary and by both local and foreign discourses (e.g., Wilmore 2008; Fujikura 2013; Kunreuther 2018; Toffin 2016; Greene and Henderson 2000; Liechty 2008). Some of these studies have stressed relatedness as a key notion in the formulation of ideas of well-being and in the negotiation of moral ways to achieve it, in other words approaching well-being as a negotiated moral experience. In some contexts, when individual goals are not attainable within the old kinship ethics, these need to be contested and reformulated. For example, for the young Chinese people studied by Jankowiak (2009) well-being often entails the contestation of established social duties.

Among studies of moral consciousness in Hindu societies, emphasis has often been placed on the control and modulation of individual emotions and instincts. In the Hindu world, well-being is conceptualized as a psycho-physical state that involves harmony within one's own self (Salagame 2013) through the observance of dharma. For example, in the Indian context, Kakar (1978) suggested that individual psychological dimensions are shaped through childhood socialization. Along these lines, Derné (2009) has argued that among young Indian men in Banaras there is a generalized belief that marriage choices should be made by conforming to the will of one's parents rather than following a romantic media imaginary, which while promising wellness and happiness is described as illusory and unattainable. Elsewhere,

Derné (1991) has pointed out the need declared by these men to be guided by their parents in order to tame otherwise dangerous impulsivities. Based on his research in India, Mines (1988, 1994) contributed new nuances to this approach, arguing that even within social contexts marked by decisive cultural conformity, people do not completely suppress their individual desires and often hold on to them until a late age when social judgment lessens and they can express themselves more freely. These and other similar studies such as that by Lim (2008) in Nepal emphasize the reflexive and dialogical nexus between ideas of well-being and their means of achievement. Well-being emerges in these studies as a process of self-shaping through the attunement of emotions and personal desires to social expectations.[9]

In a sense, a notion of well-being was long since strictly related to a notion of dharma. This is because the attainment of physical, psychological, and social well-being was understood in major Hindu scripts as deriving from the observance of the moral way of life (Salagame 2013). The question, however, is whose well-being was encompassed in the notion of dharma underpinning the broader social and cosmological order? Strong hierarchies based on age, gender, and caste-belonging, sanctioned by religious and political figures, established for centuries that the well-being of those enjoying a superior social standing should be prioritized. So a young couple's private desires would have to be subjugated to those of their in-laws, a wife's will to that of her husband's, a son to that of his mother and father, and so on. For centuries, the social order reflected the moral codes dictated by the predicaments of dharma whose main promoting voices were those of the local religious, political, and social elites. In present Nepal, new material and ideological possibilities enabled by unprecedented cultural and material stimuli overturn these frameworks, creating the premise for new contestations and new horizons of well-being at the hands of most people. The moral codes then, need to be revised, and with them, old and new concerns and norms. In this context, modern dharma is the complex entanglement of all of these pressures and practices and of the values associated with them; an entanglement that, to be sure, is not defined once and forever, but is ever-changing, in a constant process of revision as individuals bring their lives together and reflect on their own private needs and desires.

Scholars exploring the relational dynamics and consequences of pursuing well-being, the adjustments involved, and the implications for the local ethos (see Thin 2009, p. 38) have also started to highlight how these encompass several dimensions of social suffering. That is, when new ideas and behaviors are embraced, conflict and emotional distress become ubiquitous. Several authors have pointed out the inextricable connection between emotional states and moral processes, particularly in relation to cultural conformity (Levy 1983; Throop 2012). As such, some have started to argue that studies of emotions and morality in contexts of sociocultural change are becoming more urgent as societies are impacted by waves of globalization and socioeconomic transitions (Zigon 2007; Robbins 2007; Levy 1998). More specifically, social and psychological studies addressing dramatic social change have often stressed distress and conflict due to issues of mutual understanding between distinct groups, for example generations (de la Sablonnière, French Bourgeois, and Najihb 2013; de la Sablonnière 2017; Scheper-Hughes 1982; Kleinman 1999). In the anthropological field, developing an understanding of how people negotiate or rebuild their moral worlds after and through experiences of intense distress is the aim of the field of study initiated by Mattingly, Das, and Kleinman. They approach the everydayness and the microcosmos of people's daily lives as "moral laboratories" (Mattingly 2014), framing these processes in contexts of accelerated social changes that lead to social suffering (Kleinman, Das, and Lock 1997).

Distress is a recurrent theme in the literature on well-being in developing countries experiencing accelerated social change. Here, people might have to rebel against old norms and to problematize domestic relatedness in order to achieve those ideals that directly challenge domestic ethics. Research suggests that distress is often involved in these circumstances due to both the experience of conflict and to the perception of disapproval from one's kin. In fact, as Gammeltoft and Oosterhoff (2018, p. 534) postulated, individual "psychic states are inseparable from the states of mind of intimate others." In countries like Nepal, India, and Bangladesh that are characterized by sharp contrasts between aspirations for the good life and socioeconomic vulnerabilities, another dimension of distress derives from economic precarity caused by the structural conditions of the middle classes (see, e.g., Chua 2014). Gammeltoft and Oosterhoff (2018) have examined the negative consequences of perceived distress in relation to fulfilling one's expected domestic role (based on either or both old and new standards, which often are in conflict) in Vietnam and India. As I introduced in the previous section, well-being is hindered in modern Nepal by a strong dimension of vulnerability, which encompasses at once the spheres of the social, the economic, the physical, and the psychological.[10]

The impact of social transformations—driven by colonization, modernity, capitalism, economic liberalization, globalization, and, more recently, neoliberal economic policies and late modernity on kinship, marriage, and family—on concepts of the self and personhood in South Asia is a critical and popular theme among contemporary scholars of anthropology and sociology. More specifically, anthropological studies focusing on changing family realities in South Asia have started to approach well-being as a moral experience in contexts of social change (Bhandari and Titzmann 2017; Seymour 1999). This book builds and expands upon these studies.

In India, some of the important books already published on the topic of class, social mobility, modernity, and the problematization of social identities (which present very similar findings as those I discuss here) include, for example, those by Osella and Osella (2000), Donner (2008), and Saavala (2012). Still in India, studies exploring youth practices and gender roles contestation include that by Aengst (2014) on adolescent dating, elopement, and youth policing, and by Kantor (2003) on women's empowerment through home-based work. Additionally, studies addressing more directly ideas of the good life in India and the interconnections between aspirations of well-being, social mobility, and middle-class identity have proliferated in recent years (e.g., Chua, 2014). Similarly, among studies of the Pakistani middle class, the books by Maqsood (2017) and Walter (2021) on intimate relationships and marriage present findings very close to those of my study. In particular, Maqsood (2017) engages with the idea of "mutual understanding," a key theme also present in *Modern Dharma*. In a Sri Lankan context, other sister books include Abeyasekera's (2021) work on modernity, morality, and the indissolubility of romantic relationships, and the study by Lynch (2007), who examines gender and cultural politics in the garment industry. Other recent comparable books with a specific focus on well-being include the work by Kavedžija (2019), which focuses on the condition of older people in Japan.

In the Nepali context, research focusing on well-being and the good life has examined themes of health and mental health (e.g., Kohrt and Harper 2008), and it has generally remained separated from other areas of enquiry focusing on social change. On the other hand, studies exploring social change have addressed the link between economic and political transitions and dramatic transformations in family dynamics within the major cities of the Kathmandu Valley (Goldstein and Beall 1986; Kaspar 2005; also Skinner, Pach III, and Holland 1998). Domestic negotiations have been investigated in relation to male out-migration, particularly the ways in which migration contributes to shaping ideas and practices of modern masculinity (Sharma 2008) and in relation to the links between migration, remittance, and kinship (Zharkevich 2019); to the deteriorating conditions of the elderly (Speck 2017; Speck and Müller-Böker 2020; Brauner-Otto 2009; Bennett and Zaidi 2016); and to women's empowerment (Kaspar 2005; Becker 2021; March 2002; Rankin 2001). Other emerging studies have started to explore sexual behaviors and beliefs, particularly through the lens of youth cultures (Liechty 2008, 2009, 2010; Wilmore 2008). Some authors have examined marriage transformations, showing that individual preferences are gradually challenging preexisting social norms (Ahearn 2003, 2012; Gutschow and Michaels 2012, p. 33; Sakya 2000; Ghimire & Axinn 2013).

More specific literature focusing on the explicit interconnection between topics of well-being and social change in the Nepali context includes *Invitations to Love* by Laura Ahearn (2012), which discusses changing marriage practices and gender dynamics; *On the Edge of the Auspicious* by Mary Cameron (1998), which discusses issues related to land ownership and contemporary family and work dynamics; and *Himalayan Households: Tamang Demography and Domestic Processes* by Tom Fricke (1986) on joint and nuclear household transitions among the Tamang ethnic group. While these studies have focused on rural areas, another growing wealth of studies have examined these dynamics in urban areas, particularly Kathmandu, which is considered by local people to be comparatively more "modern" (Brunson 2014, p. 612), in practice allowing for different lifestyles and moral licenses. Among these, in *Planning Families in Nepal*, Jan Brunson (2016) unpacks the challenges of modern life for multiple generations, their relationships, marriages, and households, including for the young generations of daughters and sons who experience what the author calls "social vertigo," a theme that resonates with the topic of distress that *Modern Dharma* raises on multiple occasions.

With a closer focus on youth and modernity, particularly the condition of women, Brunson (2014) discusses elsewhere how the new mobility possibilities granted by riding a scooter enable women to problematize gender norms and dynamics. Nonetheless, other studies point out the perdurance of issues of honor damage when a woman is "too open." For example, Barbara Grossman-Thompson (2017) examines the dangers and related anxieties of modernity in urban Nepal; while linking well-being with moralities and relationships, a recent study by Francis K. Lim (2008) on a village in the Himalayas discusses community perspectives on changing social roles in relation to the emergence of new jobs and the possibility of making money through modern-style lucrative activities. Lim shows how local people actively reflect on how to embrace such changes in a moral way that does not disrupt the order and well-being of the community. Finally, looking at other agentive dimensions of social change

Figure 3. An interview session.

in Nepal, Amanda Snellinger's (2018) work focuses on the involvement of young students in Nepali national politics as they fight for democracy and change; Jeevan Sharma's (2018) research examined the experiences of young men migrating abroad and shaping their destiny away from their families; while Toffin (2016) examined new collective imaginaries.

My research draws from and expands on these works, showing that issues of "openness" (also referred to in terms of "advanceness") recur in Bhaktapur, and that, while being more relaxed than in rural and village areas, social control might be stricter than that found in the urban context of Kathmandu, creating problematic and painful situations of distress that social actors need to navigate on a daily basis in the name of (and in some cases at the cost of) well-being, where the notion of well-being itself is defined intersubjectively.

Outside of the Asian context, this book resonates with Jane Collier's (1997) *From Duty to Desire: Remaking Families in a Spanish Village*, which traces social change through institutions of intimacy and social relations (i.e., parents and children, marriage, and kin). Similarly to *Modern Dharma*, Collier's work grapples with the question of modernity and morality. Akin to the case of my informants, Collier (1997, p. 151) found that local people were concerned with "life as a trajectory of development" and at the same time with kinship continuity, while feeling the tension between the need of doing one's duty and following one's desire. These transitions include what local people in her study call "changes in mentality" (pp. 4–5), through which they seek to produce themselves as modern by fighting against inequal relationships that are seen locally as "traditional."

Some directly and some indirectly, all these studies touch upon the importance of ideals of the good life for these middle classes in their own contexts and outline the centrality of ongoing moral dilemmas for the social actors involved. By providing a relational perspective on the making of moral modernities in Nepal and with a focus on the urban context of Bhaktapur, this book contributes to this scholarship by centering the entanglements of kinship, self, and ethos and their impact on individual and group well-being.

Ethnography

The methodology of this research is ethnographic, involving in-depth interviews and participant observation. My husband and I stayed in Bhaktapur for fifteen months, residing in a small family-owned hotel in the neighborhood of Khauma, just outside the city gate, where a studio apartment was set up for us by the owner and his family with the addition of a table for my writing sessions and a stove-top burner. This local family, with whom we became very close, introduced us to many other local families and became crucial in helping me build my network of informants. While spending time with local people provided me with the possibility of observing many of the local rituals and daily life practices, I was not able to witness the most intimate aspects of family relatedness and conflict, which are generally hidden within the privacy of domestic walls. Yet, these aspects were often readily recounted by people during the interviews and were central to many personal narratives. Collecting these narratives was crucial for understanding local perspectives as well as the diachronic evolution of intersubjective processes through which a lifeworld is constructed.

As noted by White (2010, p. 165), paradoxically, the dominant approach to the study of subjective well-being in governmental and nongovernmental, medical, and most social studies has been quantitative, with the consequence that "despite the emphasis on individuals, the individual person in practice gets lost" (White 2010, p. 165). With the intention of understanding the entanglements between individual and relational dimensions, in my research I did not only use qualitative research to collect individual accounts, but I also paid particular attention to the stories that account for "the processes of well-being," that is, for how well-being comes to be identified as a goal in itself and associated with specific values intersubjectively.

I adopted a "person-centered" research approach to the interview process as conceptualized by Levy (1975) in his ethnopsychological studies of the Tahitians (see also LeVine 1982; Levy 1994; Levy and Hollan 1998; Hollan 1997, 2005). As Levy suggests, by focusing on the ways in which people select or discard topics of conversation, reflect on their own faults and on those of others, and participate with their own senses in creating a reflexive and narrative experience, it is possible to investigate how mental states stem from culture and relatedness as a cognitive filter for individual behavior.

As scholars across many fields have pointed out, narratives can play a crucial role in shaping personal identities (see McAdams 2019; Peacock and Holland 1993; Skinner, Valsiner, & Holland 2001). More specifically, as Parish (1998, p. 56) reminds us, "like other South Asians, Newars use stories to construct moral arguments" (see also Shweder and Much 1987). Furthermore, I agree with Mark Liechty (2008, p. xvii) that the modality of the interview can be of crucial importance in collecting the voices of middle-class people in Nepal, as a device that allows us to grasp the making of discourses of identity through the narrative act of telling. Finally, the narrative approach is particularly suited to studying well-being. In fact, as stated by Hollan (2009, p. 224), the perceptions of well-being change during a life course: "People do not encounter the world as blank states; rather, their experience of the world unfolds epigenetically." Well-being is thus a changing state of mind that personal narratives can grasp and present in critically mediated ways.

The research team was composed of myself, several research assistants who worked alternatively, and the additional presence of my husband and some local friends when appropriate. My local research assistants provided translation support, particularly with the elderly who often speak the Newari idiom rather than Nepali, and very little English. Nonetheless, since many people in Bhaktapur do speak English, I was able to interview them without the help of the translators. My research assistants belonged to different gender, caste, and religious backgrounds, providing easier access to different social groups. The majority of the interviews were conducted in the area of Khauma, while others were carried out in several places both inside and outside of the city walls, in old and new houses, and in public spaces and cafes.

Data collection involved informal conversations and in-depth interviews with 150 adult participants at different stages of their life. While all of the interviewees were adult Hindu Newar people of Bhaktapur, they belonged to a diverse range of caste and economic backgrounds, although most of them had a background in farming. There were farmers, artisans, taxi drivers, sculptors, writers, doctors, teachers, housewives, shopkeepers, tourist guides, and so on. Given the difficulty in defining and classifying the middle-class group as a whole, I decided not to limit myself to any specific group and socioeconomic features of the participants. In most cases, people would define themselves as middle class. In other cases, at some point during the interviews, I assessed (through either direct questions or deduction) the economic assets of the participant and their caste and educational background. But it was only later, during the analysis process (when I brought together their narratives containing themes of aspiration, uncertainty, and negotiation of moral selves from a relational perspective), that I would further develop my interpretation of them as a growing middle class. Therefore, while recognizing diversity, a "moderatum generalisation" (Williams 2002) was attempted in the process of selection of the material collected, bringing together a group of people who live similar experiences. Thus, while each recounted story is faithful to a real person, it is also more than a simple portrait, speaking to the broader societal processes within which these people live.

My original aim was to understand local ideas of health in relation to domestic relationships and transformations, particularly around nutrition, but this aim evolved as the research progressed.[11] People recurrently commented that health and well-being derive not only from an absence of illness in the body, but also from a state of peace in the heart and mind (*man ko shanti*). As they repeated, a balance between these dimensions descends from harmony in the family, as well as from fulfilling one's appropriate social role. It is in the balanced pursuit of these two key dimensions that moral selves are broadly understood as well as notions of well-being itself. While I encountered many disparate life plans, dreams, and ambitions that shaped personal horizons of wellness, there was a recurrent golden thread found in the compromises made between individual goals and those of others to achieve domestic harmony (*ajur ajur*). When this theme of "balance" emerged, I was intrigued by the similarity with the emic notions of "suitability" and "moral middle" that Liechty (2008) collected among informants in Kathmandu as they are involved in the process of fashioning a middle-class identity. The suitable middle was articulated in his study as a moral discourse through which people navigate between local and foreign ideas, and between upper- and lower-class groups' practices. I soon became interested in understanding if and to what extent that quest for balance that Liechty had studied in Kathmandu was unfolding in Bhaktapur in the domestic context, and how it was working in the shaping of kinship dynamics and moral creativity.

During the first half of my fieldwork, I discussed a broad range of topics with various local people. This brought my research assistant Binod to frequently ask me during our breaks with a friendly, yet puzzled, smile: "I am not sure that I understand what you want to study, Paola, sometimes you ask about food and health, sometimes you ask about the *guthi!*" As themes had started to recur, I had began to ask people to tell me more about them. These included *guthi* transformations and domestic conflict and fission. The last six months of my research were allotted for an explanatory investigation. Having established the frequency of phenomena such as household fission and the emergence of friendship *guthis*, I started to examine the reasons behind these events and refined the main question guiding this research around the recurring notion of well-being (which was articulated through a broader emic terminology encompassing notions of emotional happiness, peace of mind, health, balance, and so on) and around the dialogic processes through which people shape their lifeworld and establish moral personhood by harmonizing individual desires with those of others.

Due to the sensitive nature of the information collected, I chose not to make audio recordings. Nonetheless, translating and annotating on the spot gave me the possibility to verify certain aspects with the interviewees straight away and enabled me to continue interviewing following their replies in a more spontaneous way than if I was following a script. The dynamic nature of open-ended interviews also made it possible for people to recount their lived experiences in their own ways. Some would recite poems or show me photographs. An elderly *guthi* singer spontaneously began to sing the folk stories that he had been practicing since he was a child. This interview format allowed others to draw the structures of their houses in my notebook with me when they wanted to explain the unfolding of their lives and conflicts. When the interview was joined by other local members who wanted to take part in the discussion, after having obtained the interviewee's consent, I proceeded with a formal written agreement and I introduced new questions to the group. While there was a potential for reciprocal influences, I found that this dynamic was very productive because the members could discuss, often animatedly, contentious topics with each other. Relevant insights also emerged when I interviewed husbands and wives together. In many cases, I attempted to overcome the risk of people's discomfort through private follow-up interviews. Repeated interviews with some informants were useful to capture in-depth perspectives on different topics as well as the evolution of domestic dynamics. Furthermore, the collection of multiple points of view on the same stories helped me to gain a broader perspective on conflictual situations.

My relationship with people continued outside of the interview setting. Women dressed me up with saris and jewelry, while men brought me historical and political pamphlets and books. In our small apartment we received daily food gifts, poems, and special dishes according to the calendar occasion. I was myself part of the ongoing conversation between people and their moral worlds, unavoidably influencing the way people recounted their stories. Despite my best attempt to not force my opinion on them, their idea of me as a Western person might have influenced their way of presenting their accounts and perspectives. Also, as a woman, it was relatively easy for me to access women's spaces and to learn more about their views on family conflict, their suffering due to inner troubles, their emotions about their relationships with their husbands and in-laws, but also with their children as mothers and their parents as daughters. While I also interviewed a large number of men, their first interest was more often to tell me about their *guthi* tradition and the importance of rituals. However, many men also opened up on family matters. It is possible that the presence of my male research assistants, and in some cases my husband and some local common friends, allowed me to access male spaces and to get to know their thoughts more intimately than if I was alone.

When going through the stories collected, I selected narratives that reveal moments of "moral breakdowns" (using a notion by Zigon 2007) that challenge "one's taken-for-granted mode of being-in-the-world" (Throop 2012, p. 158). My ethnography reveals that these moments are navigated as an opportunity for self-reflexivity, enabling a transition between "moralities of reproduction" and "moralities of freedom," using the terminology by Robbins (2007). To analyze the stories collected, I first divided them into two main groups of recurring themes and exceptional circumstances. I also paid attention to the emergence of a local moral vocabulary and the recurrence of moral emotions in people's speech. In particular, the notions of "mutual understanding" (*āpasī samājdari*) and "lonely heart talk" (*mane-khanlhagu*) made the core analytical ground for discussing self-making and social change from a domestic perspective. Throughout a year and a half spent analyzing

Figure 4. Market in Taumadhi Square.

this material, I presented my research at conferences, discussed my findings at seminars, and made use of visual methods. Among these activities, the use of visual methods in the form of drawing and painting was especially essential to support my thinking, and this is motivated by my preexisting artistic interest and practice. I have discussed this in detail elsewhere (Tiné 2021a, 2021b, 2022a, 2022c, 2024).

Theoretical Orientations

For a long time, kinship studies did not encompass an investigation of the domestic realm, instead focusing on marriage contracts and alliances, political power, and the exchange of goods and money (Carsten 2004, p. 11). While "kinship is [still] conventionally defined as relationships between persons based on descent or marriage" (Stone 2018, p. 5), the notion is nowadays taken in a broader sense that encompasses peoples individual perspectives (see, e.g., Carsten 2000, 2004).

My concern in this work is to examine how all of these dimensions on kinship with their entanglements are intersubjectively problematized and maintained through careful adjustments by individual actors, in a constant tension toward the attainment of group and personal and interpersonal well-being.

Intersubjective Conversations

At the time of Parish's research in Bhaktapur in the early 1990s, social change was already starting to become evident. In fact, while he did not address this directly, several of his reflections hint at conflicts of modern times (see, e.g., Parish 1994, p. 177). Similarly, an earlier work by Nepali (2015), a comparative study on the Newars of Bhaktapur, Patan, and Kathmandu, suggests that the social order was in fact already being problematized at the time of Levy's study (1957–1958) (see, e.g., Nepali 2015, pp. 421–24). In fact, while domestic transformations were not a primary focus of Levy's research, he eventually wrote a follow-up paper reflecting on the problematization of the local culture, which he perceived as ongoing (see Levy 1998).

To enquire about social change and how emic notions of moral modern personhood are constructed in Bhaktapur, in this book I explore domestic interactions through the lens of Husserlian intersubjectivity, that is, as a process of mutual understanding through which people shape their lifeworld (see Husserl 1970b). As summarized by Duranti (2010, p. 17), intersubjectivity can be seen as a process through which "one actively works at making sure that the Other and the Self are perceptually, conceptually and practically coordinated around a particular task." Scholars following Husserl's legacy have further explored intersubjectivity as the very ground of nomos negotiations (see, e.g., Duranti 2010; Sawyer 2003, p. 9; Prus 1997; Schegloff 2006). The people that I interviewed used the notion of mutual understanding (*āpasī samājdari*) as a form of intersubjectivity in the Husserlian sense, in other words as the making of an agreement regarding one's role in the social world in order to make being-in-the-world possible through the establishment of social harmony (*ajur ajur*). While achieving mutual understanding was a recurrent preoccupation of most of my informants, this did not necessarily coincide with empathy, and in fact these understandings were in some cases "forceful" (*jabarjasti ko bujhai*) or were marked by avoidance of confrontation.

To conceptualize interactions in the domestic sphere, I adopt the notions of "constructed reality" for how it is shaped in conversation between people (see, e.g., Schutz and Luckmann 1973; Berger and Kellner 1964). Building on Husserl's social phenomenology as the study of things as they appear and are experienced by people, through the notion of "conversation" Schutz and his associates (Berger and Luckmann 1966; Schutz and Luckmann 1973; Luckmann 1983; also Berger and Kellner 1964) aimed to create a framework to understand how people come to establish a new nomos on a mutual ground of consensus with other parties. This conversation, Berger and Kellner (1964, p. 17) remind us, is what makes it possible for a lifeworld to be "stabilised," that is, when "ambivalences are converted into certainties." Let me now turn to the specific case of the Newars of Bhaktapur.

A Lifeworld in Transition

Virtually all human societies are concerned with the definition of the "right way" of life, and they establish order through rules, norms, laws, and ethos. As I already introduced, Hindu societies have referred to this right way of living as dharma. Dharma is the principle that brings order among discordant ideals, coordinating individuals around an intersubjective experience of reality in which moral personhood is possible. Having encountered this notion both in its explicit and implicit form in my informants' comments, I use it here to explore the ongoing process of agentive reflection upon, and negotiation of, ethos itself. This definition of dharma as a process qualified by the experience of the modern escapes discourses that see it as a set of contents enforced from a dominant—generally Brāhman—perspective. While some elements from dominant discourse are navigated, new values are generated and negotiated to make sense of changing desires and possibilities. Thus, in many ways this book traces the persistence of cultural ideals in a new social logic.

I look at the role of media and material possibilities in propelling change through the creation of imaginaries and opportunities. As I mentioned earlier, while recognizing that traditional forms of social control still operate in Bhaktapur, Levy (1998, p. 328) also observed that the advent of increased stimuli and possibilities in contemporary times is leading to the emergence of new moral questions: "The larger complex and contradictory world, the generation of a sense of paradox, unfairness, and imaginable (if not feasible) choice, impels a transformation of 'consciousness,' a sense of an 'I' which questions and directs and controls its constituted self and its outer world, and which asks, 'Why am I what I am? What might I be? What in this world of unfairness

and alternate possibilities should I do next?'" As Levy argues here, when individuals identify new needs and desires, the moral order needs to be adjusted,
while at the same time individuals constantly revise their own moral selves.

From an ethnopsychological viewpoint, Kohrt and Harper (2008) have
explained at length that the self is conceptualised in Nepal through several interconnected dimensions that root it to the social world. The mind
is commonly thought to be composed of *man* and *dimāg*; the first located
in the heart, the second in the physical brain. In Newar ethnopsychology,
the heart (New. *nuga*) is the locus of the true self, it is divine in nature and
never lies (Parish 1994, p. 191). The emotions from the heart are filtered by
the *dimāg*, allowing the individual to act "in accordance with collectivity and
social norms" (Kohrt and Harper 2008, p. 469). The other components of
the self are *jiu* (physical body), *atma* (spirit), and *ijjat* (social status). Finding
harmony between these dimensions is needed for moral personhood to be
properly established, and rules need to be defined by family members and by
"society" to guide this process and to ultimately validate the self.

The moral emotion preventing people from acting in unacceptable ways
is known as *lajjā* (shyness), which is described by local people as "being a
step back," "reserved," and "not seeking attention" (see Parish 1994, p. 206).
My informants recurrently used the notion of being "advanced" (used in
its English form by people of different ages) in opposition to the local term
lajjā, and it is conceptualized emically as the force that encourages the urge
to express and realize one's own desires as an attribute of a modern individual. This adjective is used with both positive and negative connotations
according to the speaker's view, and many people commented that a balance
needs to be found between concurring dispositions to cultural conformity
and "advanceness."

Modern Dharma

What I have suggested so far is that in contemporary times, harmony is
attained through both the observance of dharma and its active negotiation.
In fact, emerging values might at first appear to generate *adharma* (as the
Sanskrit antonym of dharma) because they often involve the contestation of
traditional norms such as domestic unity and a hierarchical ethos. Differently, these tend to coalesce with preexisting local cosmologies, contributing
to shaping what I shall call a "modern dharma." Dharma is thus taken here

as an ensemble of values that people internalize and revise to attain well-being. In fact, while it is based on shared principles, "different actors project different worlds around the base concept of *dharma*" (Parish 1994, p. 99). As such, not only is dharma "subject to processes of meaning construction" (Parish 1994, p. 99), but the emergence of new discourses creates the conditions for these processes to be accelerated and to be more conflictual on both an interpersonal and intrapersonal level due to the affirmation of clashing values and practices around the pursuit of well-being through a "modern dharma" logic.

Before continuing, I will need to briefly explain how I am taking the notion of modernity. As noted by Stacey Pigg (1992, p. 496), *bikās* (meaning "modernity" and "development") in Nepal is filled with local meanings that interweave with the fabric of social relations. Moving along these lines of investigation, in this book I explore an emic acceptation of the interrelated concepts of modernity and tradition for how these were portrayed to me by my informants. As demonstrated by Liechty (2008) and Pigg (1992, 1996), modernity is an emic notion that is used by local people to reflect on their own experience of social change as a moral experience. It seems to me that by using notions of modernity and tradition, local people demonstrate awareness of their active role in social change. As such, the main usage by the people of Bhaktapur seems to be oppositional in so much that the substantive meaning of traditional is in contrast to their experience of what they understand as modern. In this sense, traditional and modern only exist and have meaning in relation to each other, and they have varying meanings depending upon the context in which they are used.

Domestic Ontology

As I introduced earlier, in the mesocosm discussed by Levy (1990), the family had a crucial role among the various forces of "society" in ensuring social conformance under the guidance and control of the *guthi*. I shall add here that "attachment" in the form of love (*māyā*) is another important dimension in the making of moral personhood in Newar society. *Māyā* is the principle that roots the self to the world through belonging, in virtue of its embeddedness within a net of webs of relatedness (see also Parish 1994, p. 125). Attachment plays a crucial role in the ongoing negotiations between advanceness and shame, and between moral reproduction and creativity through intersubjective processes. I believe with Gray (2008, p. 23) that the household itself is involved in an ontological relationship with dharma. This is because the sacred duties of a householder define "the essence of the household and the fundamental mode of being in the everyday world." While Gray's study explored the case study of the Chhetri, this is also true for the Newars. Building on this, the findings discussed in this book show that the household is not only a reproduction of that cosmos, but rather becomes the ground of an active reflection on the right way to pursue this moral equilibrium. In discussing these aspects, throughout the chapters I explore how ideas of family and household are negotiated alongside ideas of self, and how these in turn engender social change.

Most accounts of kinship in Nepal have treated the family as a "system of substances" (Dumont 1980), that is, defined by kinship networks, living conditions, and material forms of exchange and duties (see Gray 2008, pp. 14–23). Other scholars have stressed the permeability of kinfolks in Hindu societies and the shaping of personhood through the exchange of bodily and nonbodily substances with kin (e.g., Marriott 1976, p. 111). However, to ask what a family is, is to also ask an ontological question that goes beyond the contingency of substances. Evidence in many societies including Nepal shows that substantial attributes might not even be necessary in some cases, and not sufficient in others, for the purpose of making a family (see, e.g., Zharkevich 2019). What makes a family, thus, has also an ontological dimension. This refers to that sphere of family belonging that is so intrinsic to the individual that it pervades all aspects of self-identity and social expectation. I take the notion of ontology as akin to that of "mutuality of being" as developed by Sahlins (2013, preface):

> Kinfolks are persons who participate intrinsically in each other's
> existence; they are members of one another. "Mutuality of being"
> applies as well to the constitution of kinship by social construction as
> by procreation, even as it accounts for "the mysterious effectiveness
> of relationality," as Eduardo Viveiros de Castro put it, how it is that
> relatives emotionally and symbolically live each other's lives and die
> each other's deaths.

As commented by Zigon (2014, p. 22), Sahlins' mutuality of being forms "the ontological basis for understanding the diverse modes of kinship locally constituted around the world and throughout time." Thus, the notion of mutuality of being should not be taken unproblematically, but rather should be

seen in constant revision and linked to ever-changing processes of moral reasoning and negotiation. For Newar people in Bhaktapur, the intersubjective
world of kin is conceptualized in a net of *māyā*, which generates the sense of
mutuality of being by rooting people to the phenomenological world (Parish
1994, p. 157).[12] Here, substantial and ontological dimensions of a family can
be profoundly intertwined, and the conditions for being involved in the net of
māyā might also derive from the sharing of bodily substances, from marriage
alliances, from specific living conditions, and so on. While I have emphasized
here the ontological dimension of family, some other kinship groups might
locally be referred to as "families" even when only possessing substantial
attributes. As such, groups residing in the same households are in most cases
also considered families and addressed in Nepali as *pariwars* (or in English as
"families") regardless of the type of relationships involved between members.
The same can be said for extended groups of relatives that are also called
"families." Therefore, following people's own definitions, in some cases I use
"family" and "household" as synonyms, and the meaning will be made clear
in each context.

As this book will demonstrate, the negotiations of personal and group
desires and of social norms in order to establish a modern dharma take
place in large part in the context of domestic life and in relation to kinship
networking.

CHAPTER 2
———

Envisaging "Better Lives" Across Three Generations: The Rise of the Middle Class in Bhaktapur and Its Existential Perspectives

The Blue Bus

Around seventy years ago in Bhaktapur, a young Newar farmer named Ratna Prajapati left his natal household following quarrels with his brothers and moved to live in a separate house with his wife and their newborn baby. Having worked as a farmer for nearly twenty-five years, Ratna was eventually able to save enough money to buy a bus with the intention of starting a new transportation business. This was a promising perspective given the rise of tourism and increased mobility of people working in other cities of the Kathmandu Valley after the fall of the Rana regime in 1951. I was told Ratna's story by his son Vishnu.

Toward the end of autumn 2018, I interviewed Vishnu and his wife, Devi, at their candy shop just outside of Durbar Square gate. Sitting at the edge of the open door at the back of the shop, I asked them to tell me if and how Bhaktapur had changed since they were children. They both commented that things were drastically different, but the most evident change was that "people can have better lives." Then Vishnu started narrating his personal story to me, recounting the time when his father, Ratna, bought the bus:

> My father worked hard for many years. Then one day he brought me outside of the city walls, where there was a blue bus parked. He told me: "This is our hope [āśā], Vishnu. With this bus we will start a transportation business, and we will have a good life [rāmro jīvanī].

With the income made we will no longer have to work in the fields, and you will be able to go to school."

At that time, I was around eight. I was excited to see my father so happy.

For the following two years, he worked in this business, and I helped him after I finished school in the evening. The bus route followed the newly built road Haraniko Highway, which linked Bhaktapur to Kathmandu passing through Patan. I helped him to collect the money from the passengers and I cleaned the dust from the bus after the last ride. During Dashain, we performed an animal sacrifice to the bus as a sign of worship. As we had seen others doing in the city, my father sprinkled a goat's blood over the motor to improve our chances of success over the next year, and to avoid accidents.

It was during those years that Vishnu's father, Ratna, changed his surname from Prajapati (a surname that denotes belonging to the farmer's caste) to Shrestha (an upper-caste group) to avoid future discrimination against his farming heritage. Things seemed to be going well, but despite these achievements, his family was still about to suffer hardship. The quality of life in Bhaktapur was still low at the time, with rampant illnesses such as rabies, malaria, whooping cough, tuberculosis, and measles, all of which were leading causes of mortality. Malaria took Ratna's wife away, and then Ratna himself within the turn of two years. In the year before he died, he had remarried and had a baby girl. On his deathbed, he made his new wife promise that she would leave the bus to his son Vishnu, a promise that she never maintained. As a consequence, Vishnu grew up and had a "very difficult life" (*kathina jīvana*):

After my father died, his new wife sold the bus and kept the profit. She did not respect the will of a dying man; this is a very bad action [*pāp*]. Also, she did not care if I went to school, so I stopped going. I played all day with the other children of the neighborhood. She then got another husband, so we had to move away from my father's house. My uncles sold my father's house and shared the profits among themselves.

To perform the yearly *śrāddha* for my dead father—which was my responsibility as I was the first son—was not possible in the house of my stepmother's new husband. People were talking a lot. I started to think that it was not right for me to stay there anymore. Besides, I was nothing to them and I felt sad [*dukhī*]. My stepmother only cared for her own daughter. One night, I did not come back and they did not look for me. That night I understood in my heart that I had to leave and make my own life. So I went to Patan.

The years that followed were marked for Vishnu by several encounters, including that with his wife Devi in Patan. Together, they gradually experienced a rise from a farming background to a middle-class status through hard work, and they were eventually able to buy a shop in Bhaktapur. Thanks to their efforts, they could provide an education to their children, which they considered an unnegotiable responsibility to ensure that their children would have better lives. A few days after our first interview, Vishnu and Devi introduced me to one of their children, Binod, and to his wife, Beena. Binod and Beena's account provides an added nuance to understanding important social changes and continuities in comparative perspective. Taken together, the stories of these three different generations reveal the affirmation of varied aspirations and ideologies of life betterment, and are examples of social mobility after the regime's fall.

For centuries, first under the Newar kings and later under the Gorkha rule and the Rana regime, the farmers (*jyāpu*)[1] in Bhaktapur were strangled in a feudal-like system known as *beth begar*[2] and were subjugated by economic hardship. In those years, social control was carried out by the funeral institution of the *siguthi*. At the eventual conclusion of the Newar rule in 1768, religion, caste divisions, and *guthi* power were strengthened. This was pivotal for ensuring that control over people could be maintained, in this way fulfilling the goal of limiting influences from the Western world and from the Indian nationalist movement (Liechty 1997, p. 53), and as such avoiding increased social and political awareness (Shrestha 1999, p. 87; Liechty 2008, p. 42). The ensuing century-long isolationist policy of the Rana regime (1846–1951) facilitated the maintenance of social fixity in Bhaktapur by enforcing both social and economic subordination of the farmers. Yet, due to the absence of ethnography and historiography of subaltern social groups in Nepal in those years, the existential perspectives of those people remain rather obscure.

Before the opening of Nepali borders in 1951, the only sources of information on Nepali society came from the Capuchin missionaries (see Lévi 1899),[3] who were the only ones allowed in Nepal throughout the period of closure to the Western world during the Rana regime, alongside some British colonialists who worked as administrators (e.g., Oliphant 1852; Hodgson 1874) and physicians (e.g., Wright 1877). While they were able to account for some of the events preceding the fall of the regime and outline certain social dynamics, this was exclusively from an upper-caste perspective (see Onta 1994, p. 1).[4] Only from 1951, following the fall of the Rana regime, were researchers allowed into the country and ethnographic accounts began to flourish. An exceptional source on the lives of local people in the years that preceded and immediately after the fall of the regime is the work by Raj (2008, 2010), which is based on the autobiography of a Bhaktapurian revolutionary named Caguthi (1928–2011). By putting the lives of farmers at the center of enquiry, Raj's account decisively departed from the tradition of studies focusing on the upper-caste perspectives. Other relevant sources include the accounts by Bhaktapurian scholar Krishna Hachhethu (2007), who vividly described the rise of the farmers during his childhood, and the records of foreign reports such as that of the Bhaktapur Development Project (Haaland 1982).[5] Building on this, the oral testimonies from Bhaktapurian contemporaries that I collected during my research provide a valuable account of the more recent history of the country and on the existential perspectives of the middle class, together with the anthropological studies of Newar society that have flourished in the last decades (e.g., Nepali 2015; Levy 1990; Rankin 2004; Parish 1994; Gibson 2017b; Grieve 2003, 2006; Shrestha 2012; Toffin 1984), as well as studies of Nepali society more broadly (Liechty 2008; Toffin 2016).

While we do not know what people thought and felt in the past, we know that there were active mechanisms in place to attempt to control people's behavior through religious ideologies, economic dependence, and fear of the law (see Khatiwoda, Cubelic, and Michaels 2021).

According to Rosser (1966, p. 96), a degree of social mobility was occasionally permitted in Newar society. This is the case of the Shrestha status, which could be obtained in exceptional cases by *jyāpu* people through strategic marriages, membership in higher caste *guthi* groups (locked behind payment of large fees), and a series of social steps including segregation of former peers. While this practice was relatively rare and discouraged through strong social judgment and household control, the case of Ratna introduced earlier is exemplary of its enactment.

Ratna's activities first, and then those of Vishnu and Devi and of Binod and Beena were made possible by specific historical events that enabled

Figure 5. A local woman drying wheat stalks.

material and cultural transformations. Drawing from the life stories of these three generations, this chapter outlines changing possibilities as well as the emergence of new imaginaries that shaped—through active negotiation—ideas of well-being and life betterment in Bhaktapur. The remaining chapters will turn to the intersubjective dynamics enacted to achieve well-being among middle-class families and how ideas of tradition and modernity are involved in this process.

The Rana Regime

Ratna's actions, such as separating from his brothers, changing his surname, and embracing a new profession, problematized the caste and hierarchy-based social fixity that had been perduring for centuries and, in his own words, were motivated by a desire for "good lives." Before moving on to examine his story, I will need to provide some notes on the caste systems and on the role of domestic structures in maintaining the social order in Bhaktapur.

Social Order in the Mesocosm

Bhaktapur was founded as a royal city in the Kathmandu Valley in 1150 by the Newar king Ananda Deva Malla (1147–1166). In 1355 CE, King Jayasthiti Malla introduced caste regulations, which included sanctions for people that did not follow the profession that was delegated to them at birth. Caste regulations also established penalties for intercaste marriage and forbade upper-caste groups from accepting food or water from lower-caste members (Hasrat 1970, p. 56). Following the Hindu principles of the Varna system, the caste system constitutes the "social, economic and religious life of the city" (Parish 1998, p. 54). The Varna system divides society into four strata in descending order of purity: Brāhmans, Kshatriya, Vaisya, and Sudra, which correspond respectively to specific forms of social engagement and service, that is, priests and rulers, administrators, farmers and artisans, and the so-called untouchables (e.g., sweepers and butchers).[6] Lying between the polarities of the Brāhmans and the untouchables was the block of the farmers (*jyāpu*), which made up 80 percent of the population up to the 1980s.[7] The farmers were strangled in a feudal-like system known as *beth begar*,[8] and their socioeconomic subordination was maintained by law, underpinned by the aforementioned caste system.

Supported and enforced through legislation over the centuries by Hindu kings, social division based on caste was also perpetrated by the Malla kings of the Saha dynasty, which ruled Nepal between the twelfth and eighteenth centuries, and by the Rana regime (1846–1951), maintaining the legal status of caste hierarchy (Parish 1998).

Adherence to social rules and the perpetuation of social fixity was based on the Hindu belief in the *samsāra*, by which social order would be necessary to maintain the broader cosmic balance. The *samsāra*, meaning in Sanskrit "the ever-turning wheel of life," is the Hindu belief in metempsychosis, a continuous process of reincarnation toward a final release (Nep. *moksha*). According to this belief, a person's reincarnation to a higher or lower state of existence corresponds to deeds conducted in their previous life (Nep. karma). That is, each individual has the duty to follow the correct dharma, the religious morality including ritual and social actions associated with a person's caste or stage of life. Dharma regulates both domestic interaction and socialization outside of the household through the observance and management of certain social behaviors between castes. Further, adherence to dharma can also produce positive results during one's lifetime, including the maintenance or enhancement of one's social prestige (Nep. *ijjat*), albeit within one's appropriate caste group. For centuries, by providing offerings (Nep. *dana*) to local priests, performing correct rituals, and observing appropriate social practices, Bhaktapurian people could improve their chances of achieving a better reincarnation, while they could not expect to change their living conditions in their current lifetime.

According to Witzel (1997, p. 502), Bhaktapur is "a sample representation of 'medieval' Hinduism in a traditional monarchy, and in an urban context" in which influences from the Vedic period continue to persist. Thus, Witzel (1997, p. 502) believes with Levy (1990) that Bhaktapur's social order is based on the idea of the mesocosm, a middle ground between people and gods, in which the observance of dharma plays an essential role in maintaining the cosmological order. In this context, a dimension of public judgment intertwines with the working of the intimate world of moral sentiments to guide people's behavior toward ideas of right and wrong.

The mesocosm itself could thus be seen as a world suspended between the living and the dead whose order is maintained through domestic relatedness. Researchers such as Levy (1990), Parish (1994), and Witzel (1997) provide insights on the links between dharma and domestic life, suggesting that it is not the order of the cosmos that matters to the wider society, but rather the maintenance of appropriate relationships between family members, both the living and the dead. Within the household, a hierarchical structure contributes to control individual actions through the perpetuation of a domestic dharma. As observed by Levy (1990, p. 110), "the household is the setting for intimacy, for the education of the young, for preliminary (and usually effective) attempts at controlling deviant behaviour, and for much family religion." In fact, it is not only through caste observance that the order of the cosmos can be maintained, but also by perpetrating asymmetry through notions of respect in the household (see Gray 2008, p. 52). And if the social and the cosmological orders are deeply linked, the family and the *guthi* are the practical venues of ethos maintenance, while the caste system provides the framework within which these dynamics are conceptualized. Within a domestic hierarchy, individual roles are interconnected and ensure a family's location in the religious order. That is, by following the age-appropriate sacraments, all of the household members are bound together through complementary roles and duties.

What I have introduced so far is important for understanding how social control acted as a guarantee of rigor in Bhaktapur's social order and that domestic dharma played a crucial role in its articulation. In this context, a dimension of public judgment intertwines with the working of the intimate world of moral sentiments to guide people's behavior toward ideas of right and wrong. In the next section, I trace the historical events within which Ratna's existential perspective developed, with a focus on the tensions that led to the fall of the Rana regime (1846–1951) and to the emergence of new possibilities for and understandings of the notion of the good life in Bhaktapur. All of these enabled the active problematization of the status quo at the hands of the local intellectuals through communist movements, and the gradual participation of the stratum of the farmers to political activism.

The Malla and the Gorkha

According to historical sources, the Malla dynasty emerged after the fall of the Licchavi dynasty in the ninth century and of the subsequent Thakuri rule (ninth century–1200), marking the beginning of the so-called "era of the Newar kings" (1200–1768) (see Levy 1990, p. 40). Niels Gutschow (1980, p. 137) suggests that royal Bhaktapur was founded by Newar kings through the assimilation of preexisting small rural villages, creating a centralized urban area. The foundation was completed with the introduction of icons of the Ashmatrikas goddesses throughout the town since it was commonly believed that only through regular animal sacrifice to the bloodthirsty goddesses and the observation of rituals could cosmic order be maintained. After nearly 700 years, the Malla era was violently interrupted in 1768 by the invasion of the Gorkha warriors under the rule of Prithvi Narayan Shah (1723–1775).[9]

Over the following century, Gorkhas and Newars remained largely distinct through the practice of intracaste orthodox marriages. While high-caste Newars received special admissions within the government services, their role in the army was strictly prohibited, possibly due to a fear of rebellion, although the official explanation given was that they were shy and cowardly (Nepali 2015, p. 19). Caste divisions acquired more rigidity after the Gorkha conquest, with the introduction of fines or imprisonment for infractions (Gellner and Quigley 1995, p. 12). The fear of foreign (particularly Western) interference was addressed through the strengthening of religious ideologies. Prithvi Narayan Shah saw himself as a protector of Hinduism against the "mussalmans" (Liechty 2008, p. 11), by which he meant all non-Hindu people. In that phase, "foreign" and "immoral" "were all more or less

synonymous concepts" (Liechty 2008, p. 11), and Prithvi Narayan enforced a
"quasi-ascetic" (Burghart 1984, p. 115) discipline on the country, banishing
musicians and foreign imports, and encouraging local manufacturing.

In 1840, following a series of court murders and intrigues, a young sol-
dier and personal attendant of the young prince named Jung Bahadur Rana
started plotting against the king, Rajendra Bikram Shah.[10] In collusion with
the queen, he first killed the prime minister and then was involved in organizing the Kot massacre in 1846, in which more than one hundred men
from both noble and lower ranks were shot down in an ambush. The queen,
who had been hoping to establish her power with the help of Jung Bahadur
(Wright 1877, p. 58), was instead forced to leave the country, and Jung Bahadur nominated himself Rana prime minister of Nepal.[11] Since its inception,
the Rana regime established a strict autocracy that lasted for a century, enforcing oppressive and unequal treatment of civilians, carrying out isolationist
foreign politics, and reacting to British colonialism through a strengthening
of caste rules, the promotion of religious activities to prevent emancipatory
movements, and the limitation of foreign cultural influences for non-Rana
elites (Liechty 1997, p. 41). Jung Bahadur instated his brother Dhir Shamsher
Rana as the governor of Bhaktapur.

The Condition of the Farmers Under the Rana

During the years of the Rana regime, Newar farmers endured an extremely
difficult life. While *jyāpu* people living in villages sometimes owned land and
enjoyed a somewhat higher social status (Toffin 2016, p. 122), in the Newar
cities of the Kathmandu Valley they lived in arduous conditions, strangled
in the previously described caste-based feudal-like system. In Bhaktapur,
the rental price of land was not regulated, and it was based on agreements
between the landowners and the tenants, generally set at half of the produced crops (Hachhethu 2007, p. 78). There was a 25 percent interest rate
per season applied for every four *pathi* of grain borrowed. In addition to this,
offerings had to be given to show deference to the owners in the form of
fruit, eggs, sweets, and butter (Rankin 2004, p. 108). In that period, taxa-
tion powers over the farmers and lower-caste people who rented lands for
their activities (such as the butchers, *kasai*) were granted to local function-
aries (such as the Brāhmans) "in exchange for administrative oversight and/
or political patronage" (Rankin 2004, p. 112). Farmers were often forced to

dig the pits to extract the clay soil (*kamka*) that was widely used as fertilizer in the Kathmandu Valley, and often remained trapped in the underground tunnels (see Raj 2010, p. 142). They were also expected to provide services for their landowners that were considered undesirable and of a subordinate nature, such as carrying lamps (*musyami*) during their funeral processions (Hachhethu 2007, p. 74).

During those years, farmers fell prey to moneylending at the hands of local merchants (*sau*). Having earned fortunes in Tibet (Rankin 2004, p. 105), merchants provided loans to people so that they could perform compulsory social and religious activities such as festivals, feasts, and marriages, and so that they could buy the white cloth necessary to cover the deceased for funeral rituals (Rankin 2004, p. 107). A Nepali saying, "*Newar bigranchha bhosle*" (lit: "the Newar is ruined by entertaining") (Fürer-Haimendorf 1956, p. 31), stresses the importance of performing feasts on special occasions as a way of maintaining one's reputation (*ijjat*) (see Rankin 2004, p. 120). Exploiting these needs, the merchants become richer and the farmers poorer year by year. Despite (and perhaps because of) the hardships they endured, Levy (1990, p. 64) suggests that the farmers came to develop class consciousness at a relatively slow pace. The next sections trace the emergence of these feelings of injustice and the establishment of ideals of rebellion and life betterment that challenged caste fixity. The fight came first from the intellectuals belonging to the upper-caste groups.

The Fall of the Regime

The foreign policy of closure to Western goods and knowledge during the Rana regime was largely motivated by the fear that the local people might rebel, a fear that grew with the expansion of the British colonial empire in India (Liechty 1997, p. 9).[12] However, after the death of Prithvi Narayan, the dream of total autonomy decayed, and Western materials and objects gradually became "important elements in the language of status and social rank in Kathmandu" (Liechty 2008, p. 42). Additionally, the Rana wanted to manipulate European influences to their own advantage. For example, while limiting education and banishing foreign teachers from schools was a primary tool of the Rana to maintain the status quo, at the same time Western education was seen as a desirable practice that could be used to pursue further the interests of the royal family (Sharma 1990, p. 3).

After a trip to England, inspired by the British education system, Jung Bahadur Rana founded the first school in Kathmandu (the Durbar High School), which only Rana children were allowed to attend. As noted by Bista (2020, p. 118): "From the beginning, there was an awareness of the potential of the educational system as an instrument of change, so that an attempt was made to control its effects by keeping the school under close scrutiny." In 1880, Ranoddip Singh Rana opened schools to the non-Rana children, including Newars, yet still restricted access to the higher-caste groups (Bista 2020, p. 119). Education in this school became a prerequisite for employment in government positions, contributing to limiting the advocacy power of the subaltern groups.

During those years, the Rana also repressed Newar language and literature and the work of Newar intellectuals. They saw the Newars as dangerous, "possible antagonists who might strangle them any time" (Shrestha 1999, p. 87). Nonetheless, Newar literature flourished through underground routes and embraced topics of social change and political awareness during what Shrestha (1999, p. 87) has defined as the "Nepal Bhasa literary renaissance age" (1899–1940). Among the writers who led this movement, Siddhidas Amatya discussed social issues and inequalities, including gender and caste-related discrimination, and the importance of education for social emancipation (Shrestha 1999, p. 88; Raj 2010).[13] Some young writers inspired by Siddhidas were persecuted, tortured, and hanged by the Rana regime. Others managed to escape and to continue their work from India where they came into contact with foreign literature and political ideas. In 1936, a group of Nepali intellectuals founded the Nepal Praja Parishad movement, which plotted against the Rana regime. During those years, King Tribhuvan (the descendent of Prithvi Narayan Shah who was being kept with his family in a state of captivity in his palace in Kathmandu) secretly supported the anti-Rana activities of the Praja Parishad (see Leuchtag 1958, p. 139). The leaders of the movement were arrested and sentenced to death in 1941.[14] The king then took refuge in the Indian embassy, from where he continued to support the making of a constitutional democracy.

Gradually, people started to act on their sense of injustice. Take for example this quote from the local revolutionary leader Caguthi (as reported in the account by Raj 2010, p. 71) when he heard the speech of a local intellectual who was harshly criticizing the taking of hay from the peasants in 1951: "I was flabbergasted [. . .]. We had been feeling a wound, but we could not say where. It was Sribahadur Dai who pointed the spot to us. I could not sleep that day. I felt overblown with excitement." As noted by Gibson (2013, p. 99), "this dawning consciousness transform[ed] Caguthi's view of peasant life," leading him to write: "I began to understand the tragedy of it all [. . .] my mother would wash the blood stained undergarments of [the landlord family's] female members [. . .] she could not imagine that there could be a different life to that" (Raj 2010, p. 123).

Eventually, following the success of the Indian independence movement, the Rana regime was overthrown in 1951 by a nationalist revolution led by educated people (including many of the upper-caste Newars who had been in exile in India) and some dissatisfied members of the regime itself. On the wave of these events, the Shah king was reinstated as the head of state. In the following years, upper-caste Newar intellectuals continued to play a crucial role in fostering the political awareness of the farmers and as such promoting social and political change. Soon after the fall of the regime, they founded an organization called Akhil Nepal Kisān Sangathan (ANKS, lit: All Nepal Peasant Organization) with the goal of defending the farmers' rights (Raj 2010, p. 71). This led to the establishment of the land reforms in 1964 that improved the condition of the *jyāpu* dramatically, as I will further explore in a moment. At the same time, while the initiatives of ANKS certainly played a role in influencing the political awareness of the farmers, Levy (1990, p. 64) asserts that the results of the land reforms slowed down their emancipation, having provided them with improved lives and having therefore mitigated their perception of injustice. In fact, while the farmers only gradually started to actively seek a mediation between old and new ideologies, the story of Ratna displays one such case of emancipation, showing that there were some who, on the wave of the land reforms, were already daring to change their profession less than ten years after the fall of the regime, and who imagined better lives for themselves and their families.

Becoming Middle Class

After ten years of mediations and increasing tensions between the monarchy and the government, King Tribhuvan Bir Bikram Shah passed away and was succeeded by his son King Mahendra (1955–1972) who in 1960 put an end to the democratic experiment, dismissing the government and establishing a one-party Panchayat system (1960–1990). The Panchayat banished all political parties and imposed exile on political dissidents, enforcing heavy censorship, while at the same time promoting several infrastructure projects and supporting the rhetoric of development. The latter was founded on the three pillars of the national identity, that is, Hindu religion, Nepali language, and monarchy, according to the "one nation, one language and one religion" policy (Shrestha 1999, p. 91). But the concurring initiatives of the intellectual-led communist parties and the growing grievance of the farmers were about to push for more concrete socioeconomic transformations.

The Land Reforms

In the early 1960s, a communist-led project promoted the cleaning of Bhaktapur at the hands of the local people. The absence of a sewer system and the disposal of garbage, excrement, and animal blood on the streets had not only given the city the reputation among other people in the country of being a "dirty city" (Dhakal and Pokharel 2005, p. 182), but it was also a plague on the people themselves, causing the spread of chronic diarrhea, gastroenteritis, and worms, often leading to malnutrition. Other diseases, such as measles and whooping cough, were fatal to children, especially in combination with malnutrition. Activities of sanitation were started in 1962 by Comrade Narayan Man Bijukchhe[15] during the Panchayat rule. His ultimate goal was to make people "aware of their real constraints and possibilities" (Dhakal and Pokharel 2005, p. 184).

These activities became a way for the farmers and intellectuals to meet and discuss current problems and pressing social issues. During the meetings for the *safai abhiyan* (lit: cleanliness campaigns), Bijukchhe and other members of the Youth League spoke to the farmers about their condition and about the need to react (Dhakal and Pokharel 2005, p. 184). Using these meetings strategically, the communists and the farmers led the Bharpai Āndolan (a movement through which they asked for a receipt of land tax from the landowners) and various protests for the reduction of the *kut* (the land tax to be paid to landowners). These movements eventually contributed to the establishment of the tenancy rights instituted by the Land Reform Act by the Nepali Congress in 1964 (Hachhethu 2007, p. 187), which included the *mohiyani hak* (a law granting tenants partial ownership of the land they were working on). The promulgation of land reform marked a significant improvement in the farmers' lives. It guaranteed tenant rights through legal registration and fixed the land rent at 23 *pathi* of *dhan* (paddy) per *ropani*.[16]

Figure 6. A blue bus covered with animal blood as an offering to the gods during Dashain.

Concomitantly, the ability of upper-caste people to secure their food in the form of offerings declined as the farmers started to sell their own produce.

Similar to Caguthi, the ideology of Ratna Prajapati was largely influenced by the ideas spread by communist groups. As Vishnu commented, Ratna brought him to the activities of ANKS, and it was thanks to the land reforms that he could own a produce surplus that he could sell, in this way making money that could be used to purchase the bus in 1970. Ten years after the land reforms, the initiatives and rhetoric of life betterment of a foreign initiative called the Bhaktapur Development Project (henceforth BDP)[17] contributed to establishing the ideological and socioeconomic ground for the affirmation of Vishnu and Devi's business.

The Rise of a Family

Also known as the German Project, the BDP was conducted in Bhaktapur between 1974 and 1986. With the slogan of "improving people's lives," a team of architects, anthropologists, and health care workers carried out a series of activities in the town, renovating buildings and monuments, and addressing pressing sanitation issues (see Haaland 1982). High rates of tuberculosis, child mortality, social discrimination, poverty, and poor hygienic conditions were identified as major areas of concern. The BDP built a drainage system, started paving the city roads, and provided individual households within the old town with the monetary support of 500 Nepali rupees to build private toilets. People were instructed about the link between sanitation and health after a BDP survey had revealed that more than 90 percent of the local population wanted to receive health education (Haaland 1982, p. 42). After concerted local requests, the BDP started involving local people in the second phase of activities. The local participation in the BDP was crucial for the structural changes that were about to come, and some of the core principles of the BDP were later embraced by the Bhaktapur Municipality (BM) itself.[18]

In the following years, possibilities for social mobility in association with a sense of injustice began to increase, particularly under the influence of local political parties and foreign initiatives. In 1975, Newar intellectuals introduced the communist Nepal Workers' and Peasants' Party (NWPP) in Bhaktapur.[19] This party had greater success among the *jyāpu* than ANKS, due to its support for equality and advocacy for tillers' rights, claiming land for the landless and a regulation of land taxes. Importantly, the communists did not stand for collective ownership, which would have lost them farmer support (Gellner 1997, p. 175).[20] The activities of the NWPP in conjunction with the land reforms enabled entrepreneurial farmers such as Ratna to gain access to capital and to begin to think about changing professions. While Ratna was not successful in leaving his transportation business to his son Vishnu due to the interference of his second wife, he was able to pass on to him his tenacity and outlook for a better life.

From being subaltern, ideas of well-being eventually became dominant among a middle class, as contemporary researchers (e.g., Liechty 2008; Pigg 1996; Zharkevich 2019; Sharma 2013) have been able to assess firsthand. These ideas added to growing desires for improved livelihoods that despite the isolationist effort were spread through the work of intellectuals in exile and political dissidents, in large part through the model of the upper-caste groups. Western materials and objects gradually became "important elements in the language of status and social rank in Kathmandu" (Liechty 2008, p. 42). Well-being desires among lower strata became unstoppable when economic conditions started to ameliorate.

For Vishnu, that sense of hope in his father's words had materialized in a glimpse of a brighter future, one that had allowed him to go to school even if for only a short time before his family fell apart. It had given him a sense of how hard work can lead to concrete results and, even if only for a moment, this feeling had started to shape his dreams and would guide his next moves. This was evident in Vishnu's own words:

> When I ran away from my stepmother at the age of thirteen and went to Patan, I met a distant relative who introduced me to a shopkeeper. The shopkeeper gave me a job as a seller in the shop and let me sleep there. It was a small grocery store, and the shopkeeper was an honest old woman. During those years, my dream became to open my own shop. After a few years, the shopkeeper started inviting me to her house for dinner. There I met Devi, her niece [he and his wife smile, then he continues the story].
>
> One night, I was sitting on the floor having my meal with the rest of the family, and she was serving the food to us. I looked at her and she was smiling at me and I thought that I liked her. We were from the same caste, Shrestha, so it was a good match [jata tu]. We did not talk much with each other, she was too busy helping her aunt to cook and serve dinner, and I was very hungry every evening, but our eyes were connected through the space of the kitchen. So I asked her aunt if she could help me as a mediator [lamē].
>
> After two months, we celebrated the wedding. There was not a wedding procession though, because we were poor. But we did not want to live in her aunt's house and wanted to be independent and to start our own family. So we moved back to Bhaktapur. But it took a while for our plans to come true, and lots of hard work [gahro kam].

Vishnu and Devi moved to Bhaktapur in 1978, four years after the BDP started its activities. Devi continued the story:

> It was a very difficult life. We rented a small house and started a tailoring activity. We made mainly topi [black Newar-style hats]. After the first two years, things started going bad. We had a baby girl who soon died, and the tailoring machine broke down. We changed business and began selling products on the street; it was only the two of us, and our small bamboo tray.

On the first day, we only had three pieces of candy and one cauliflower. On the second day, we had twenty small chocolates, two *pappadams* [thin bread], and two cauliflowers. We bought goods from wholesalers in the morning with credit and paid them back each evening. For the next five years, we added to the business roasted almonds and soybeans. We could roast and sell 35 kilos of almonds daily; I was always so hot and covered in sweat and smoke all day. We were struggling, feeling stressed and desperate through these years. During a tense period such as this, you talk to your own heart, you feel *mane-khanlhagu* [lit: "lonely heart talking"], you feel alone and do not see an escape. We were so desperate that we would sometimes act violently with each other [they look at each other and laugh]. Eventually, especially after having children, we were able to control these strong emotions.

One night, I had a dream. A bus stopped in front of Durbar Square, near the usual spot where we sold daily our goods. A woman got off the bus and came towards me, while I was sitting on the floor selling some almonds. She smiled at me and gave me a towel bag full of goods to sell. Soon afterwards, the business increased dramatically, and I became pregnant with our first son. After five years of profits and savings, we were able to rent a small shop and then eventually buy it. The woman in the dream was the incarnation of Indrayani. The help of Indrayani in addition to our hard work has been fundamental to the success of our business.

Vishnu and Devi's story demonstrates the belief in the possibility of attaining social mobility through hard work. It also shows that a narrative of agency can be in productive tension with preexisting religious beliefs. Because of Devi's dream, they have been devotedly worshipping the goddess Indrayani, and they believe that the circular bamboo tray on which they put their products (*hasa*) is a materialization of the goddess Indrayani herself. They keep the original tray that they used in their business hanging on the wall in their shop to remember their origins, and they pray to Indrayani during Dashain by worshipping the bamboo tray through the offering of coconuts. In the material form of the bamboo tray, they put together the pieces of their story of socioeconomic rise, thus combining the memory of hard work and the practice of devotion. Perduring religiosity could also be seen in Ratna's sacrifice to the bus performed for Dashain. Offerings (*prasad*) such as these are given on the ninth day of Dashain (*Maha Navami*) to the gods to protect those items that sustain a person's livelihood (in their case the truck and the tray). The object themselves are seen as gods and are associated with some specific gods or goddesses that are particularly important for a given family, although the main divinity worshipped on this day is Durga. During my research in Bhaktapur, I saw such offerings being given to the gods to protect trucks, cars, motorbikes, and schoolbooks. For children, schoolbooks are considered the vehicle for a better life through education.

Education can lead to social mobility and improved well-being by opening up a future of possibilities. As Vishnu and Devi commented, they are proud (*garva*) that they have achieved better well-being than what they had in the past, proud of having been able to buy a house and two shops, and to provide their children with a good education.

Vishnu and Devi's experience was nested in the context of increased economic and entrepreneurial possibilities. When Nepal was opened to political and economic relations with Western countries following the fall of the regime, international imports of products that were once only reserved for elites entered the market, and tourism began to increase. Occupations changed dramatically with the emergence of new needs and desires, and different professions started to be established on the wave of the rising tourism sector and other services. During those years, Vishnu and Devi were able to get credit from a local merchant and to repay him each day thanks to the increased demands for goods (including both vegetables and sweets that were becoming more popular). In turn, children's access to school was helped by improved economic conditions, which allowed them to take time off from working in the fields, shops, or as helping hands at home.

But achieving better lives also involves the experiencing of intense distress. Needing to save money, Jyāpu families such as that of Vishnu and Devi still had to make sacrifices and even younger informants remember times of hardship, including Vishnu and Devi's children. Their son Binod told me that they would only eat eggs on their respective birthdays and meat only a few times per year during annual occasions such as the Tihar festival. Children would be excited to go to their relatives' houses, when secret passages were opened up between adjacent buildings and all households became one: "Each house's food had a different taste and it was exciting to try it, while nowadays children have everything they want and no longer even want meat. And new clothes that were given only for festivals, they now tear them on purpose." In comparison with those years of struggle, as Vishnu's wife Devi told me, "these days it is a paradise" (*sworga*), even if their grown-up children still need to make sacrifices to maintain or further improve their middle-class status.

Dimensions of Class

Tertiarization and Aspiration

As outlined in the previous pages, the BDP was responsible for conducting activities of sanitation in the city, which dramatically improved people's life conditions and helped in reducing mortality rates. The BDP also provided the farmers with new agricultural technologies that significantly increased their productivity. Chemical fertilizers, improved seeds (*bikāśe*), and machinery (such as threshing machines, hand tractors, and rice mills) were at first given to the farmers for free.[21] Initially, new agricultural techniques led to a productivity boom and to the beginning of a centralized money economy. That is, when the farmers owned a surplus, they could sell their own vegetables and gain monetary capital through which they could invest in new businesses and in their children's education. But over the years, the farmers needed increasingly more money to sustain productivity and fulfill other economic demands. When productivity increased, they needed cash to buy more fertilizers on which they became dependent. They also needed cash to rent machinery to sustain market competition and to pay for service workers.[22] This increasing demand for money could not be sustained solely by agricultural activities when productivity eventually started to slow down. This happened for several concatenated reasons. The new improved seeds became unproductive as they were not resistant to drought and insects. This was followed by an increase in the use of pesticides and chemical fertilizers. This in turn impoverished much of the land of important nutrients, making it acidic and thus less productive (Haaland 1982, p. 25). Additionally, the emerging trend of household fission into small nuclear families in some cases made farms too small to maintain both subsistence and income.

Agricultural unproductivity led many people to abandon the farms altogether. When these issues led to critical unproductivity, people started to sell their plots, which were widely used for building new houses or for brick factories.[23] However, as noted by Ishii (1980, p. 168), this transition was not clear-cut at first, and men who went to work in Kathmandu (which had quickly become the business district hosting shops and offices) left their

Figure 7. Election campaign in Taumadhi Square in 1991 (Gutschow 2017, p. 41).

elders and women to work on the small plots of land. Besides agriculture, artisanal production also started diminishing dramatically, with the growth of competition from Chinese and Indian manufacturers that sold cheaper products. Additionally, in the follow-up phases of the project implementation, the BDP supported local people in finding new jobs, strengthening their construction skills, and encouraging the creation of small businesses such as women-led cooperatives and *thanka* painting shops.[24]

Favored by the agricultural boom and by the new jobs created by the BDP, including in construction and small businesses, and by selling their land, people from a *jyāpu* background could start financing their children's education with the ambition of obtaining "higher status" jobs. In fact, as noted by Hachhethu (2007, p. 77): "To get exposure to modernization through educational attainment or other means is an expensive process. For parents, it is not only a question of meeting the cost of tuition fees but also of having to bear the expense of other associated activities." At first, the *jyāpus* were inspired by the middle class of professionals that had arisen from the upper-caste Newars. Haaland (1982, p. 28) describes the "brain drain" to Kathmandu through a vivid image of the upper caste going to work, waiting at the bus stop in their high-heeled shoes and ties, an image that must have also entered the minds of the *jyāpu* people of the city. Similarly, Hachhethu (2007, p. 77) recalls the period in which his *jyāpu* friends actively started differentiating themselves from the *jyāpu* lifestyle and aesthetics by following the model of the upper-caste Newars: "educated *Jyāpus* were the catalyst in bringing about changes within the family that moved it away from the traditional inherited ways of doing things." In those years, children's access to school was helped by improved economic conditions, which allowed them to take time off from work in the fields or at home. Also, women's education and access to the workforce started to increase.[25] But new political turmoil was about to shake the country for the next two decades.

From the People's Movement to the Civil War

During the years of the Panchayat, "the gap between the government rhetoric of democracy and development and the reality of economic stagnation, ecological degradation and political opportunism, became ever wider" (Gellner 1997, p. 165).[26] This led to the establishment of the People's Movement (Jana Āndolan),[27] which in February 1990 started leading the Nepalese Revolution to force the king to accept constitutional reforms and to establish a multiparty democracy, eliminating the Panchayat system. The movement was created through a joint effort of the Nepal Congress and ten major communist factions united in the United Left Front (ULF). Strikes spread quickly around the country, and the smashing of a statue of King Mahendra by the protesters in November 1990 led to a violent response by the police. Among the protesters, the farmers of Bhaktapur were particularly angry about having received fewer economic opportunities from the government compared to the commercialized urban centers of the nearby cities Kathmandu and Lalitpur (Gellner 1997, p. 167).

The king eventually agreed to establish a new government of Nepal. While the events that had led to the fall of the Rana regime were directed prevalently by the work of upper-caste intellectuals, a young and educated middle class constituted the main new feature of this movement (Raeper & Hoftun 1992, p. 79). Having lived "long after the hierarchical and deferential days of the Rana" (Gellner 1997, p. 165), these youths were animated by different existential conditions from those of their parents and grandparents, and their ideas were largely shaped by media influence (Gellner 1997, p. 169).[28] While the movement received the support of Indian political parties and student groups, the participation of the farmers of Bhaktapur, Patan, and Kirtipur proved decisive (Gellner 1997, p. 166). Also, the role of female farmers was crucial in Nepal's political fight. This was possible due to the relative freedom of women belonging to lower-caste groups compared to their upper-caste counterparts (Gellner 1997, p. 170). According to some scholars (e.g., Tamang 2009), the fight for democracy also meant the beginning of women's political participation and awareness about social inequality within and outside of the household.[29]

Despite the initial success of the pro-democracy movements, the internal divisions among the various communist parties soon became evident. Some of them did not approve of the alliance of the ULF with the Congress in the Nepalese Revolution and started to envision a new democratic revolution. From this group of dissidents a more extremist fringe emerged, the Communist Party of Nepal (Maoist) (CPN-M), which wanted to abolish the newly formed government of Nepal (as well as the remaining monarchy) and establish a people's republic. In 1994, the CPN-M started violent demonstrations, which were soon opposed by the Royal Nepal Army. It was the beginning of the Nepal civil war, marked by massacres and purges, kidnapping and torturing of dissidents, and other crimes against humanity, causing over 17,000 deaths (Douglas 2005, p. 54).

In June 2001, during a family dinner party, King Birendra Bir Bikram Shah Dev and his family members were killed in a royal massacre. The king's brother Gyanendra Bir Bikram Shah Dev took up his role until 2008 when the interim parliament voted to abolish the monarchy and declared Nepal a federal republic.

In May 2005, a Seven Party Alliance (SPA) was formed, including the Nepali Congress, the Nepali Congress (Democratic), the Communist Party of Nepal (Unified Marxist-Leninist) (UML), the NWPP, the Nepal Goodwill Party, the ULF, and the People's Front. They joined the CPN-M against the king with a pact ensuring that the Maoist rebels would renounce using any more violence. One year later, the SPA and the CPN-M signed the Comprehensive Peace Accord, which put an end to the civil war and led to the election of a Constituent Assembly. In 2008, Nepal was declared a federal democratic republic with the victory of the Nepal Communist Party (NCP)[30] in the ensuing elections, and a new constitution was promulgated in September 2015.[31]

As a consequence of these events and of the transition to a federal republic and on the wave of the development of a free market and the growth of the private sector, Nepal became part of the global economy and of a competitive capitalist system. These transitions followed from a gradual transition from an agrarian society to a cash-based economy made possible by the "open door" policy (Liechty 2008, p. 47) initiated after 1951 by the Nepali state, which facilitated unregulated commodity imports and exports, the introduction of international development money, the establishment of local and foreign investments, and new flows of cash through remittance and the growing tertiary sector with its orientation on services and tourism. As suggested by Fujikura (1996), a transition from a feudal rule to a modern bureaucracy was in fact often the result of a need to channel flowing cash introduced by foreign aid. It was through the affirmation of new economic possibilities and ideas of life improvement, which gradually become dominant throughout the historical process seen so far, that the modern middle class could finally emerge with its "shifting registers of social value and prestige" (Liechty 2008, p. 47), which were dictated by the example of consumption practices of the upper strata as well as an idealized as much as dreaded "Western style."

Despite the emergence of private hospitals, schools, industries, banks, and small businesses, the corruption of companies in association with political powers and the concurring lack of government support and start-ups increased the gap between rich and poor, and only benefited a handful of wealthier people. Additionally, while historical conditions following the fall of the Rana regime had enhanced local aspirations and the possibility of establishing businesses and other entrepreneurial endeavors, more recent historical events, such as the Maoist insurrection, the civil war, and the resistance to investing in the agricultural sector (due to historically engrained stigma attached to farming and the concomitant emergence of new professional ambitions),[32] created the conditions for a state of economic precariousness experienced by a modern middle class (as I discussed in more detail in Chapter 1). As noted by Liechty (2008, p. 51), "it is this kind of local monetary economy—where cash is relatively plentiful and opportunities for investment limited—that serves as backdrop for the cultural economies and social formation" of present-day Nepal. This generates anxiety and a sense of vulnerability in the growing middle class. This was evident in the reflections expressed by Vishnu and Devi's son Binod and his wife Beena.

Figure 8. Dog, sheep, and motorbike in a street of Khauma.

Binod and Beena studied business at Tribhuvan University in Kath-mandu and now manage a shop near the Siddha Pokhari pond on the out-skirts of Bhaktapur. They told me about a sense of insecurity in maintaining the better lives that they have thus far achieved in comparison with the lives of their parents, and the difficulty they face in improving their social and economic standing further. Binod commented: "While we run a reasonably successful business, we still feel like we are on a precipice. Educating our children is expensive and it is difficult to get ahead. We are better off than many people that we know, but we could still lose everything quickly. We are relying on our business going well and we have no safety net." The per-spectives of several other informants revealed similar perceptions about the reality of middle-classness as a condition of precarity. These reflections speak to a broader experience of middle-classness in Nepal. Other informants, for example, discussed how easy it is to have a business fail, to become poor, or to lose one's house. As revealed by the comments by Binod and Beena and by the reflections of many others, it appears that a combined perception of aspiration and vulnerability frames a middle-class existential perspective in contemporary times.

Negotiating a Modern Dharma

Based on the stories of the people of Bhaktapur and through the sourcing of historical material, in the previous pages I traced a social history of the idea of a "good life" or "better life," using my informants' terminology, and I unpacked its importance in the emergence of a middle class in Nepal. As a consequence of the historical evolutions outlined, ideas of life betterment continually circulated through various avenues, and the education of children progressively became a moral duty of middle-class parents and the way *par excellence* to attain good lives. In turn, the possibility of acquiring and spending cash started creating new needs and supporting consumer desires in Bhaktapur, influencing domestic moralities. Gradually, ideas began circulating, no longer just through books, but also through the emerging media world, which spreads ideals of a Westernized lifestyle (see, e.g., Liechty 2008) and development discourses (Pigg 1992) by which well-being would be a right of all people and should be pursued by fulfilling one's own desires. Visual landscapes of development pushed by the media play a role in shaping local discourses of well-being. Advertisements of private education in the United States, Australia, and Canada feature on most buildings in Kathmandu, contributing to building new perceived parental responsibilities and new imaginaries in children's eyes.[33]

While we do not know what people thought in the past (whether they were resigned or not, were silently dissident, or even agreed with the status quo), we know that there were strong limitations to enabling one's well-being through socioeconomic advancements such as job change and educational pursuit. Unorthodox behavior was sanctioned by the law and religious institutions with fines, imprisonment, and physical or social death. Today, social mobility is possible. Ideas of life betterment are more diverse due to the influx of media messages with their power to instill desires through their many channels, and they are portrayed and perceived as attainable due to improved livelihoods. In this context, economic possibilities are mainly bounded by class discourses and practices rather than caste-based limitations.

The desire for improved well-being, both in terms of tangible living conditions and of greater autonomy in pursuing one's future in terms of job choice, spousal relationships, and family structures, creates complex webs of desires and expectations, which in turn generates domestic conflicts in the process of redefining dharma itself. Navigating these sometimes contradictory pressures and ideologies can be a challenge, and making adaptations often leads to conflict in one form or another, whether within or between households, family members, friends, and the like.

If, as suggested by Appadurai (1996, p. 3), the media "offer new resources and new disciplines for the construction of imagined selves and imagined worlds," one could wonder what selves and what worlds are being imagined and enacted in Bhaktapur. While, as I introduced in Chapter 1, a notion of well-being has always been a part of dharma, its meaning has now changed vis-à-vis the new possibilities that make old hierarchies crumble and new social categories rise and center their own well-being. This is because different karmas, as personal destinies, are now allowed. In fact, nowadays, karma is seen as something that can be found, achieved, built, and transformed within one's lifetime, much like the story of the young son of the merchant with which I opened this book. Yet this has to be done through intersubjective processes within which individuals make sure that they are attuned to dharma and fulfill their own goals while maintaining connections with others.

In other words, while there are more possibilities for people to achieve their desired lives in terms of logistics, economic opportunities, and better access to education and health care, these new possibilities generate clashes with the old ideologies perpetrated for centuries, and people still fear—as will become evident in the next chapters—being judged badly by "society" and incurring social death. Harsh conflicts arise within families about how each individual should act, and these intersubjective processes ultimately lead to new definitions of the very notion of well-being, its goals, its means of attainment, and the factoring of family needs. All of these issues are situated in a larger context of economic precarity and of capitalistic logics and competition dynamics, through which services and commodities are measured and compared for their potential to provide better lives. For example, private schools are considered superior to public schools and only the wealthier or those who sacrifice other expenses (such as those for annual religious festivals, funerals and marriages, and *guthi* fees, among others) can access them. This paradoxical situation in which the economic potential of each individual has improved and yet faces significant precarity is one of the main features of the Nepali middle class. In this complicated lifeworld, individuals have to navigate among their own desires and those of others; face the dilemmas posed by clashing needs and moral frameworks with their often dissonant values; and find ways to maintain economic stability while also pursuing unnegotiable priorities. For example, providing education in the pursuit of an improved life is understood by many parents as a shared project, and it is expected that it will be the children's responsibility to cooperate with their parents' efforts (see Chapter 7). Ideas and practices of well-being involve both personal desires and relational duties, where the latter are being redefined within old and new moral codes.

From the following chapter, I will begin to explore the motivations and actions that are shaping, reinforcing, or breaking down relationships (particularly those within households and family units) in the name of well-being. I will start by looking at parent-child and child-peer relationships, examining what emotions and relational strategies are employed to negotiate divergences and affinities. I begin by describing the mundane occasion of a birthday party and its contestation, to start unpacking different priorities among family members, and to discuss how people deal with these in ways that influence their moral selves. As this book in its entirety will demonstrate, while the family remains central in the construction of a local moral world, a modern dharma needs to be defined for well-being to be attained and domestic harmony preserved. In this balance lies the making of moral personhood.

CHAPTER 3

Parent-Child and Child-Peer Dimensions
of Friendship: Making Moral Selves
Between "Advanceness" and "Shame"

A Contested Birthday

On a winter day at sunrise, a man in his forties named Dor Bahadur Bhakta was jogging in white clothes[1] around the Siddha Pokhari pond on the outskirts of Bhaktapur's old town. Josh and I had met him before; we often chatted with him after our morning jogs while drinking a glass of aloe vera bought from a street vendor. After his run, when the usual early morning fog had been replaced by the sun, Dor Bahadur generally would go back home to get ready for work. On that day he was off duty, and he invited us to his house for breakfast. While he was boiling some water in his kitchen, his teenage daughter passed by to grab a snack before going to school. Just before leaving, she casually said: "Bye, dad. Vishnu and I won't be at home for dinner this evening. We will go to the cinema with our friends, and we were also thinking of having a cake later on. . . . You know it's Vishnu's birthday tomorrow."

"What?" Dor Bahadur snapped out of surprise. "You know that we are in a mourning period! You cannot throw parties in our house!" The daughter rolled her eyes with impatience and replied: "Yes, I know, but we'll go to *paju*'s [maternal uncle] house. I have also bought a present for Vishnu with my savings, it is our birthday tradition and—" "Enough!" he yelled again. "I don't want to know anything about this present, bye now!" The girl left the house, and Dor Bahadur recomposed himself and served us tea, while explaining: "You see, I am a modern father and I treat my children as friends. I believe that since they are about sixteen, children start to be able to think with their mind and make good and wise points. So we need to listen to them and have mutual understanding, and consider each other's point of view as *pāsā-pāsā.*" When using the term *pāsā-pāsā,* Dor Bahadur performed a gesture that I had seen before when talking to local people in Bhaktapur. He first moved his hand right and then slightly left with the palm facing down, each of the two movements accompanying one of the two repeated words, "*pāsā*" and "*pāsā.*" Repeating a word two times is a common way in Newari to express the resemblance of two things.[2] In this case, through the repetition of both word and gesture, local people stress the equality of the relationship between parents and children.

"But ...," Dor Bahadur continued gravely, "even if we are like friends, there are things that are unacceptable, such as this."

Dor Bahadur could not accept that his son Vishnu celebrated his birthday in their house that year because they were in a mourning period following the death of the paternal grandmother a few days before.[3] Local people say that attending a ceremony during a mourning period is considered improper (*anuchit*), let alone organizing a party and sharing gifts. Yet, for Dor Bahadur's children, celebrating the birthday mattered a great deal, enough to act against the conventions. In the end, Vishnu shared a cake with some friends at the house of his maternal uncle. This kind of behavior is not contemplated within preexisting norms, posing a dilemma for the whole household. In a sense, the role of the maternal uncle in spoiling and nurturing a child as opposed to the strict control of the father is somewhat expected in Newar society (Levy 1990, p. 126). At the same time, something like this would have been unlikely to have happened ten to twenty years ago due to rigid control over mourning social norms and to the fact that Western-style birthday celebrations have only become popular over the last ten years (N. Gutschow 2021, personal communication, June 7).

During a later interview with both the parents, Dor Bahadur's wife, Tika, explained that they did not even want to know what the birthday gift bought by their daughter for their son was, "because it is not proper to give presents during a mourning period" and, differently from the previous years, they did not provide any presents themselves. Despite these decisive incompatibilities, after this first incident in the kitchen, both the parents and their children did not argue openly about this issue, treating it instead as a taboo. This situation was thus prevented from escalating through the avoidance of dialogue. Considering that the daughter willingly brought up the topic, it appears that she was interested in negotiating on this issue; however, her father quickly blocked her attempt. Nevertheless, while he was openly angry at the circumstances, he did not go so far as to forbid his children from celebrating the occasion altogether, and he did not discuss the matter with his brother-in-law.

This story sums up a recurrent theme that I encountered when researching parent-child relationships in Bhaktapur, that is to say an ongoing reflection on the boundaries of acceptability within the sphere of domestic moralities and on the relational dimensions of the making of moral selves. What does being friends with one's own child mean among middle-class Bhaktapurian parents and why does it matter? And if, as Dor Bahadur said, friendship means the reciprocal sharing of individual points of view, what are parents and their young children willing to negotiate to maintain kinship in the reciprocal pursuit of well-being, and why is confrontation often avoided? These are some of the questions that guide this chapter. These need to be addressed in the framework of colliding temporal values whose clash leads to moral breakdowns. In a context of accelerated social change, the making of moral identity for both young people and their parents involves the problematization of old and new norms.

As I introduced in Chapter 2, domestic relationships are traditionally based on a strict hierarchy, and in turn the domestic cosmos itself is the central sphere where the social order is scrutinized and implemented. In principle, authority is held by the oldest man of the family, at least until he is able to work and provide for the family. The oldest woman too holds a central place in the domestic hierarchy, controlling the movements of the younger women (the wives of her sons) in the household. The relationship between parents and children is thus of a "vertical" type, using a notion by Srinivas (1976). Father-son and mother-son dynamics differ, for a father is generally harsher and more distant from a son and a mother more nurturing and more demanding of a son's attention and devotion, also after his marriage. The relationship with daughters is generally more relaxed for both parents.

Nowadays, with the emergence of nuclear families and with the delay of age of marriage and establishment of middle-class lifestyles, new clashes are emerging as parents and children have to navigate different problems as well as different possibilities from what previous generations of families experienced. Their conflicts and adjustments involve a revision of the basis of their

relationship, as well as a negotiation of their life plans and a broader reconsideration of societal values at large.

Conversations with people (both parents and young adults) revealed that
ongoing discordance between parents and children coalesces around discordant ideas of well-being. Parents widely consider themselves to be guides for
their children in the process of seeking a moral balance between new values
and preexisting social and religious beliefs and practices, ultimately helping
them to attain well-being for themselves and the whole family. Many called
themselves "friends" to their children, thus enabling them to "open their
heart" and embrace advanceness rather than "hesitate" to express themselves
due to a feeling of shame (lajjā). Yet, parents were also very firm in defining
what they expect their children to do. This involved achieving socioeconomic
improvements for the whole household and respecting social and religious
norms. On their side, children understood their parents' perspective and
appreciated their efforts, but had a different idea of well-being, which was
articulated in terms of "emotional happiness" and "emotional well-being."
Among ideas of emotional happiness, a great space was dedicated by young
informants to the discussion of intimate relationships as an important path
toward improved well-being, and yet it was an area of confusion and lack of
direction. Nonetheless, the youth hid their moral doubts from their parents
due to a feeling of shame and turned to their peers instead, who, as many said,
"think alike." The role of friends was considered essential by young people in
navigating moral ideas and defining a "stock of knowledge" (Schutz 1970)
around intimate matters. This was counterbalanced by parents' unwillingness
to discuss these issues with them, instead only giving space to other priorities
and topics of discussion.

By examining how parent-child and child-peer relations play a role in the
making of moral selves through articulations of aspirations and fears, this
chapter contributes to the broad aim of this book by presenting the relational
dialogues through which modern moral selves evolve. It shows how different,
converging, contested, shared, or hidden ideas of well-being circulate and are
negotiated between these social actors. These findings contribute to Liechty's
scholarship on the making of a moral middle in Kathmandu by highlighting
changing understandings of the roles of parents and ideal parent-child relationships and how these affect the making of moral selves. This chapter is
complementary to Chapter 4, where I will explore how new crises arise on the
occasion of marriage, where parents and children negotiate traits of a Newar
ethos in the name of their emotional well-being.

Spoiling Children

Anthropologists and historians have long since demonstrated that notions of childhood and youth are the result of cultural constructions and as such are treated differently across societies and time.[4] The Newar people of Bhaktapur are no exception in this process of reflection on the appropriate treatment that should be given to children at various stages of life.[5] My informants recurrently stressed the role of parents in guiding their children toward the "right balance" as well as fostering their moral agency. A discussion with our local friend Dilip started to clarify some of these aspects.

When he joined us on the rooftop terrace, Dilip was holding his grandson, a baby who had no official name yet because of his young age, so they temporarily called him Hiraa (diamond).[6] While the baby was playing under a bamboo shelter, I asked Dilip about what the difference was, in his opinion, between children and grown-up people. He replied:

> Young children [bacchā] need more love than grown-up people [vayaska] due to their innocence [nirdōsta], which makes them vulnerable [āsurakshit]. Because they don't understand [bujhāunos, lit: don't know and understand], it is all right to pamper [pulpulyaunu] them.

His idea resonated with what several other people told me, and it was associated with the belief that parents should be more permissive toward young children than toward teenagers, who should already be further along the path to full maturity. Many commented that this is a major difference from the past. For example, an older woman reflected upon her grandchildren's attitudes and commented on how children were treated when she was younger, with an emphasis on food practices:[7]

> My grandchildren make me angry [uthalaputhala, lit: "upside down"] as they are fussy [sokhin] and do not want to eat biscuits that have already been opened the day before. They request a new pack of biscuits every day. So we scold them, and tell them that in our time we had to make many sacrifices. Now the economic situation has improved and more can be given and so the parents give more. We gave love to our children too, but the food that we gave to them was very different. In the past, we could only afford meat once per month.

Now they eat it every day. In the past we were so poor that we only
had maize. We had to chew the maize to make it softer before giving
it to the children.

The comment of this woman also reveals an attempt to make the children
understand the value of things (in this case food) by stressing the sacrifices
that they had to make in the past and that have allowed them to obtain the
lifestyle that they enjoy today. Dilip's comment confirmed these themes by
stressing the role of the media and other influences in shaping children's
desires:

Children are pestering [jiddī] because they want the things that they
see on TV or from their friends at school, such as sweets and toys,
and parents spoil them as a consequence. This is a big transition
from the past, when such behavior was not tolerated and children
were scolded or spanked.

Comparing with the past is a common practice among local people based on
both personal experiences and the comments of the elders. Yet, most of these
people are from the Jyāpu background and therefore their experiences of the
past need to be understood as caste-specific. Among the farmers, children
started to work from an early age (Onta-Bhatta 2001, p. 246),[8] in some cases
well before their initiation to adulthood, while they were often more spoiled
and nurtured among the upper castes (see, e.g., Lewis 1989).[9]

Broadly, these days middle-class children are expected, at least in principle, to be treated according to a "modern model, in which children need to
be protected" (Snellinger 2013, p. 77) and spoiled. This means that parents
are more "friendly," as my informants said, and pamper their children as
much as they can. It seems to me that because children "do not understand,"
that is, they are not fully aware of the social and moral world, parents feel
comfortable, and also in a sense required, to spoil them without fear that
they will become immoral adults. This is considered the first dimension of
friendship.

Nonetheless, economic considerations are also made, and some parents
would not tolerate insistence when requests are considered beyond their possibilities. As I could see and as many said, some parents would give harsh
lecturing, slaps, or other forms of punishment should the children insist.
Some parents tell their children that if they misbehave they will be reborn

in a lower-caste status. Children are also expected to fulfill some responsibilities, particularly related to school activities. In fact, emphasis was put by parents on education as a commodity that is offered to the children in order to provide them with better future lives. This emerged, for example, in the comment of a forty-year-old father, who said:

> In the past, families were very poor, there were no facilities, and there was a lack of money, so families didn't allow their children to study. The time of difficulties [*kaṭhināiharū*] has now passed, so now we can enjoy and give more education to the children to make them suffer less than what we did and help them to stand on their feet [*afno khuttama ubhinu*].

Seen as necessary to attain better futures, education is considered a nonnegotiable matter and parents do lecture their children if they do not do their homework or go to school.[10]

From puberty onward, children start to be considered independent moral agents and more expectations are placed on them as they become "able to understand," as many people said.[11] A thirty-nine-year-old man reflected on these transitions, and while criticizing his children's lack of understanding about the value of hard work, he also stressed that they would understand "in the future":

> My children do not care if I get annoyed at them when they do bad things. They simply do not listen. They lack practical experience in everyday activities. They do not understand the value of things. For example, they do not understand the hard work [*dhāvanti dhāwanti*] that is required for them to have the things that they own. How did the water arrive in their house? Or how a plant came to be in the house? They do not understand that the dirt in the pot has to come from the countryside. However, when they have issues in the future, they will finally understand the things that their parents tried to teach them.

"Understanding" is only possible according to the maturity of the *dimāg* (that dimension of the self involving the brain-mind connection), a local priest (*purohit*) told me. The *dimāg* of children is considered immature (*aparipakwo*) and therefore they are not seen and treated as moral agents.[12] When very young, children are considered to not have mutual understanding and empathy for the world of adults and their struggles toward life improvement. As I will show, however, their existential perspectives eventually diverge as they embrace and experience new imaginaries and ranges of the possible.

Before growing up and empathizing with their own parents' existential condition of struggle, there is a phase of negotiation. This involves the maturation of the youth, which is said to occur under the strict guidance of their parents. When children start to grow up and are gradually treated as moral agents, the idea of friendship changes as well, creating a very specific and nuanced dimension of parent-child mutual understanding. In the past, maturation was marked decisively by life passage rituals, while now it also involves the intersubjective shaping of the very idea of modern youth itself.

The "Maturation" of Children

Rites of Passage

Several scholars of Newar society have stressed the importance of rites of passage in the making of moral adults (see Allen 1982; Vergati 1982; Emmrich 2014; Gutschow and Michaels 2008; Toffin 1975; Parish 1994). According to traditional beliefs, rituals of puberty mark the loss of innocence and the transition to a full social personhood (Parish 1994, p. 247). For boys, the first of these rituals is *chudakarma*, which involves the first shaving of the head between the ages of five and nine. The second is *bratabanda*, performed between the ages of ten and twelve. During *bratabanda*, boys are given their first pair of underwear in the form of a loincloth (*kaeta*). Through this ritual, they become full members of their fathers' clan and caste. There is a moral transition occurring here, which includes establishing shame of the boy's body, where the loincloth symbolizes sexual restraint (Parish 1994, p. 256). Shame is a relatively new moral emotion for the growing-up child. From that point onward, young boys will be expected to treat others according to social conventions, particularly demonstrating respect to the elders and observing caste distinctions (see Parish 1994, p. 249; Gutschow and Michaels 2008, p. 57).

Rites of passage for girls include two ritual marriages, which precede a marriage with a human being. The first is *ihi*, performed between the ages of five and eight, which is a collective celebration marking the marriage to the god Vishnu Narayan, symbolized by a bel fruit. The second is *bahrā*, which is performed just before (or right at the beginning) of the first menarche, and which involves confinement in a dark room. The isolation ends with the symbolic marriage to Surya, the sun (see Gutschow and Michaels 2008, p. 93). Originally, the confinement would last twelve days, but I found that for most families this is now limited to one to three days due to school commitments. While spending these days in her room, a girl is told how to become a good grown-up woman by the other women of the house. This instruction includes how to take care of her own appearance and health, about hygienic practices, how to put on makeup appropriately, and how to use oils and creams. She is also told how to talk and behave toward the elders in order to show respect, and to be more careful of the things she says and does in public, that is, demonstrating a sense of self-control (*lajjā*). The topics of discussion and the manners through which such knowledge is passed vary from family to family and have been modified over the years to adjust to new needs. For example, Sabita, a forty-two-year-old woman, commented that when she was a child the women of her house told her not to talk to boys outside of the family and never to leave the house alone, otherwise she would "look bad":

> We taught very different things to my daughter. She goes to school, she has to learn how to talk to anyone, and while she needs to be polite [*mijāsi*], she also has to be balanced, because girls nowadays can be vulgar if they only follow the magazines. You can see groups of girls looking and making calls to boys around the pond; sometimes girls are more advanced than boys. We explained to my daughter how to avoid looking vulgar, and this is by following the right goals. For example, if you want to have a good marriage, it is better not to act in a superficial way. But since she first will have to finish her studies and get a job of her own, it is also good to postpone these problems for later. So there is less need to talk about intimate matters to girls nowadays, because these are problems of the future. I mean dating, marriage, fertility aspects. All these aspects come later in their life, otherwise their future life will not be good. In the past, girls and boys got married early after puberty rituals, especially two generations ago, but now they can do these things later and dedicate themselves to other things first, such as getting an education and finding a good job.

As noted by Sabita, the social role of young unmarried people has radically changed from fifty years ago. On the one hand, they are still deemed responsible (at least in principle and whenever possible and required) for respecting caste distinctions (Hachhethu 2007, pp. 73–74), and are requested to follow specific rules of pollution (Gutschow and Michaels 2008, p. 57). On the other hand, following the rituals boys and girls are no longer immediately treated as adults (*vayaska*) in terms of domestic roles, which in the past would have involved getting married and starting their gradual path toward the *Grihastha dharma*, that is, becoming householders. They generally live with their parents until much later without marrying, often until their late twenties or early thirties. Marriage is generally delayed until they have completed higher education and/or found a "good" job (see also Liechty 2008, p. 211) in order to enhance the socioeconomic status of the whole family. A man commented:

> Nepali youth is becoming similar to Western youth, but there are
> some differences. In the Western world when children are sixteen
> they start being independent and go to live on their own. Here
> people take more time to become mature before being independent.

The notion of "maturation" of the children recurred among my informants. It is in this phase that "understanding" becomes possible, and therefore moral guidance is essential to carve the *dimāg* to meet social expectations. This parental perspective resonates with what was found by Collier (1997, p. 153) in her research on changing domestic relationships in Spain. She noted that children are considered locally to be "parental projects." Similarly, among parents in Bhaktapur, children are perceived as being in need of guidance to achieve preestablished life plans.

During these years of cohabitation between parents and young unmarried adults, expectations remain that the children will establish their professional career and start thinking about having an appropriate marriage. This is a crucial matter in the family that will be examined in Chapter 4. During these years, young people are also exposed to alternative moral systems and ideas (for example, the magazines mentioned by Sabita and peer influences) that contribute to shaping ideals of well-being, but also to fostering a sense of discomfort and shyness (*lajjā*) when going against the will and expectations of their parents.

Parental Guidance and Control

The concept of "youth" is generally described in Bhaktapur as a phase of life occurring gradually after childhood in which there is a strong will for freedom that would generate a sense of "advanceness." Through this newly coined Neplish term, my informants described a disposition for change and an attraction toward "Western influences." On the one hand, people provided several examples of how they often learn from their growing children, particularly about "modern matters," for example in the areas of finance and education. On the other hand, while the youth's will for freedom is seen as a push toward cultural creativity, which can benefit the whole family, it is also described as a potential path to immorality that could cause various ills such as the decline of traditional values or the loss of social status (with the extreme consequence of the breakdown of kinship relations). For example, a man commented negatively about seeing his neighbor's teenage children going to a local cinema instead of going to school. He claimed: "The problem is that their parents do not control them enough!" Like this man, several people commented that young people need to be "controlled" regarding the choices that they make.

Informants often compared teenagers and young adults to a plant that needs to be nurtured to grow well. A middle-aged female farmer used the expression "*hune biruwa ko chillo pat*," which means "to fertilize the children like a plant to make them grow in a good way." In other words, while parents are not entirely opposed to the ideological changes occurring around them, they are concerned about helping their children to find the appropriate balance to become "good persons." When I asked people what they mean by a "good person" they usually told me that this means becoming a respectable member of society by both observing the cultural and religious requirements of a moral Newar (e.g., supporting rituals and festival expenses) and fulfilling new expectations (e.g., obtaining a good job that earns enough money to be able to finance their own children's education and to support their aging parents). Differently, from their perspective young people talked about money as that commodity that will enable them "to enjoy themselves" and fulfill their own private desires, as I will discuss in a while.

In parents' own words, to make a "moral" or "good" person (*rāmro mānche*) is the main responsibility of a "good parent" (*abhibāvaka*), and this is achieved through certain steps. In all cases, this first and foremost meant providing children with a good education, which was usually considered the main role of the father. Both boys and girls are educated and families work hard, whenever possible, to send their children to private schools that are considered better than public schools in terms of education and future possibilities. Second, parents felt responsible for passing on traditional moral norms to their children, such as respecting the elders, celebrating important religious domestic occasions (such as death rituals), and performing the *samskāra* steps. Socialization in the traditional Newar ethos (including rituals, religious and cultural norms, caste and social distinctions) has generally been described as the role of the mother. While these values are passed on to the children from an early age, the ways in which these are imparted change when they grow up and are considered ready to embrace more responsible behavior aimed at affirming a sense of balance and self-control. The role of parents thus is to guide their children to find the right balance between different ideas and practices.

To initiate their maturing children into this sense of balance, parents put more limits on their behavior and requests compared to when they were younger. This often involves controlling the acquisition of commodities in order to shape a sense of responsibility and respect for their parents' hard work. Other, stricter limitations are often put on social interactions outside of the household (including friendships and romantic relationships). As Sabita commented through the use of a common metaphor, "a fruit that ripens too early will ruin their future life, and will also appear inappropriate and vulgar." This controlling approach was demonstrated by most parents and shows their understanding of well-being as a gradual process of maturation in which certain values need to be prioritized over other interests.

The way in which parents communicate these values of balance to their growing children and restrict their behavior is, in their own words, not coercive, so the message is not conveyed by raising the tone of their voice or through violence, but through a dialogue in which they are "like friends." They call these "open talks," in which the two parties can speak their minds. It is a common idea that this is possible because the parents do not demand respect (*ādar*) in the old way, and therefore children have no hesitation (*hichkihaot*) as was common in the past. Many people gave examples of these open talks by referring to their chats during dinner. However, in almost all of the conflictual issues that I encountered during my research, parents did not hesitate to demonstrate anger regarding certain topics even if they often avoided additional confrontation. While this might be a way to avoid an escalation of such a conflict, this also means that, in practice, open talks and negotiations

Figure 9. A young man on his phone in front of Tribhuvan University, at the out-skirts of Kirtipur municipality.

can rarely occur, and dynamics of hierarchy and authority are reaffirmed. Thus, while many parents felt that they were having open discussions, in reality their children were acting to please them, were often suppressing their thoughts, and did not make any reference to many of the things that had happened to them on those days.

The contradictory and "controlling" approach by the parents contributes to an increasing sense of frustration in the youth, who instead conceptualized their situation as in need of "direction" rather than "instruction" in their path toward the making of their moral identities between feelings of advanceness and shame.

A Theater of Shadows

For Vishnu, the celebration of his eighteenth birthday was not up for discussion. He had been waiting for that day for the entire year. Usually, in the early morning before bringing him to school his parents would put a *tikā* on his forehead, would perform a small *pujā* by offering a lit lamp to Ganesh, and would serve Vishnu a small copper plate with a dry fish, a fried egg, a piece of ginger, and a goblet of curd (to substitute for alcohol as is commonly done for children).[13] They would also have a cake for dinner after school and would invite some relatives and schoolmates. In truth, as Vishnu explained, they did not buy a cake every year as this depended on what his father could afford at the time. This year, Vishnu knew that since his grandmother had just died, they would have skipped these traditions altogether. He was also expecting that they would not have allowed him to have a cake with his friends in his house. At the same time, he did not expect that they would have been so disappointed if he went to celebrate this occasion in another house, such as that of his maternal uncle. For how mundane, perhaps frivolous it might seem, celebrating his birthday was for Vishnu much more than a cake and some gifts:

> My birthday was the occasion to finally have fun and relax with my friends. Yes, grandma had died, but I still wanted to celebrate and did not see how this could impact the situation. Traditions are not always right, here it was about me, my birthday, and also my own friends . . . after so much study and stress during the year, we could finally meet up and enjoy ourselves. I don't think that it was disrespectful, it just seems unnecessary to skip something so important to me.

Vishnu's reflection reveals a self-reflective scrutiny of what was right and wrong. There are precise reasons why celebrations are not allowed in a mourning period. Festive occasions are considered dangerous because they can attract the spirit of the dead back to the house when they should be leaving for the afterworld. During a mourning phase, gifts in the form of food and previous belongings of the dead are only given to *purohits*, who will pass them to the deceased by enjoying them through ingestion or by using them as new items in their daily life. This is believed to be necessary to help the deceased to establish their own permanence in the afterlife.

While celebrating a birthday in another house in a sense overcame these issues, it still was a new behavior that created uneasiness in the parents, who therefore preferred not to know anything about it. In so doing, he allowed them to follow their own preferred line of action and to experience an alternative moral world from that of his own. This story is thus an example of how a dichotomy of perspectives is dealt with through avoidance as the preferred mode when individual needs strongly undermine the potential for an open agreement. Other stories of disagreement and avoidance that I collected recurrently revolved around certain personal desires, such as traveling with friends or buying a new motorbike, or else concerned contested attitudes toward others outside of the household (for example, seeing friends late at night or talking with them in an appropriate way in front of older people, consuming alcohol, and so on).

Like a theater of shadows, dynamics of avoidance often become a common reality during the years of maturation of the youth. From the perspective of the children, avoidance involves the establishment of alternative moral worlds in undercover dimensions, as I will discuss in the next sections.

Life Plans and Emotional Happiness

The young interviewees were also involved in an active reflection on becoming moral adults and seeking a sense of balance. They often mentioned the notion of "emotional happiness" as a crucial part of their ideal of well-being. This was described as being undermined by perceived pressures and anxiety around study and work responsibilities, and yet it was still seen as necessary to build a better future.

Those who had completed their studies or were looking for a job while studying recurrently referred to perceived pressures and responsibilities as a major cause of anxiety. Some expressed a sense of dissatisfaction when discussing how they had made choices about their study disciplines. They often had to sacrifice what they wanted to study and instead were forced to do what their parents considered more suitable for them or reputable in society. Rajit, a twenty-five-year-old university student who wanted to study fine art and instead studies architecture and works part-time in a restaurant, reflected on this aspect: "Many young people do not choose their study path, which is instead chosen by their parents. This might lead to conflicts with the parents, but more often children are submissive to their parents' choices in matters of study and job. After a few years, you realize that it is hard to find your real path." What Rajit calls a "real path" is in fact a quest for one's own self-construction that needs to be balanced with other economic considerations. Other informants referred to this quest in terms of "emotional well-being." For example, Shuvam, a twenty-six-year-old business student working in an office in Kathmandu commented: "I do not particularly enjoy studying, but I must be forceful in order to get a job. If you study, then you can have a good job. Then you can have enough money to buy what you want. But I also know that things are not everything and I do not know how to achieve emotional well-being. I wish I had more time for myself. I would like to go into nature. And adopt a healthier lifestyle, but I have no time to take care of myself." Alongside the widespread sense of uncertainty and of collision between different values and goals, there is also a sense of duty toward following the life path initiated by one's parents. This is due to both a sense of indebtedness for their efforts and as a necessary way to become economically independent and be able to achieve their personal desires. For example, for Shuvam being "forceful" is the only way he envisions to overcome his perceived struggle, which is taking time away from his deeper desires.

Both parental pressures and media messages can play a very important role in shaping the youth's imaginary and commitment to a life plan. For instance, watching vlogs[14] that track the daily life of both local and international personalities, such as influencer Logan Paul, is a very common practice among the youth that I encountered. These videos are often related to themes of success, to traveling, and to the making of "new experiences," as several people said. By skimming through YouTube, they select what they call "creative YouTube." This is based on their own judgment of what is good and desirable, which departs from what they call "copy-culture" attitude, that is, an unmediated approach to Western influences. By consciously selecting videos to consume, the youth demonstrate agency toward the media, although what is deemed interesting and desirable is itself often shaped by external ideas, particularly the influence of peers. This behavior is relevant insomuch as the practice was very common. Almost every informant aged twenty-five or younger mentioned that they at least occasionally watched these vlogs, and they usually justified it by an interest in discovering what they would like to achieve in life or what kind of lifestyle they wish to eventually obtain. Many of them watched them daily.

Often, desires instilled by the contents of the vlogs, such as traveling or purchasing expensive items, are unobtainable in the short term, especially when parents impose limits and priorities as discussed earlier. While it was often acknowledged that such commodities were not necessary for emotional happiness, it was evident that through the act of identifying their innermost desires, the youth of the city were actively crafting their own sense of personal and social identity.

For many, emotional happiness was strongly linked to themes of intimacy, romance, and sexuality, which were also recurrent in media content. This emerged as an area of great interest, and yet was usually discussed in terms of a lack of direction and strong moral doubt. Matters of intimacy and sexuality are particularly problematic as they are situated in between contrasting traditional discourses of partner avoidance and modern desires for romance and companionship. At the same time, modern ideas discussed among the youth themselves pass contradictory messages, with values of intimacy and exclusivity being counterbalanced by emerging "carnal economies" (Liechty 2005), of commodified food and sex. Following the spread of a capitalistic market, these factors contribute to the criticism by many parents of Westernized ideals of modernity. These contradictions were evident in a reflection made by Shuvam:

> I think it is taken as a taboo to talk about sex in our society with
> elders. It is something that elders and parents do not talk about
> and prefer to avoid any such talks with their children. This is one
> of the huge differences with Western culture. I think it is an open
> topic to talk in Western culture. People are open about sex and find
> it a casual thing in the Western countries. They even hug and kiss
> to greet each other, whereas here people find such activity as a bad
> influence in society. People might want to talk about it, but I think
> they suppress such talk. Elders and parents could find such things
> related to sex, and sexual queries offensive. In particular, this is the
> topic which is not talked about often within the family. But if we look
> into our ancient monuments and architecture, we can see carvings
> and sculptures with such representation. Maybe it should not be as
> open as it is in Western culture, but I think at least it should not be a
> taboo. But things are changing and with time these thinking patterns
> might change for good.

Shuvam shared here the perceived need to find a moral balance and expressed criticism of explicit sexual messages exaggerated in Western influences that are "too open." But on another hand, he believed that such matters "should not be a taboo as they are necessary for a person's well-being." There seems to be a problem of communication present here when parents avoid communication and children "suppress it," as Shuvam says, because they are not comfortable.

For both parents and children, discrepancies between ideas of what is right and wrong cause anxiety in relation to the emotions experienced in one's heart. This was often to the point that they questioned and reflected on their moral selves, on the righteousness of their feelings, and on the appropriate way to either vocalize or suffocate them. These differences were sometimes articulated in discourses of resentment. For example, take Rajit's comment, which while resonating with the reflection made by Shuvam, adds criticism to parents' attitudes: "When I will be a parent, I will make sure to let my children speak their mind." According to him:

> Good parents should provide the right environment for their
> children to have good mental health. This means ensuring a secure
> and open relationship in which problems can be talked about,
> suggestions made, and solutions found. But this is not common to
> see these days because parents and children have relationships of
> respect rather than friendship. It is true that parents do not beat their
> children like in past families, so this is a big change, but parents and
> children still are not like friends; and therefore children keep every-
> thing in their heart.

This perspective, which was in fact common among young interviewees, collides drastically with that of many parents whom I interviewed, who, as I discussed earlier, described themselves as "friends" with their children and believed that they did conduct such daily talks about their problems. In fact, in those same families where parents made efforts to talk to their children (as they told me and as I was able to witness firsthand), these talks had nothing in common with those that the same young people had with their own friends (including myself in some cases). In a sense, within joint families this type of confrontation between parents and children might be even harder to accomplish, but it does not seem to be much easier in smaller nuclear families either. This is despite an ongoing ideal that nuclear families would enhance intimacy (see Chapter 5). It appears as if topics and modes of conversation are shaped by a sense of what parents are willing to hear based on a pre-made script, an intersubjective ground that, while shifting toward a more open dynamic, seems hard to negotiate in practice.

Here the adoption of what moral and psychological anthropologists have called "opacity of minds" can be seen (see Robbins and Rumsey 2008; also Feinberg 2011). This takes the form of an active avoidance of both sharing one's private thoughts and making an effort to understand those of others. Several young people explained to me that this state of avoidance is due to both feelings of shame of doing something inappropriate and of guilt for one's parents' efforts and sacrifices to give them a better life. If they were to open up on certain issues it would be seen as if they lacked the expected *lajjā*. This notion is felt for both going against parents' ideals of domestic dharma, but also for engaging with topics that are considered taboo.

Sita, a twenty-five-year-old girl who is completing her master's degree in business, gave her view of why young people prefer not to share their suffering. According to her, "children should not create trouble, be respectful, and not upset the parents." She then noted that it is easier to share with the parents on social media than face to face: "Nowadays children are more free to decide about their life, but it takes many years to realize this in practice. Some prefer to share it on social media and this is good because they can have more interaction with their parents, while face to face they hesitate to share about their lives." Since confrontation is not direct here, parents do not need to respond and this makes avoidance easier, while the transmission of ideas and feelings can still occur. Some young informants told me that they received harsh comments from extended relatives on social media, while the parents can pretend not to have seen what could be considered controversial behavior in order to mediate their own relationships on both sides. This included the case study of a boy who shared a post about traveling to Australia (even though he knew that his parents were against the idea of him traveling), and of others who made frequent references to romantic movies (whose topics they would never share directly with their parents). This might be taken as a form of "half opacity," where confrontation is initiated but in a mediated and indirect way. Furthermore, the internet can be used as a space to answer questions or get feedback without the fear of being shamed. For example, Quora (a question-and-answer website) is used frequently for various questions by local youth. These include matters of intimacy and romance, for example on how to communicate messages to lovers or potential lovers without being disrespectful. Social media such as Facebook and other internet platforms such as Quora can be seen here as an alternative space of confrontation, as well as a place where a stock of information can be acquired in an anonymous way.

Several young informants said that they often seek support from their peers rather than from their parents. Only with good friends "one can open their heart," Shuvam commented. The expression of private feelings and ideas is deemed necessary to feel content, so trying to share with parents on social media or more often sharing with friends become necessary "to feel complete," said Sita. Here we can start to see how *lajjā*, as the sense of moral restraint and a negative emotion of not conforming, no longer necessarily leads to the suffocation of one's feelings and ideas as Parish (1994, p. 206) observed some thirty years ago, but rather to hiding them from their parents and sharing them with their peers. As children grow up, their interactions become a "private" matter from which parents are often excluded. As I discuss in the next section, what I shall call "public spaces of intimacy" become privileged venues where young people can experience the shaping of their moral selves in relation to their peers.

Public Spaces of Intimacy

It is common for young people from Bhaktapur to hang out in Kathmandu and vice versa, so that they can escape family control in a place where people do not know them and cannot judge them personally and report them to their parents. There are also several fast-food restaurants in Kathmandu that are used by many as a place where they can escape from daily stress. Coffee shops and fast-food restaurants are examples of what Oldenburg (2001) has called "third places," that is, spaces other than the household and the workplace. While also in the past there were restaurants (*bhatti*) and tea shops (*chiapasal*),[15] new social places allow for new social rules to be established. Here people are more anonymous, the cooks are often not known to the customers, and their caste background does not matter, as well as that of the customers who no longer have to wash their own dishes should they belong to a lower caste group as was the case in the past (see, e.g., Parish 1998). Also, people might attend these places in the more chaotic business district in Kathmandu where they are less likely to know other customers.

Birthday celebrations in popular cafes are an occasion for friends to gather.[16] A nineteen-year-old boy discussed how the practice of birthdays celebrations in his friend group started to change as they turned eighteen to avoid parents' involvement:

> When I was a child, we celebrated our birthdays at home and invited both relatives and friends. As we turned eighteen, we stopped celebrating our birthdays in our homes and we started going to cafes instead. Everybody does this. Even if our parents are friendly to us, we do this because we do not want our mothers to cook for so many

people and also we want to be able to say whatever we want without feeling worried [*dhurukka*] and shy [*lajjā*]. Furthermore, friends from different caste groups can participate outside of the home.

In these more anomic spaces, increased intimacy can be established for groups of friends of same or mixed gender, and for couples, as well as families with young children. For example, stressing the importance of public spaces of intimacy to share their problems, Shuvam commented:

> Young people go to cafes and talk with their friends about anything, which could be related to their family, other friends, or any other content. Some of the topics they might find more comfortable to talk about, which they wouldn't feel comfortable to talk [about] with parents, can include family problems, school/college/office issues, girls or girlfriend, health matters, and sexual queries.

Something similar was noted later on by Sita: "We might discuss private stuff, such as sentimental matters, or about conflict in our families, and we do not want to be heard by our parents or friends' parents. We are shy and don't want them to listen." By providing reciprocal support to each other, young people navigate and articulate their ideas while seeking a moral middle ground in several matters, such as those of love and intimacy. Friendships are also an important link to the development of actual romantic relationships. Several people discussed the help that they received from their friends in these matters, for example, finding a compatible partner or exchanging dating advice. Sita commented that she formed her ideas on how the right balance should be articulated in romantic matters by talking with her good friends:

> These days one has to be careful how they act because there is more freedom, but also you can be judged more harshly. It is very difficult to be a good person when you want to know more about becoming an adult, if you don't have some examples. For example, I think that marriage should be a personal choice, but I also have a friend that thinks this but she also does not want to upset her parents, so she says that caste matters are still important for her even if she is modern, because of her parents. So each person makes up their mind by considering several factors, but the thing is you should find the right balance. For example, I think that it is too early to go out on a date

when you are less than twenty, but after that I think it is normal, and
it is good so you know the other person better. I also get opinions
from boys who are good friends. One of my good friends says that
these things take time to fully develop, he has been in a relationship
for three years and then they broke up, so he says it is good that they
did not get married. At the same time, it is difficult to go on dates
without looking bad, and also you don't know what to say and how
to talk to them if you are not friends with each other yet. But I guess
everyone has their fears and also curiosity, so everyone just tries to
keep going and trying to be good while also being modern.

As this reflection demonstrates, "to be good" means to be accepted, to find
the right partner, to fit in the friendship group, and to not be judged badly by
society and by their families. Yet, to achieve this balance one needs guidance,
that is, what Sita calls "examples." This guidance is sought from those who are
in a similar state of mind. "Young people find it more comfortable to share
a lot of things with their friends who think alike," said Shuvam while sitting
with me alongside the pond. However, parents often demonstrate worries
over their children's relationships with their friends, and this is one of the
reasons why the youth hide these encounters in such public spaces of intimacy. As noted by Shuvam:

Young people prefer to meet in cafes and talk because people of the
same age group think alike and understand each other much better.
The same occurs with parents. They also have friends from their own
age group to share and talk with. But parents think that children are
too young and may not have the proper understanding of how things
work and so they could be taken advantage of or be given bad advice.

Along these lines, Rajit commented that parents are worried about the influence that friends can have on their children (which is a theme that I had
already encountered when talking with the parents):

They do not like their children having friends because they think
that their influence might change their behavior or thinking process. They are worried that friends could eventually drag them away
from the family's responsibilities by pushing ideas of modernity into
their minds. But this might be due to their lack of understanding

about their son's friends. The friend could be sincere and helpful but parents may not understand it in that way. This could be a different way of thinking from the parental perspective. But the son knows that he has an understanding friend. Also, the friend might be just pretending to be helpful and in fact be manipulating the son. So, in these cases a parent not wanting their son to be with that friend seems valid. In most cases, I think that parents believe that their son's friends are misleading and manipulative. This is probably the main reason why parents don't want their son to be with his friends.

He then made some considerations of these problems in terms of both a clash of points of view and a concomitant lack of communication:

These are the situations that appear if there is a lack of communication, understanding, and sharing between the parents and children, due to a different way of thinking. In some cases, parents may be right and in others their children. Basically, parents want their children to receive good influence and it is a valid point from their end. If a child has a good friend who has good influence in terms of behavior, thinking, and so on, then parents may not have any issues.

Friendships are also seen with suspicion by the elders of the family. According to Rajit, this is because "young people support ideas of modernity that do not suit the elders' points of view." Similar issues were encountered by his own parents against his grandmother: "The elders would like to control modern ideas, because they are scared, and that's why they don't like friendships." "What is it that they fear?" I asked, and he replied:

They are scared that friends will push their children and grandchildren away from them. They are scared of losing their youth, that they won't return home after traveling to another country, and that they will leave them alone. They worry that nobody will understand them anymore and that they will remain alone and misunderstood. For example, my parents did not get along with my grandmother, especially in the context of becoming modern. They argued about many things, such as building a new house in Kathmandu, my dad going to Dubai for work, and my brother going to Australia and settling there. My grandma didn't like the idea of change.

Here Rajit seems to reflect on how from their side, parents also have to mediate their own desires and those of their children with the pressure from their own parents and society itself. Later in the conversation, he commented that parents should play a more active part in the process of mutual understanding with their children:

> Parents and children have their own point of view and are correct
> in their own way. But if things are done in balance with mutual
> understanding, it could result in a better environment where parents
> themselves could be a friend to their children. Parents also could
> play a part as their friend if both of them have an understanding
> relationship.

As his words suggest, parents and children could be friends if parents acted in a different way.

Finally, during these years, young people also start dreaming about their own families in terms of independence. Some expressed anxiety over the ways in which independence will actually be achieved when there will be two families to take care of. For example, Rajit commented: "How will I take care of my family? Of my own family one day and also of my parents? How will I be able to do all this if I don't find a job and things don't go as planned?" Nevertheless, as if they were looking for the right balance between the will for independence and interdependence, some young interviewees criticized those young people who do not care about their families of origin, but still reflected on the way in which they could achieve the right balance themselves. One of these interviewees was Shuvam, who observed:

> I think that too many people don't care about their family. They
> go abroad and don't want to return. I personally would like to go
> to study in Australia and then come back to look after the family
> because I need to take care of them as they took care of me. But for
> now I could not go because I am not economically independent and
> I have not finished my studies yet.

As revealed by Shuvam's words, many young middle-class people experience a moral sentiment of indebtedness for their parents' efforts, and also a sense of economic dependence that limits agency and causes an ambivalent sense of guilt and responsibility.

Shifting Values and Opacity of Minds

In the previous pages, I have examined how parent-child and child-peer interactions play a crucial role in navigating and affirming different ideals of well-being. While the notion of life improvement as a middle-class mantra recurred in conversation with both parents and their children, two broad different ideas of well-being emerged. Parents placed particular emphasis on education as a pathway toward future socioeconomic improvement. As pointed out by Liechty (2008, p. 215), in front of an uncertain future, education becomes an "almost mystical commodity that represents the only avenue to a modern future that middle-class parents can imagine for their children."

From their side, the children stressed the importance of "emotional happiness." Children's and parents' perspectives are negotiated within a "life plan" that is conceptualized as a "'supreme system' of overall objectives and guidelines for an individual's life as a whole, in contrast to plans for limited periods and objectives" (Schutz 1970, p. 319). In fact, as noted by Schutz (1970, p. 319), a life plan "does not have to be deliberate; it may be imposed; and it may change in the course of a person's life." Such changes might follow from the emergence of new doubts and self-questioning, acting as "markers of transitions" (Mines 1981, p. 100), that is, "periods of questioning and doubt about what the person perceives as his or her life direction" (Mines 1981, p. 100).

As Liechty (2008, p. 211) elucidates, the moral articulations of sexuality, love, and intimacy are particularly problematic for the Nepali middle-class youth. This is because, on the one hand, there are external pressures through the media on such topics, which contribute to the shaping of a negative idea of modernity in the eyes of parents and elders. On the other hand, the reality of the difficulties in accessing a job market means delays in independence and with it marriage. This delicate equilibrium might be influencing the way in which a dialogue is avoided between parents and children. This is a common scenario for young middle-class people in Nepal who, as Liechty commented (2008, p. 210), "must pioneer a new social identity that forces them to reconcile images of themselves and their futures according to state and commercial narratives of progress and abundance on the one hand, with the real world of scarcity and precarious claims to social standing on the other." Similar to what was found by Liechty in Kathmandu, the young people that I interviewed perceived a sense of uncertainty and, while they reflected on their need for direction, at the same time they also demonstrated a concomitant resistance to sharing their feelings with their parents due to concurring feelings of shame and guilt toward the expectations that they have from them. As pointed out by Levy (1996, p. 139): "The emphasis on childhood learning (and life in general) on hierarchical interdependence (allied to doctrines and teaching about the learner's responsibility and indebtedness to the people who have constituted him or her) tend to predispose someone who has done something 'wrong' to guilt." The findings discussed confirm this interpretation. The tension between advanceness and shame as two complementary moral emotions framing the existential condition of the youth in Bhaktapur causes a perception of discomfort in experimenting with new moral codes and ideals, particularly around interactions outside of the household. This might be due to the parenting style discussed here, which, while professing a will to adjust, is in reality very strict on some points.[17]

Experienced as painful and shameful situations, open conversations are generally avoided by both parents and children, who instead create opacity when they perceive that empathy for their perspective (and as such any mediation) would not be possible. Parish (1994, p. 305) suggested that empathy is a process of "identification with cultured others." That is, empathy is filtered and adjusted based on what contents one is willing to take. This becomes particularly critical when parents and children have different existential perspectives and also diverging ideas on how mutual understanding should be established, which can range between empathy, sympathy, and avoidance.

In psychological and anthropological studies, empathy means imagination of the other's feelings and states of mind, where sympathy means bringing the other to understand one's mental state. Empathic processes are thus imaginative, cognitive, and emotional in nature (Halpern 2001, p. 85). But imagination can be manipulated or avoided, as in the case of many parents who resort to opacity of minds. Here interpersonal sympathy between parents and children might be avoided due to a willingness to avoid harsh conflicts and suffering (and the associated shame). Concomitantly, younger people only open up with those that they feel more close to and in the contexts that are considered appropriate and safe.

Experienced as a "shamelike affect" (Parish 1994, p. 208) shaping the boundaries of empathy between parents and children, *lajjā* becomes here a motive for seeking alternative venues of sociality and moral creativity rather than completely suffocating individual desires. Alternative dimensions of expression carried out through dating, socializing in public spaces, and virtual engagements demonstrate the affirmation of a different shade of the moral emotion of *lajjā*, which rather than suffocating "unauthorized feelings," restores them in alternative contexts. This is made possible by the desire for advanceness, which enables a new dimension of expression outside of the domestic sphere. As a moral state advanceness brings about the manifestation of a new dimension of *lajjā* that differs from what was observed by Levy (1990) and Parish (1994) thirty to fifty years ago in Bhaktapur.

After years of avoidance, confrontation between parents and children often becomes inevitable, particularly around marriage practices, involving the contestation of social norms, as I discuss in the next chapter.

CHAPTER 4

"Mutual Understandings" and "Lonely Heart Talks": Self-Making and Social Change Through Conflict and Adjustment Around Marriage Practices

Turning Points

Marriage constitutes a crucial step in the making of the moral self in Newar society, being a religious sacrament that marks a necessary passage in the affirmation of the householder's path, and a fundamental moment of social and emotional attunement to the expectations of "society." A marital union is thought to ensure the maintenance of a family's progeny, which is necessary for the support of the dead and the continuation of the cycle of rebirth (Nepali 2015, p. 198). In practice, for a woman getting married means leaving her own household and becoming part of her husband's family, where she will be expected to serve her in-laws and to perform a number of rituals throughout the year. For a man, it is the beginning of a new phase of social, religious, and economic responsibilities, and of delicate negotiations between his own interests and those of his brothers and parents, through which he should ideally be guided by the intention of fostering harmony in the household by respecting hierarchical principles.

Established cultural norms prescribe certain criteria for partner choice at the hands of the bride's and groom's families, and predicate spousal avoidance. In fact, a marriage is customarily conceptualized as a religious and social occasion that does not emphasize the bond between the spouses in terms of emotional attachment as is generally found in Western marriages. Differently, according to orthodox views, a marriage should not be based on love, nor should affection between spouses be manifested. Love in Newar society is traditionally considered a potential inconvenience to the well-being of the whole household, and a marriage was (and still often is) considered "incorrect" if a husband and wife were too close (Shepard 1985, pp. 211–12). Therefore, as literature and people's commentaries suggest, in the past when spouses were in love with each other, their reciprocal affection should not be shown to the other family members (Levy 1990, p. 115), running the risk that if found out the in-laws might decide to terminate the relationship altogether. For example, Levy (1990, p. 115) noticed that manifestations of love between husband and wife, such as the exchange of gifts, had to be avoided or at least kept secret because any expenditure motivated by affection was considered to be a "diversion of household income" (Levy 1990, p. 115). Detachment between spouses fulfills domestic hierarchical expectations including subordination of the wife to the husband and of the young husband to the eldest man in the household, and ideally prevents them from supporting each other against established social norms. This is necessary to guarantee social order and to avoid the negative scrutiny of "society" and the relative loss of status.

In contemporary times, new ideals are emerging among younger generations, which challenge both established expectations within the household and marriage norms by emphasizing mutual understanding between spouses rather than between their families of origin. As such, mutual understanding is becoming increasingly important for young people as either a factor for marriage inception or as an aspect to develop later in a marriage. These transitions create new grounds of competition within the families of origin and also push toward the problematization of individual versus parental choice in marriage inceptions and in the unfolding of spousal relatedness. They also have the potential to cause further social disruptions when going against preexisting social codes, including caste distinctions, religious expectations, and status and economic considerations.

While much has been written on the emergence of new ideas around marriage in Nepal (see, e.g., Ahearn 2012; Williams 2010; Maharjan 2013), it remains to be explored how these choices involve the adjustment of various social actors to different and often discordant discourses, and how moral selves are shaped in this process, particularly when notions of individual well-being arise. Several scholars have been pointing out in recent years the need to unpack processes of conflict and adjustment following moral breakdowns in contexts of accelerated social change (see, e.g., Robbins 2007; Zigon 2007). In addressing this scholarship, in this chapter I examine a collision of perspectives and desires, and the follow-up conversations between family members, suggesting that these processes act as motors of social change from a micro perspective. According to Berger and Kellner (1964), marriages are "conversations" that aim to shape a couple's nomos, enabling their being-in-the-world under shared as well as negotiated moral circumstances and, as such, form the very basis for the intelligibility of the spouses' life experiences. Berger and Kellner (1964) also noted that the role of external "others" in this process is crucial. This is particularly true among Newar families, where several layers of mutual understanding need to be established between different social actors, including the young couples and their families, in order to dialogically redefine a constructed reality.

The people that I interviewed articulated their own experiences by using the notions of "mutual understanding" and "lonely heart talk" as two concurring psychosocial dynamics through which they conceptualize their struggle to shape their moral selves between desires and expectations. As introduced in Chapter 1, with the notion of "lonely heart talk" people refer to a condition of extreme suffering in which one perceives that there is no escape. The stories discussed demonstrate that self-making processes and dynamics of social change are deeply interconnected and unfold through family negotiations. This chapter contributes to this book's main aim by examining how individual ideas of well-being are negotiated around preestablished norms framing a domestic dharma, including ideas of tradition, hierarchy, and individual choice, and how moral selves are shaped in this process. Ultimately, by revealing people's changing perspectives of domestic relatedness, which challenge a preexisting family ethos, this chapter complicates dichotomies between social pressure and individual desire.

The Role of Marriage in Maintaining Social Order

Customarily, spousal choices in Bhaktapur are scrutinized by the *guthi* institution and by the local astrologists (*joshis*) and priests (*purohits*) who weigh the suitability of the bond based on caste and astrological considerations. Acting as a form of social and moral control, the *guthi* has the capacity to deny membership and the associated benefits regarding death rituals to those performing nonorthodox marriages such as intercaste marriages (see Fürer-Haimendorf 1956, p. 30). The Hindu belief in the cycle of rebirth makes the need for a strictly defined funeral procedure fundamental for the believers. In fact, only through an appropriate ceremony and a purifying fire can the soul be ready for a new life in a superior state of existence. Due to this fear, many people remain tied to family decision-making and to the *guthi* power, seeking the approval of "society" for their own marriage practices. Because of this, despite the abolishment of the caste system in 1963 and its criminalization in 2011, caste discriminations are still a reality. Furthermore, before finalizing a marriage agreement, the families exchange the *cinā* of the potential spouses and consult with their family priests. The *cinā* (New. *jatā*) is a birth certificate provided by a *purohit* that contains horoscopic information about the life of a person.

Alongside caste and astrological considerations, new socioeconomic interests are also taken into account. For example, I found that it has become more common for families to share an additional document called *bio-data*, which in South Asia is the equivalent of a curriculum vitae. This outlines the particulars regarding the education, attitudes, and professions of the spouses themselves, and sometimes of their parents and relatives. It can also involve a description of physical attributes and subjective values and perspectives. Young men who have a university degree, possibly in the IT sector, business, medicine, or engineering, are preferred. For girls, education is generally seen as a positive trait to foster the status of the whole family, but they are also expected to balance modern values with traditional norms, particularly by guiding their children to the establishment of a "moral balance." Some still see female education as a threat to the joint household's harmony because women might refuse to be "collaborative," that is, respecting their role in the domestic hierarchy. From their side, younger generations that I inter-viewed stressed that mutual understanding between spouses is necessary for a successful marriage, which is a marriage in which the partners are happy and free to act in accordance with their own desires (see also Williams 2010; Maharjan 2013). This is considered essential whether or not it is established before a marriage, and companionship is considered a goal of many young couples even within arranged marriages. The emergence of these values is largely influenced by the spread of new cultural forces.

Following the end of the Rana autocracy and the opening to economic and cultural contact with other countries, new ideas around marriage have started to circulate from disparate vehicles, including the media, education, migrants returning from abroad, tourism, and nongovernmental organization campaigns. These processes represent new constraints and opportunities, new limits and possibilities, new pathways of desire and models of success and well-being. These ideas have contributed to shaping new interests and desires around marriage and intimacy among younger generations. In turn, changing ideas of marriage and concomitant emerging ideals of individual and family well-being form an important part of the process of social change in Nepal.

Envisaging "Modern Marriages" Through Ideals of Companionship

I agree with Parry (2001, p. 816) that romantic love is not a new concept in Hindu societies, a fact that becomes evident when one looks at the rich folk-loric heritage of Indian and Nepali songs, poems, and tales (see Parish 1994, p. 161; Ahearn 1999; also Lienhard 1984). Yet, recent scholarship (Maharjan 2013; Williams 2010; Sakya 2000) and my own findings suggest that the dis-course of love is becoming more central and that ideas of companionship are progressively seen as essential for the making of a good marriage by younger generations. In fact, the growing literature on marriage practices in Nepal and India (see Ahearn 2012; Donner 2016; Bhandari 2021) has been system-atically pointing out that the dichotomy of love/arranged is too rigid, and that there are several shades in between these two typologies of marriage inception, such as "love-then-arranged," or "arranged-then-love." The desire for companionship is a generalized trend that can be observed across all of these typologies, as can also be seen in other Asian societies (see Fuller and Narasimhan 2008, p. 75; also Gilbertson 2014). As noted by Ahearn (2012, pp. 70, 257), a shift has occurred in Nepal in the last decades in the meanings and values of marriage with the emerging desire to find a "life friend" with whom a better life can be pursued.

New demographic dimensions of marriage and the concomitant intro-duction of the practice of dating are coming together to construct new ide-als of companionship. At the time of the comprehensive research on Newar society conducted by Nepali (2015) in the 1950s in the major Newar cities of the Kathmandu Valley, people were generally arranged into marriages no later than their twenties. As I explored in Chapter 3, this is largely chang-ing for the Newar middle class, for which education and the attainment of a good job are a priority before marriage and people are more commonly getting married between their mid-twenties and early thirties. Marrying at a later age means that spouses have matured expectations over the years, both from increased social contact with peers occurring in educational and work environments, and from media exposure, as well as from premarital romantic experiences. As people told me, in the past, if any contact before an arranged marriage occurred between spouses, this was often only a furtive look or the exchange of a few words through the small holes of the houses' carved windows. Even a love marriage was generally based solely on eye contact, or on brief secret meetings, which would lead to a formal request by the young couple to their respective parents to follow up with a formal arrangement. Older informants recounted that a brave young man would throw little stones at the foot of the girl that had touched his heart to catch her attention while she was collecting water at the fountains. He might then sing the verses of a bird to call her outside of the house to meet him on full moon nights.

Differently, nowadays dating is becoming a common practice (Regmi et al. 2011). Young couples go to sit at the back of a temple's steps after school, or walk by the holy ponds at sunset. More intimate couples go for a ride together to sacred spots on the outskirts of the city, such as the Surya Binayak temple, Boudha Koja, Doleshwor Mahadev, Jamchen Gumba, Gorakhnath temple, and Bhundole. Major festivals in the town are another occasion for couples to meet, holding hands while hidden in the crowd.[1] During a date, a couple might go to add their "love lock" with their initials in a spot called "love wall" in Jawalakhel, or go shopping, eating *momos* and drinking bubble tea in the streets of Kathmandu. Shops are equipped to respond to people's growing demand to celebrate romantic occasions such as anniversaries and Valentine's Day.

As Gutschow and Michaels (2012, p. 33) commented in their study of Newar marriage practices in Bhaktapur, "newspapers and magazines became important tools of communicating and legitimising the 'language of love.'" The practice of dating becomes a further step toward consolidating these dreams through the gradual establishment of mutual understanding. Dating is in some cases promoted by the parents between an official marriage arrangement and the wedding day, in order for the spouses to establish compatibility for the years to come. However, even when premarital dating is not practiced, my findings suggest that mutual understanding is generally sought in the years following a marriage.

A marriage based on mutual understanding is also a way to ensure that other modern desires and needs of a young spouse can be protected. Men stressed the importance of safeguarding their freedom to travel and spend time with their friends, while women pointed out the importance of being able to pursue the job that they have studied for, rather than being forced to

Figure 10. A marriage procession in Pottery Square.

abandon it (Williams 2010, p. 13). In fact, the notion of companionship might lead to a revision of the social norm of spousal avoidance and the refusal of old ideas of subordination of a young man to his parents and of the wife to the husband and her in-laws, emphasizing instead the exclusive relationship between "two intimate selves" (Parry 2001, p. 816) that can support each other's well-being. In the next sections, I examine selected stories to explore processes of adjustment and creating mutual understanding in relation to both marriage choices and postmarital dynamics and unpack how "advanceness" is dealt with by various actors. I first look at two cases in which children deviate from parental expectations in relation to marriage choices, and then move on to examine forms of postmarital adjustment.

Love Is Stronger Than Society: Dewa and Tika's Elopement

During the night of Bijaya Dashami in 2018, the white horse of the Taleju temple was taken for its ritual walk around the city, just like in every other year, to bring its blessing to the local people. According to popular beliefs, this occasion is the best time for couples to elope. Knowing this, twenty-four-year-old Dewa and Tika left their houses and spent the night together away from their families, an act that by Newar standards constitutes marriage. Their union was being contested due to Tika's lower-caste status.[2] When Tika returned home the day after, her mother cried over how miserable their lives were about to become, not only for the humiliation that her daughter was about to undergo if she had to be admitted into a higher-caste family, but also for herself, who would be looked down on by the boy's mother. However, the final decision would be made by the boy's family since they were expected to live in his parents' house.

At Dewa's home the discussion was assuming different tones, with the main issue being that a girl of a lower caste was impure and could not cook for them in their house without the social penalty of lost prestige. What followed was a consultation between Dewa's parents and their direct relatives (from both the father's and mother's sides) that lasted several days. When I interviewed her, Dewa's mother, a fifty-year-old housewife, explained: "We did not talk to our son for a month, but then we made peace because our love for our son is stronger than society. When we started to talk again, however, his young wife was initially not accepted into our house." Dewa's uncle, a man with a thick moustache, the owner of a textile factory, revealed to me other dimensions that guided their final choice: "We agreed that these days, with modern thinking, these things of tradition are less important and it only matters that she is neat and clean [safa sughar] in order to gain access to the household; and we also want the couple to be happy." Here a discourse on modernity as a superior episteme and the fact that such a transgression is an increasingly common practice was the final justification through which the union was accepted and Tika was permitted access to Dewa's house. Other considerations included acknowledging that Tika was not "very low-caste," belonging to the farmers' caste, and as such not as impure as would have been lower-caste groups (such as butchers or sweepers). Second, it was pointed out that she was educated, and her parents had good economic assets. But a crucial point on which all members agreed was that "these are the new generations," as the uncle further explained, and that "these things are more common in modern times." These points ultimately proved to be enough to motivate the family's choice to let them "be happy." The family then consulted their purohit and the members of the digudhya guthi, who accepted the final decision made by the relatives in order to make the union socially acceptable.

In all the comments and versions of this story that I collected, it was the idea of the inquisitive eye of others, articulated by the emic notion of "society," that created the most tension. This was a common theme among other informants' narratives as well. For example, a man reflected on the practical punishments that society can inflict and that are difficult to navigate: "Now intercaste marriages are becoming more accepted, but in my time, they were not accepted by family and society. People were less educated and afraid that society would point the finger at them [*tiniharulai aunla dekhaunu*]. I personally think that there is no difference between castes, men are all the same, they have the same blood. But I also could not accept it myself because I am afraid [*darāunu*] of society." "What can society do to you?" I asked, to which he replied: "You host various events for festivals, weddings, birthday parties, and no one would come to participate. Also, a wife has to perform several functions in case of death of a parent and if we were forced to separate households, then my wife could not perform these." As this man's comments reveal, one member can bring social death to the whole family by lowering their status and creating limitations to the performance of religious duties in the domestic context. These fears might have brought a middle-aged woman to make this consideration: "If my sons had a low-caste marriage I would have separated from them. I would have separated so much that I would not have cared if they died." While such a strong affirmation can often be negotiated through the gradual modification of social norms, moral breakdowns need to be carefully weighed on each individual occasion against any potential repercussions and the willingness to support one's child. Parish (1994, p. 154) was right when he noted that "by setting aside the norm, you assert that something else is more important." In the story of Dewa and Tika, what seemed to matter to the family was that they understood the young couple's situation and established mutual understanding by providing an explanation for their choice through the critical addressing of local norms and expectations. In other words, while the bond between parents and children was ultimately considered more important to strengthen the family unit and preserve harmony, a "modern" conceptualization of society also played a role in decision-making. In other stories that I gathered, religious orthodoxy was discarded in order to accommodate favorable arranged marriages. For example, in one case a family did not consult with the astrologer to verify the suitability of an arranged marriage, and instead they asked the potential bride and groom to put each other's *cinās* under their pillows for a night. Since they did not have any nightmares, the marriage could be arranged.

Additional conflicts often occur after a marriage when they involve the contestation of domestic roles, often against the views of the families of origin.

Toxic In-Laws and Modern Buharis

Issues with the families of origin are a very important arena of gender contestation in Nepal, and social media is becoming a powerful venue to share ideas on these themes in an anonymous way. This can be seen vividly in the stories collected on Tales of a Modern Buhari (*buhāri* means daughter-in-law in Nepali),[3] a social media platform available on Facebook and Instagram, where primarily young women share experiences of conflict with their in-laws and discuss gender issues and the willingness to promote social change. The stories shared by the users reveal stress surrounding such mediation, in some cases also from the perspective of young men. Similar anxiety is also seen in stories of people who have moved to live in nuclear households and who have to deal with their in-laws on festival occasions. Difficult relatives are defined in the posts by English terms such as "toxic" and "dysfunctional." These terms hint at how these relationships, which challenge women's ideals of domestic symmetry, are perceived as a threat to the health of the couple and of the women themselves. In fact, there are also several accounts of attempted suicides. The general consensus here is that people want to be friends with their partners, emphasizing the notion of symmetry and shared ambitions. In this way, they also expect the partners to protect their needs and desires in relation to both family and spousal dynamics and other areas of life, such as work, relationships with others, and so on.

There is a video on this platform taken from TikTok in which a young groom readily stops his new bride from touching his feet in an act of ritual submission during their wedding, and instead proceeds to touch her feet. The bride laughs at this unusual act, which breaks a centuries-old tradition of ritual submission. Seeing this scene, the aunt of the boy, who is standing behind him, immediately starts hitting his back to make him stand up. I take this as an eloquent visualization of social change as a relational process, as a "conversation" between people. The young groom publicly overcomes social shame (*lajjā*) by doing something inappropriate; the wife probably laughs because she is happy, perhaps a bit shy too, and surely surprised; while the aunt tries to block this act, which might create a precedent for an illicit social dynamic.

Figure 11. A groom touching
the feet of his bride in a
screenshot from a TikTok
video.

Other posts on the platform discuss positive cases of achieved symmetry between spouses after the marriage. For example, consider this comment
from an anonymous user: "These are my parents, they have been married for
twenty-four years. . . . And for the past few years they put on *tikā*[4] on each other's foreheads at the exact same time to signify that both of them are equally
respecting and loving each other. It's a great standard they have set for us to not
settle for anything less." This is an interesting reflection, because not much is
available in media and public discourses regarding the topic of marital adjustment outside of the in-law sphere, either in nuclear or in joint settings.

Of course, not all experiences of adjustment are successful, and some end
in divorce or in the endurance of extreme distress. While it is also true that
divorce is not a new phenomenon in Newar society (Nepali 2015, p. 239; Levy
1990, p. 134), data suggest that the phenomenon has increased noticeably.
While in Nepal love marriages are on the rise, making up 50 percent of total
marriages in Bhaktapur (Gutschow and Michaels 2012, p. 33), the number

of divorces doubled between 2000 and 2014 (Rai 2014). Although it is not possible to verify the principal causes leading to divorce, among the stories that I collected these ruptures very often occurred due to quarrelling between young wives and parents-in-law. This might at first sound contradictory to the emerging emphasis on companionship, but it could instead follow the working of the same ideals. That is, instead of demonstrating a diminished value of marriage, this data might suggest that being discontented with an unfulfilling marriage can lead to the choice of breaking up, hinting at the diminished willingness to carry on a forceful adjustment as would have been seen in the past. This would corroborate the stance by Parry (2001, p. 817) that, unlike what Giddens (1992) suggested was a trend in modern societies, companionate marriage and emphasis on intimacy do not mean a "new acknowledgment of the possibility of de-coupling," but rather "a new stress on the indissolubility of their relationship" (Parry 2001, p. 817).[5] Increased willingness to support one's partner and an emphasis on companionship might then lead to collaborative efforts to tackle inequalities in the household and to redefine gender norms.

Yet, while there is evidence that men are more eager to support their wives than in the past, or prefer to find mediations between their families and their spouses, some others might hold conservative views themselves. In fact, while the relationship with the families of origin, with its attached conflicts and possible adjustments, is a very important sphere of domestic and gender roles negotiation, there are other dimensions of intersubjectivity between spouses that do not necessarily involve direct confrontation with a young man's family.

Other Dimensions of Spousal Adjustment

Several informants defined love marriages as gradual processes of mutual understanding. For example, Dor Bahadur commented: "In love marriages people understand each other but this is a gradual process. A love marriage is not enough to be happy. It takes between two and four years to fully understand each other, the respective families, and what they really want. This is the construction of a real friendship. If this mutual understanding is completed, people can have a lifelong relationship; otherwise, the bond is broken." This reflection sums up very well the importance of spousal adjustment in further shaping moral personhood through the establishment of a "friendship" between partners. Therefore, while confrontation with the families of origin is acknowledged by Dor Bahadur as one of these steps toward the affirmation of such friendship, there are several other dimensions of marital adjustment that two spouses undergo throughout a marriage. These conflicts and the ways that these are addressed are revelatory of transitioning individualized values and ideals of companionship. Often, stories of confrontation between partners that I collected included attitudes toward people outside of the household and behaviors that go against couple and nuclear family interests. For example, both men and women mentioned the criticism received by their spouses regarding the time spent with their friends. Men accused their wives of gossiping about family problems, of being lazy and spending too much time on their phone, or of being too nice to male friends. Women were concerned about their husbands drinking too much alcohol and receiving bad influences from their friends (for example, gambling or cheating). Other conflicts were motivated by a lack of understanding of one's efforts. A couple told me that their harshest fights occurred on those occasions when the husband did not like the food that the wife had made. She accused him of not respecting her hard work, while he expected that she would cook something that he would like after a long day at work.

Over time, at least in most cases, couples come to accept or change behavior in order to solve their differences. For instance, some men told me that they have agreements in place with their wives "to make them happy" and mediate between their requests and their own desires. Some told me that they commonly eat two dinners, one with their friends at a *bhatti* (local restaurant serving mainly Newar meat-based dishes and alcohol) and then with their wives and children. Another couple instead agreed that the wife would not wait for her husband each night to have dinner together, as he usually came back from work late and this initially made her angry. Many men also came to accept that their wives would go out and gossip with their girlfriends. But these adjustments were commonly the result of harsh confrontations. Overall, I found that many conflicts were solved through more violent dynamics in the early stages of marriage. During these years, people often go through that same feeling of "lonely heart talk" that was experienced in many other conflictual dynamics seen so far in this book. Differently, confrontation is completely or preferably avoided in later years. Some older people told me that they sleep in different rooms during periods of tension.[6] During later stages of a marriage, when people "learn how to control their emotions," as

Vishnu and Devi described (see Chapter 2), "lonely heart talks" are experienced more rarely.

Having undertaken a dating period can be a strong factor in both shaping expectations (and therefore avoiding possible frustrations) and in facilitating adjustments in later years. Still, the clash between expectations cultivated before a marriage and the reality of married life with all its problems might be a cause of distress, particularly in the early years. This might involve the negotiation of expectations of the respective families and the ways in which partners will support each other, but also, as I described, the negotiation of behaviors that are perceived as a threat to one's nuclear family. While emotional participation in a relationship was discussed by many informants as a cause of more conflict, many others stressed that people in such relationships have more chances to establish mutual understandings that allow for individual desires to be fulfilled. In modern marriages, the notion of adjustment in more intimate couples comes to be taken in a completely different way from the past, as a more intimate "conversation" between the spouses. An older woman used a metaphor that I think is useful here to put these occurring transitions in the right perspective: "In the past, the wife was the mirror of the husband. If the husband died, she remained with no face. Nowadays, they have mutual understanding, the wife is more free, and they try to understand each other's emotions better." This metaphor reveals that mutual understanding is now conceived on different grounds in terms of attunement to each other's existential perspectives, and it is no longer conceived of in terms of subordination of a wife to her husband to the point of losing her own personal identity (symbolized by the notion of "face"). On the one hand, from the perspective of younger couples, mutual understanding is based on shared values and also similar educational background. Being modern, open, and friendly, including with the other gender, is often a starting point for people to meet and for a relationship to emerge. On the other hand, different people have different ideals of how to reach that "moral middle," and therefore clashes might be unavoidable. Mutual understanding of each other's diversities, even when these diverge from one's imagined life, is necessary for the achievement of couple maturity and the establishment of friendship between spouses. As such, adjustments between spouses can be seen as modulations of "advanceness" and another level of social change that is enacted once again through conflicts and mediations for the purposes of shaping moral selves and attaining a sense of well-being. Here an ideal of companionship can both be a factor for increased distress due to unattended expectations and a reason for improved mutual understanding and empathy.

Overlapping Mutual Understandings

The findings discussed in the previous pages reveal that for Newar people in Bhaktapur a marriage is a crucial sphere in which individual desires and social pressures come together to negotiate new and old moral discourses. Through a dialogical process of mutual understanding between members, modern marriage practices contribute to the contestation of the social order by pushing for a reconsideration of gender norms and individual choice.

Adjustment often means distress for the people involved, who experience situations of "lonely heart talks" when mutual understanding is not possible. Yet, the present study reveals that these moments of distress can become catalysts of change. More specifically, social change is made possible by individual action that is socially weighed and judged, when one pushes between old limits and new desires, overcoming shame and pursuing "advanceness." This was seen here both in relation to in-laws and at a more intimate level between spouses. Nonetheless, as noted by Derné (2005, p. 33), "changes resulting from globalization are [...] more likely to follow from changed structural realities than the introduction of new cultural meanings." Similarly, in the context of Bhaktapur new discourses are embraced by the people themselves who weigh them against preexisting moral frameworks. Notions of mutual understanding and lonely heart talks were used by the people in the stories to account for their personal experiences of change as a relational matter.

The case studies discussed also demonstrate that spousal mutual understanding and parental mutual understanding overlap. On the one hand, I demonstrated that various social actors still enter into play even within the intimate spousal bond, with a persisting role of the families of origin in bringing about adjustments that lie between ethics of cultural consonance and moral creativity. At the same time, stories of couples' interpersonal adjustment also reveal an ongoing struggle in balancing between perspectives of companionship and gendered desires that might be dissonant from one's expectations (such as traveling with friends and spending time without the family during the week, for example gossiping or gambling). From the perspective of the adult children, marriage becomes a "technology of the self"

(Foucault 1988), that is, a device through which "individuals create their own identities through ethics and forms of self-construction" (Foucault 1988, p. 18). Here a struggle for balance and stability becomes essential in the making of modern moral selves. This shows how social change is a deeply embodied as well as relational experience.

These findings resonate with Derné's (1991) theory of the "socially anchored self" in his study of India. For Derné (1991), Hindu men conceptualize social pressures as necessary to ensure conformity and see individual desires as fundamentally shameful and unregulated. Others, such as Jankowiak (2009) in a Chinese context, reveal how opposition itself is a criterion to affirm modern moral selves. These strict dichotomies do not work in the present context, where instead several degrees of adjustment are at the base of the negotiation of moral personhood. In a way, my research both builds on and departs from Derné's theory, showing a more dialogic dimension of moral creativity. The interconnectedness of the dimensions of the self that I discussed in this chapter suggests that we should reject schematic dichotomies opposing individual desires and social order as they have been dealt with in Hindu social worlds (see, e.g., Derné 1991; Kakar 1990). On the one hand, if in the past the moral self was locally understood as more subordinated to static forms of social opinion (Parish 1994, p. 118), nowadays social norms themselves are revised, and selves adjusted, with the ultimate goal of making space for new forms of well-being and local voices.

And yet, one could wonder if the modern self is any less "socially anchored," or rather whether the contemporary self is anchored in a new sociocultural context. The case studies discussed show that while a process of breaking away from a kind of social anchoring is ongoing, a concomitant generational reanchoring in a different social space and logic can also be observed. The question then becomes, what is that new social logic? And how does it invite or compel people to anchor themselves to it? How do "modern" class logics interpolate subjects? The answer here seem to be in the need for intimacy and emotional support, which is perceived as necessary to one's well-being, even more as one seeks well-being itself within the logic of a modern dharma. In fact, even the men studied by Derné (1994) who deviated from the rule of husband-wife avoidance were animated by ideals of well-being. In sum, for the people of the stories examined, marriage practices make up a crucial link between self and society by engendering new arenas of negotiation between moral creativity and moral reproduction for how these intersect with the making of moral selves.

So far, this book has looked at how new emerging ideas shape and are being shaped by middle-class people in Bhaktapur. Ideals of life betterment in particular have had a profound effect on parenting philosophies and youth outlooks as outlined in Chapter 2. This chapter has proceeded to examine spousal choices and family negotiations and how these are balanced to maintain kinship when "modern" ideas clash with preestablished cultural norms and cosmologies. It has been argued that ideological shifts are creating space for more equal spousal relationships that are often in opposition to hierarchical household structures. These dynamics can be framed as a contest for emotional well-being, where the needs of the household unit clash with those of the individual and their family of choice, and where social norms and individualized moralities are slowly shifting toward gender and generational equality. In line with these developments, the following chapter looks more closely at household conflict and how fission may occur when differences prove insurmountable.

CHAPTER 5

A Room of One's Own:
Well-Being in the House Space

The Pillow Insect

It was love at first sight. We met at school. During the cultural program, we danced and ever since then we wanted to stay together, so we got married as soon as we turned eighteen. But love marriages are still not seen positively by many people—although this is gradually changing. From the moment we got married, I was forced by my parents-in-law to quit my job in a tailoring shop and made to cook for eighteen people and to work in the house.

Maya, a woman in her late thirties, was telling me this story sitting in the café of the inn where we were staying.[1] She seemed distressed in recounting these events but eager to tell me, as she wanted "the whole world to know that women can do more than working in the house": "There was so much work to do every day that I never had time for myself or to spend with my husband. He kept his gifts for me secret from the others to avoid arguments. I didn't even have time to eat, and I eventually contracted gastritis. When I did have time to eat, after having cooked and served them all, I always had to eat last and alone, often just the meager leftovers. Things became worse over time." Her parents-in-law were controlling her movements and her relationship with her husband, Ganesh, who had to keep his gifts for her secret from them. He told her in private that they called her a "pillow insect" (New. *phunga ki*). As Levy tells us, with this metaphor some local people refer to "the wife talking in bed at night, and [they] say] that if a man listens to his bride's opinion, everything will be over" (Levy 1990, p. 116). In fact, Maya and Ganesh shared their bedroom with two other couples (Ganesh's brothers and their wives), and their talks had to be quite furtive and brief. And what would the "whispering pillow insect" deliver if not ideals of well-being for the young woman, the young man, the couple, and their nuclear family against the world? The pillow is the center of an intimate space, a rather private corner in the shared household's highly surveilled system. But what does it take to make a woman an "insect"? An insect is somewhat of a parasite, an outsider, isn't it? In fact, Maya's story is also an account of controlled movements in and out of the joint household, of painful accesses and barriers, and ultimately the story of an escape.

Starting from Maya's account and drawing from other ethnographic material I collected, in this chapter I unpack what I shall call "spatial dimensions of well-being." I do so by tracing the ongoing transitions in household spaces, including the phenomenon of fission and nuclearization with its motivations; by describing the gendered and generational trajectories in and out of the household; and by outlining the tensions between intimacy and privacy engendered by new spatialities and mobilities. I will commence by discussing changing domestic spaces.

Changing Domestic Spaces

Household spaces play a central role in the ongoing processes of moral negotiation. As noted by Toffin (2016, p. 164), "a house is not merely a shelter, an architectural edifice. It also corresponds, in the mind of its dwellers, to a set of ideas, and it is associated with a whole series of powerful images."

The Newar traditional house is conceptualized as a sacred space, a place of worship, and a threshold of death (see Gutschow and Michaels 2005), where multiple families (the subnuclei formed by married brothers and their aging parents) live sharing one kitchen. Here the dead are worshipped periodically and supported in the afterlife to gradually return to earth with a new body.[2] Following ideas of purity, the Newar house itself is divided vertically into stories (generally four) among which the kitchen is the purest space, and as such is located on the top floor to keep it protected from both the impurity of the street and the influence of evil eyes, which are believed to make food indigestible. It is in these spaces that social hierarchy is reproduced. As noted by Quigley (1985a, p. 16), symbolisms underpinning divisions of space in Newar households "are not mere intellectual constructions. They have a very real bearing [on] everyday social life."[3] Similarly, as postulated by Lefebvre

(1991, p. 121), "the house is as much cosmic as it is human. From cellar to attic, from foundation to roof, it has a density at once dreamy and rational, earthly and celestial." In Bhaktapur, as it emerges from available literature and from my own informants' comments, the traditional house is conceived of as a space of order and hierarchy, where social norms are enforced through the socialization of the young and through the reproduction of religion-based inequality between members deriving from each person's age and gender-appropriate role. Their kitchen is a space of reproduction of hierarchy, where food is served, and where adults share their business affairs (Quigley 1985a, p. 17). Bedrooms are not romantic spaces and were generally shared between several couples and their children.

Many of these spatial features are reconceptualized in nuclear households, either when families move to modern houses or when they renovate old houses to modern requirements and standards. The kitchen areas are generally still built on the top floor beside a worship room (*pūjā kōthā*).[4] Differently, bedrooms in nuclear households host only one couple and sometimes their young children, although whenever possible children are given private bedrooms. Divisions between subnuclei in modern houses might still follow a vertical criterion, by which each nuclear household has a room on each floor, but also horizontal divisions are not uncommon. The religious practices that are associated with the household, making it the threshold of life and death, are adjusted to accommodate modern lifestyles. For example, this is enabled by not having to perform *śrāddha* rituals exclusively in the house where the dead once lived. In this way, these rituals can be performed even by sons who live in other countries, although people still try to gather together annually whenever possible.

Following a Western imaginary conveyed by the media, modern housing is both a way to achieve a middle-class status and to affirm modern practices of relatedness. In many ways, the spatial organization of modern houses allows for more intimacy and privacy than that of traditional Newar houses. The kitchen in particular is now understood as a place for intimacy, where one can "share their problems," as people say, and it is a responsibility of good householders (men and women) to make sure that individual issues are discussed when meeting together for dinner. Another architectural element introduced in modern houses is the rooftop terraces. Toffin (2016, pp. 162–64) suggests that "on these terraces, members of the household can give free rein to their imagination and spend time lost in their thoughts." Finally, while toilets in the past were shared between households, now new private toilets are installed, often with additional facilities located on lower floors that can be shared with guests.

These changes in household spaces reflect and enable a transition in relationships and relational desires. Among these transformations, the nuclearization of households is quite telling, not only of new economic possibilities, but also of the affirmation of new values that redefine the limits of acceptability. My research findings suggest that one major motivation for the joint family dispersal is conflict. I will further discuss this in the next sections by continuing the story of Maya and Ganesh, and their own case of household fission.

Maya's Escape

One night, on the day of Mha Pujā, when returning home after having been singing traditional songs *deosi* and *bailo* around the city as a part of Tihar's celebrations, the family did not allow me to enter, because, as they said, I had been in other houses. A neighbor saw me crying in the courtyard and insisted that they let me in, as it was cold and dark outside. They finally agreed to let me in, but only after a barber cut my nails.[5]

Recounting these events, Maya exclaimed: "I knew that I could not continue like that!" She eventually became so stressed that her parents-in-law claimed that she was being possessed by the ghost (*preta*) of a dead relative who would be coming back to feed from her body. According to popular beliefs, hungry ghosts can return to haunt the living, attracted by festive events such as festivals and life passage rituals. The explanation given by the shaman for Maya's case was that the ghost had been following her since that night when she went to celebrate the *deosi* and *bailo* ceremonies in front of other houses in town. Her sense of depression, anger, and stress (using her own English terminology) was manifested gradually through rebellious actions. "I was irritated that I could not work, could not go out, and could not hold hands with my husband," she commented. "Also, my mother-in-law complained all the time about me not being a good cook and not being enough neat and clean."

Maya progressively started avoiding her in-laws and stopped bending down to touch her mother-in-law's feet in the morning. During these tense days, she experienced the emotion of *mane khanlhagu* (lit: "lonely heart talk"). When she opened up with her husband about her issues, "he did not know what to do," and this made her feel "lonely" and "without escape." The experience of lonely heart talk occurred later at night when she could not get any sleep because she was "too stressed," and her "stomach irritation became more painful." Feeling frustrated, she started talking rudely to her in-laws over the following weeks and occasionally refused to perform chores. She had also found out that she was pregnant and had started to worry about her own well-being even further. One day after cooking, she sat at the kitchen table and ate food by herself before dinner time. Her mother-in-law did not accept her behavior and once provoked her, saying that they wanted to send her back to her natal home and that she would soon start looking for a new wife for her son. Hearing this, Maya felt a rush of anger, and yelled that her husband hated her, and they were going to leave and move to a new house on their own.

Maya's expectation of an intimate marriage conflicted with the harsh reality of having to share the same house with other people, but also to be treated in a different way from her expectations. Her married life was fundamentally against her idea of womanhood, but—at least at first—her love for her husband convinced her to make an effort to adjust and to stay. However, when her in-laws went as far as considering what she wanted as irrational and spirit-induced (rather than the fruit of her own independent will), a conversation could not be established, and a rupture soon followed as mutual understanding was not reached.

In that crisis of indecision, the help of Maya's brother was essential as an external influence contributing to their "conversation." He offered to them the house he had inherited from his parents, and they moved to live there, where their lives changed for the better. Maya went back to work in a tailoring shop and to volunteer in a mental health hospital.

While the help from her family of origin is somewhat expected,[6] the support received from her husband can be seen as a new feature of contemporary times. In fact, literature suggests that in the past men were more subordinated and less likely to defend their wives. This can be seen in the stories recounted by Nepali (2015, p. 241), which he collected among Newar families in the late 1950s. For example, he reports the story of a couple who had received education and wanted to "live according to their progressive outlook, enjoying freedom to move about together. But this militated against traditional Newar life. The parents of the boy did not like their

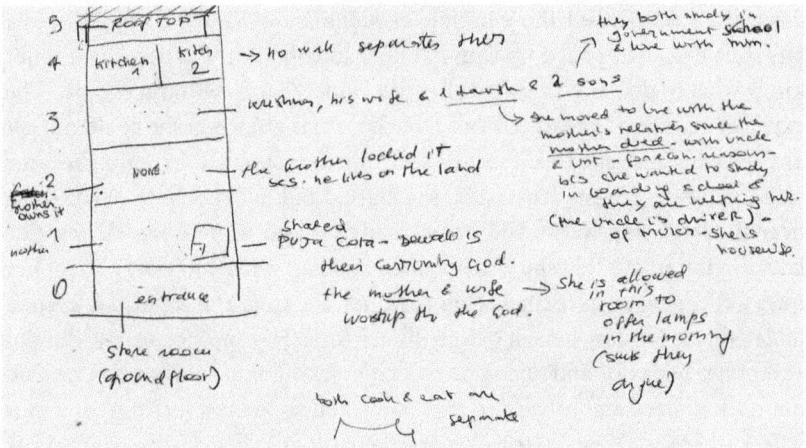

Figure 12. My fieldnotes showing a house with a partitioned kitchen.

daughter-in-law to enjoy freedom like this." The couple was then pushed to divorce. In another family, a daughter-in-law was not allowed by her mother-in-law to share the bed with her husband and so again a divorce was arranged. In the case of Maya, while her in-laws refused to adjust, a preexisting intersubjective ground established with her husband in the years before became crucial to affirm new ideas of self and gender, and to ultimately revise family and household structures. In fact, while in the past young men themselves were subordinated to the family (Nepali 2015, p. 241), they now also partake of a romantic ideology that shapes the affirming discourse of a moral husband.[7] In the story of Maya and Ganesh, we can see a link between ideas of companionship and love, independence, and gender role contestation. Their story is also an example of the increasing phenomenon of household nuclearization and of the social and relational transformations afforded by changed spatial arrangements.

To get her own house means for a woman new freedoms, new mobility in and out of the household, more autonomy on the food cooked and consumed, more time to rest, and overall more agency toward her own well-being and that of her husband and children. It means upgrading from the status of a perceived "insect," a parasite and a subordinate in a joint household, to the role of head of the household in a much more horizontal social structure in which duties and liberties are negotiated directly with her partner. I will further expand on the phenomenon of household fission in the next section.

Household Fission

Recent data on household composition in Nepal reveals that the average size of a family is 4.6 people (4.2 in urban and 4.8 in rural areas) with the majority of households composed of two to six people (84 percent in Patan, 83 percent in Bhaktapur, and 84 percent in Kathmandu).[8] While literature suggests that the process of nuclearization started at least fifty years ago (Barré et al. 1981, p. 100), recent census data show that this is progressively increasing. This trend was observed among the Newars in particular by scholars such as Levy and Parish. The 1973 census as cited by Levy (1990, p. 111) reported a majority of six-person households in Bhaktapur, and in the early 1990s Parish (1994, p. 299) recorded that 40 percent of families were nuclear.[9] My own findings confirm this trend. By surveying one hundred households in 2018–2019, I found that 56 were composed of four to six people, 21 by one to three people, and 23 by seven or more, with the largest configuration being 15. This is a considerable change from the past, when Newar families lived in more numerous households (Nepali 2015, p. 251). From an investigation of the reasons behind each household's composition, I observed that the majority of the nuclear families had been created following voluntary separation after a quarrel of some sort. Among the remaining cases where fission did not follow conflict, nearly half of the people had separated after the 2015 earthquake (when whole areas of the houses were made unlivable), while others had left the joint household due to migration to other areas of the Kathmandu Valley or abroad.

I encountered three main modalities of household fission. The most prevalent of these is what locals call the "flat system," which involves the creation of separate households in the form of small apartments each with its own kitchen. In some cases, these households still share an additional common kitchen on the top floor. Another system commonly implemented to mark separation between two households is the creation of two distinct stoves within the same kitchen. Electric stoves make these divisions easier than the old groundfire system (*chulō*), although some older people reported that in the past separated groundfires were arranged following quarrels. Bungalow-style concrete houses are also becoming very common, and the iron rods of the construction structure are left sticking out of the roofs to enable subsequent expansion of the spaces. This might make fission easier in case of quarrels, or else can be useful to add extra space for one's married children.[10] Lastly, fission may involve separating into completely different houses.

On a practical level, partitions of domestic spaces are made more viable in contemporary times by improved livelihoods and by the availability of new rental properties, which are constantly being built on the outskirts of the old city perimeter on the wave of the expanding construction market.[11] In the 1960s and 1970s, the number of houses in Bhaktapur was still limited by the old walls of the city (Hagen 1980) with the exception of the lower-caste settlements that were customarily located on the riverbanks beside the cremation sites. This was both due to reasons of security and because of the symbolic stigma directed toward areas outside of the city as places of impurity, thus relegated to lower-caste families. These ideas have now changed and living outside of the city is often considered a sign of high status.

A dramatic expansion of the city occurred between 1971 and 1981, when residential areas doubled in size (Doebele 1987). At that time, advertising of modern housing and new construction materials started to become more readily available and directed to a richer stratum of the middle class (Bhattarai-Upadhyay and Sengupta 2016, p. 90). Nonetheless, changed material possibilities alone do not explain why fission would be preferred to finding a solution for staying together, especially when the very act of leaving challenges the established Newar ethos of domestic unity. In fact, while in Western families it is generally expected that people separate from their household once they get married, in Nepal young married couples are still considered new subnuclei that are expected to join the extended household, which is regarded as the ideal form for a Hindu family (Michaels 2020).

I suggest that these negotiations need to be examined in relation to new pressures and ideals that come together to shape a modern dharma. In fact, it seems to me that transitions in domestic structures do not only represent the consequence of improved economic possibilities, but also communicate dramatic social transformations that include the emergence and affirmation of new ideas of family and self toward the betterment of members' well-being, contributing in turn to shaping intimate dimensions of social change.[12]

As I described in Chapter 4 (p. 94), in the past divorce was often the solution to these same problems. The reason for this, Nepali (2015, p. 283) commented, is that it was difficult for young men to "revolt against the decision of the elders," and therefore they seldom voiced their own desires or supported their wives' needs. Consequently, women's dissatisfaction was a "strain," using a term by Beals and Siegel (1966), one of those "areas of life in which culturally induced expectations tend to be frustrated more frequently" (Beals and Siegel 1966, p. 68). In contemporary times, the increasing number of love marriages could be the reason why more conflicts end in nuclearization rather than in forced understandings or divorce, thus acting as "stresses" (again using a notion by Beals and Siegel 1966), which is leading to ruptures. This follows changing ideas of family and a reconsideration of the role of each household member in this process. For women, this derives from the development of a stronger sense of their own rights and the affirmation of their desire for intimacy, which is greatly influenced by access to media and education. From their side, in demanding respect for their wives and making sure that they also have good lives, husbands too affirm their own selves based on their moral and emotional values.

Focusing on women's hopes in Indian domestic settings, Derné (2000, pp. 342–43) commented that "a young wife focuses on cultivating an exclusive one-on-one relationship with her husband, so that he might intervene to improve her life." Even further, my findings suggest that reciprocal care is becoming increasingly important, even to the point of going against old social rules. These processes involve a redefinition of the very notion of mutual understanding, which is made to pass from the equivalent of a forceful agreement, which was mostly unequal, to a dynamic of reciprocal care, which often leads the joint household to fall apart. In summary, in the context of dramatic sociocultural change, the use of "traditional devices" (Beals and Siegel 1966, p. 68) to solve occurring problems, such as the discourse of mutual understanding in the name of harmony, might not work due to people's unwillingness to compromise. In this process, it is the very idea of self and belonging that is involved, being redefined through conflict and value negotiation through the questioning of old and new social ideas, as I further unpack in the next section where I discuss the case of a joint family dispersal and the motivations involved in their decisions.

Two Kitchens

On a winter morning in 2019, Krishna Hada, a middle-aged man working as a hotel cook in the old town, told me that he and his wife, Geeta, had divided their kitchen into two halves to avoid sharing food with his mother. He invited me to see the kitchen arrangements firsthand. Their house, located in the neighborhood of Khauma just outside of the city's gate, is a five-story traditional Newar house of 250 square meters. The whole building had previously been divided into small apartments due to conflicts between the elderly parents and their adult sons. Despite these separations, the kitchen had been shared until that point. As we walked through the bright kitchen on the top level of the house, I could see the two separate stovetops and two sitting mats on the floor in opposite corners of the room. The two areas were not divided by a wall or any other structural element; it was the action of cooking, eating, and washing the dishes separately that marked the fission between the two subnuclear families.

In previous years, both his brothers had left the joint household to live independently with their nuclear families. A net of quarrels was at the base of these divisions. As we went out on the rooftop so that he could smoke, Krishna further explained the reasons for their conflict with his elderly mother that had eventually led to the division of the kitchen into halves:

> When my father was still alive, we separated the building into small apartments, one for me, one each for my brothers, and one for my parents. This is because we had several conflicts due to money management, and my father did not want to sell our land. When he died, three years ago, the problems continued. We wanted to sell the land, but my mother wanted a share for herself to give to her widowed sister. My brothers and I thought about it for a while, but eventually refused. The land remained unsold, and now she is angry [krōdhit] at us and she is refusing to accept our food. We do not eat together anymore; she cooks rice for herself. And we wash our dishes, while she washes her own. However, if we cook any special type of food,[13] we still share it with her, and she accepts it, but she will always eat it separately from us. And she never offers us any special food in return. In any case, we never share rice with her.[14] You see, why should we give part of the money to her sister? She has her own children. And we need funds to be able to support ourselves and our children.
>
> "So are you going to stay separated also for Dashain?" I asked.
> "Yes, although we give food to her, we eat separately also for Dashain, such is our anger for each other."
> "So why do you share special food with her?"
> "This is to show our love to her, which goes beyond the anger."

From his perspective, Krishna believed that he was right in preserving his own interests and those of his nuclear family against those of his aunt, whose

destiny is said to be attached to that of her own grown-up children. Nonetheless, demonstrating his continued affection and respect for his mother
through the sharing of special food was a necessary step for him to establish
his own self as moral. This hesitance to enforce complete household fission
might follow from the fact that his role in relation to the mother is peculiar;
he is the youngest son and is customarily supposed to take care of his mother
and eventually of her funerary rituals.

Eight years earlier, Krishna's eldest brother, Bikram, had left the joint
family while his father was still alive. I went to see him and his wife, Ramila,
in their new house, which they have built on the family-owned land. Sitting
on the rooftop terrace, partially covered by the shade of the umbrella placed
in the middle of a plastic table, Bikram described the nuances of the quarrel
that had eventually led him and his wife to leave the household. A contentious issue stemmed from the fact that Bikram is educated and works in an
office in Kathmandu, while his brothers are illiterate and work as farmers like
their father:

> There was no harmony in the family. No one had mutual under-
> standing. My wife often complained with me in private that they
> did not give her a moment of peace during the day when she was at
> home and I was at work [Ramila works in a bank and is out of the
> house four days per week], always yelling at her and giving her more
> jobs than themselves.

Eventually, different educational levels and competing desires made mutual
understanding between Bikram and his brothers impossible. Bikram's anger
gradually grew, and he kept making mental notes of his sisters-in-law's
actions, up to the point when they attacked his wife: "One day, an argument
between the wives became so heated that I could hear them yelling when
returning home for lunch, and objects of the house were being thrown out
of the window. They were arguing for who had to work in the family's fields
because the work was very hard. As I ran upstairs to see what was happen-
ing, I saw my brother's wife, Sita, hitting my wife with a wooden spoon on
her shoulder." Following this incident, Bikram went to live on the land that
they own and that they never sold due to the subsequent arguments with his
mother. His father gave him some money to build a new house on a corner
of the land. Bikram's apartment in the joint household was dismantled, and
Narayan and Krishna took one floor each of the building.

In his story, Bikram uses the notion of mutual understanding, without which harmony is no longer possible. This notion was used by many of my other informants when I enquired about the ongoing phenomenon of fission. Bikram defined mutual understanding as "an agreement" (*samjhautā*): "People have mutual understanding when they choose to stay, talk, and share. It's like an agreement, like coming to a resolution between two parties or people by agreeing upon some points based upon some discussion. When there is not understanding, there is conflict. In that case, people separate because there is no understanding between them." As discussed by Bikram, mutual understanding can be a way to solve a conflict. However, when this cannot be achieved, a breakup is often the only option. This can take various forms according to both economic possibilities and the perceived gravity of the disagreement. Several people commented that in the past mutual understanding was usually forceful (*jabarjasti ko bujhai*), which means that one person had to submit their will to another who was superior in the domestic hierarchy in the name of harmony and group well-being.

As noted by Orenstein and Micklin (1966, p. 315), within Hindu joint families "a considerable number of people may share distaste for a given standard, yet comply with it." Thus, whereas conflict challenges what Parish (1994, p. 182) referred to as the "cultural structures of empathy and solidarity," an ideal of harmony and mutual understanding facilitates the convergence of different ideas. While these days the notion often refers to an intersubjective dimension marked by ideals of equality, in the past the submission of one or more members would have been the norm for maintaining the household's unit and hierarchical harmony, which in turn provided social and economic security. In Bikram's story, the interests of his nuclear family prevailed over the ideal of harmony for the joint household. Nevertheless, as Bikram remarked, material possibilities still play a crucial role today in forceful understandings: "If you don't have a stable income and a secure prospect for the future, you will fall into poverty and life will get very stressful. In that case, you will need the help of your relatives, and that's why it is good to have peaceful relations with them. But if you have conflict with them and then you need help, then you are left alone." After making this reflection, Bikram stopped talking, looking away at the green hill known locally as "sleeping Buddha," while the strong sun of noon splashed upon his face. Sipping my tea, I smiled at Ramila and I asked her about her opinion on people conflicting and separating. She commented:

In the past, relatives lived all together. When I was a child, there was a family with one hundred people in my *tole* [neighborhood]. There were twenty-nine people in my house, but gradually everyone started to leave. They could not get along. They divided everything they had, up to the last chicken. When I grew up and moved to my husband's house, things were the same, and we eventually separated too. When there are many people put together, everyone has their own opinion and conflicts emerge. The difference from the past is that nowadays people separate, but the reasons for arguing are the same, they have been the same for centuries.

I then asked her what the reason is that people now separate more than before. She smiled and answered as if she had never been more sure about something: "It is because nowadays, if things don't go well, women leave!" Later in conversation she revealed that while conflict was the decisive factor for separating, they would have gone nuclear anyway: "We do not care what society thinks. We are modern and our views are different from society. We still take care of our elder parents, but we want to be independent."

While Bikram believes that the economic aspect is a strong factor in decision-making surrounding fission, Ramila identifies women's moral agency and a will for independence where individual desires and "society" are inevitably in opposition. Their voices taken together show how changing sociocultural values and ideals of well-being attached to an idealized nuclear family setting can be profoundly intertwined with economic drivers leading to fission.[15]

The Ideal of the Nuclear Family

Scholars of moral anthropology suggest that conflicts that arise in phases of sociocultural change are due to the introduction of new values or to transformations occurring in the hierarchy of traditional values (Robbins 2012, p. 120; Zigon 2007). Nonetheless, hierarchies of values are problematized, and complex explanatory frameworks are developed in people's commentaries on their experiences of fission. These speak to new ideas of empathy and relatedness, and to the desire to provide one's family with a good life.

Many of the people interviewed defined their nuclear family as that group among kin that is "more close to one's heart" (New. *du nughla jise*). The nuclear family was also often referred to by local people as "my family" (Nep. *mero pariwar*; New. *thache[n]*)[16] and was commonly described as the unit that provides "the highest level of trust" (*bharosa*), because relationships are based on reciprocal affection rather than on the compulsion of relatedness. "You also have affection for people in the joint family," said Geeta (the wife of Krishna Hada who had divided the kitchen into halves), "but it is different from the spontaneous feelings [*sahai*, lit: "free flow from the heart"] that you have for the people in your nuclear family." For many women, this type of spontaneous affection was also felt toward their natal household.

For men, sentiments of affection and subordination were more blended in their feelings toward their own parents. For example, Krishna said: "You have to love your elder parents, even when there is no understanding." Of course, not all in-laws have little empathy for their children and their wives. For instance, a middle-aged man commented on the difference between the relationship that his wife has established with his own mother and that of his wife with his daughter-in-law, where this difference is given, according to him, by the quality of being modern:

"My wife is respectful to my mother and they have a good relationship, but surely they are not friends! My wife greets my mother every day, touching her feet. And she does the same with other elders when she sees them. Differently, my daughter-in-law is a friend to my wife, because my wife is modern, and she does not expect respect from her and she lets her free to act however she feels more comfortable." Several informants told me that in nuclear families attitudes between members can be *pāsa-pāsa* (lit: "friend-friend"), that is, more free, trusting, and spontaneous. Further conversation with people revealed that this increased empathy (as a form of mutual understanding more in tune with the feelings of others) can also allow for enhanced moral creativity. Overall, people commented that when family members are not friends with one another, there is not the possibility to express oneself freely. At the same time, while both men and women expressed their desire to live in a nuclear household as a way of fulfilling one's true self and inner desires in opposition to strict control of the joint family, the affirmation of new ideas of family through fission has distinctly gendered aspects.

According to many of my informants, those who separate from the joint family are considered selfish and ultimately subversive of the social order. Thus, strong motivations are needed to take this significant step. In fact, as noted by a thirty-year-old man, "material possibilities and changed values

do not make leaving the joint household any easier." Revealing a problematization of fission that is not uncommon among men, the same informant
added: "It is very hard to leave the joint family because society will judge you
[*prashna garcha*]." This was also observed by Krishna himself: "Many people
would rather go to live in a nuclear household but it is not easy to make such
a big step. Even when there are conflicts, people always fear the judgment
of society. I do not like this part of society, being too judgmental, but elders
take society seriously and will judge badly. Society is a strange thing, people
prefer to respect society than following their own desires." While this form
of what I shall call here "public morality" (as a revisitation of the notion of
"public and private faces" by Mines 1994) is still decidedly strong in Newar
society, this is strictly linked to more private moralities that directly relate
individuals within a family. Thus, there is suffering when going against cultural norms and a sense of guilt often emerges. Revealing the workings of
these concurrent pressures, for men the discussion on the preference for the
nuclear family was embedded in a narration of a forceful separation. For
example, both the sense of guilt toward his own parents for having left them
and a feeling of shame accompanied Bikram's story of a necessary separation:

> When you go nuclear, people will judge you as a selfish person. Also
> as an immoral person, as a son who has not been able to maintain
> the harmony in the family, to keep the balance between everyone. In
> my case it was hard to be together, and so it is better for us to be free
> from that burden. At the same time, I felt both embarrassed [*lajjita*]
> and guilty [*dōṣī*] soon after I left them, but we had no choice. You
> need to perform several rituals and also death rituals for your par-
> ents, and living in another house makes this problematic; but also
> these days *purohits* celebrate *śrāddhas* in different houses from that
> of the deceased, so things are starting to change in this sense.

While Bikram stressed the difficulties in making this decision, Ramila high-
lighted their agency in choosing to leave, as discussed earlier. Despite an
evident problematization of fission seen in men's narratives, the duties of a
moral householder that were conceptualized by several informants as "traditional" (including the maintenance of domestic harmony and the preservation of the social order through the performing of death rituals and hierarchy
dynamics) are now challenged by new responsibilities of a "modern" type,

Figure 13. A new house at the periphery of the city.

such as funding children's education, spending time with spouses and children, and ideally caring about their well-being. All of these aspects come to shape a modern dharma. These transitions are in large part enabled by changing spousal dynamics.

A Room of One's Own: Between Intimacy and Privacy

So far I have discussed the ideal of the nuclear family and the practice of nuclearization. The tensions leading to fission reveal emerging values and desires of intimacy (whether these attempts at dividing are successful or not), and the limitations to make such a step possible are based on logistic and moral considerations. The nuclear household is thus, at least ideally, a space of intimate confrontation and emotional support. These features make it a space for moral creativity. This is because there is less control and judgment, and more intimacy between members, which is enabled by the layout of the new spaces. At the same time, private bedrooms become personal spaces for the young, where media imagery can enter one's dreams, with many middle-class houses featuring a television screen in every room.

Then, one could argue that modern domestic settings allow for more mutual understanding, in other words more openness of one's personal thoughts, but also more opacity of minds, that is, more privacy between members. Enabling a new balance between privacy and intimacy, modern houses become epistemological structures of relatedness and intersubjectivity. This "spatial paradox" of providing more intimacy and yet enabling more privacy between members could be taken as a spatial visualization of the problematic relationships between parents and children seen in Chapter 3, where more intimacy is sought and yet more opacity between members is the reality. In fact, in nuclear households the possibilities of intimacy might be in tension with desires of privacy between partners and between parents and children. These frictions recurred when I discussed household structures with younger people, who often introduced to me the ambition to form their own nuclear families. Intimacy and privacy, then, emerge as the two faces (as much as desired and in tension with each other) of modern relatedness. This was obvious in the comment of a young man in his twenties, Ganesh, who lives in a joint family and for whom his private bedroom was still not private enough.

Ganesh had been fighting for week to get a new bedroom. His bedroom is beside that of his parents, and he was hoping that when doing some restructuring to their four-story house, he could have owned a brand-new bedroom which would have replaced the small *puja* room on the rooftop, and which would have had—he imagined—windows on all the walls to see the hills from every direction for his daydreaming. This hope was dashed when his father and his uncle came to an agreement to maintain the *puja* room. While he already had a bedroom of his own, that was too close to his parents' bedroom and to that of his uncle. Disappointed about this choice, he commented during an interview: "I dream to go nuclear one day, to be free to make my own choices, without being judged and watched, being able to make mistakes, learn new things, and enjoy life." On their part, to mediate with his requests, the parents eventually bought him a new motorbike, which he uses to go to work in Kathmandu, for trips outside of the valley with his friends, and to spend time alone in the forest. This story shows how nuclear households too are intersubjective spaces in which negotiations of well-being and harmony are enacted.

In *A Room of One's Own* (2009), Virginia Woolf discussed how a writer needs her own space to be able to write creative prose, a luxury that in her time was rarely granted to a woman. Having one's own room was a desire of both young men and women whom I met in Bhaktapur. While in some cases the growing-up children enjoy these luxuries, this is not the case for their parents who share their own bedroom with each other, with the children when they are younger, and/or with other couples. For them, trajectories outside of the household can afford some kind of privacy outside of the intimacy of the domestic sphere. Unlike what was found by Brunson (2014) in Kathmandu, where women enjoy new freedoms thanks to the use of scooters, in Bhaktapur women's movements seem to be more restricted and limited to their brother's, father's, or son's vehicles. This is because for women there is still stigma in owning a motorbike or car. Additionally, the possibility of "wandering" or traveling outside of the house is also related to women's wages and to several degrees of social and relational control. Grossman-Thompson (2017, p. 494) noted that "earning precipitates a broader sense of personal autonomy" and as such mobility outside of the parental house. While my research confirms this, I also found that married women have less autonomy in these movements when they live in shared households, where their daily movements are still controlled and they often have to give up their jobs or dreams. Walking to the temples in the morning to bring offerings to the gods is a way for married women to exchange gossip and support, but this activity is frowned upon by their husbands and in-laws who worry that they might be spilling the private matters of the household. Conversely, married men visit the local restaurants (*batthi*) almost daily, where they see their male friends, but are more controlled by their wives when living in nuclear households, where they have to navigate their wives' sense of competition with people outside of the household. And if one goes even further away, outside of the valley, there they will encounter sacred and dangerous places. But it is also there that a certain license and deviance from expected social norms can be afforded, including caste considerations.[17] Areas on the edges and outside of the valley are the favorite destination for short trips as dating experience before an arranged marriage, for family vacations, and for honeymoon trips. All of these mobilities allow household members to achieve additional nuances of privacy and intimacy outside of the domestic sphere with various family members or without them altogether.

Spatial Dimensions of Well-Being

Not only are spaces regulated by social norms and relational moralities, but they can be negotiated to enable new social dynamics. In this chapter, I have unpacked what I shall call "spatial dimensions of well-being" by tracing the ongoing transitions in household spaces, including the phenomenon of fission and nuclearization with its motivations; by describing the gendered and generational trajectories in and out of the household; and by outlining the tensions between intimacy and privacy engendered by new spatialities and mobilities in and out of domestic spaces. The case studies discussed reveal that the motivations behind the partitions of domestic spaces include the protection of spouse and nuclei interests; a desire for intimacy; and the willingness to achieve middle-class ideals. Several interconnected themes run through the narratives of household fission seen here. The main points of contention included diverging economic interests between brothers and the competition for care and status between family members.

These findings resonate with literature referring to the phenomenon of dispersal in Nepal and India. Many of these studies have stressed money matters as a central element in the conflicts between nuclear families living in joint households (see, e.g., Quigley 1985a; Goldstein, Schuler, and Ross 1983, p. 721; Nepali 2015, p. 252; Pradhan 1981, p. 54; Kaldate 1962; Ross 1961; Kapadia 1959; Shah 1988; Srinivas 1987; Caldwell, Reddy, and Caldwell 1984). Others have pointed out the essential role of women's dissatisfaction in Newar joint households as a leading factor of tension in the family, especially in combination with economic matters (Pradhan 1981, p. 50; Nepali 2015, p. 260; Levy 1990, p. 116). In fact, while these changes occur in a context of new economic possibilities, the question of how to make these resources flow within the domestic sphere involves a reflection on new ideas of relatedness and on the family itself. The motivations behind the quarrels show that new limits are placed on acceptability in the domestic sphere and point towards the affirmation of new sensibilities toward traditionally established roles and hierarchies.

Throughout these processes, the nuclear family emerges as a locus where new lives are both imagined and practiced, and in which men and women collaborate dialogically to shape a modern dharma to seek family well-being. By "well-being," local people refer not only to better education, better jobs, and better economic resources, but also to systems of reciprocal care, privacy, freedom, and emotional attunement. In all cases that I came across, including some not directly mentioned in this chapter, people's rationales revolved around articulations of mutual understanding, whether in terms of forceful hierarchical acceptance or more empathetic and open dynamics. This demonstrates that regardless of whether people are for or against "modern" ideologies and nuclear family structures, such debates have become central in local identity discourses.

The stories analyzed show that through household conflict and fission, people revise their position in the domestic hierarchy, rethinking ideas of family in which preference is given to children or spouses over parents and in-laws, with the goal of enhancing family well-being. They suggest that the potential of these processes is related to changing notions of mutual understanding as a modality of intersubjectivity, which (at least ideally) involves empathy and equality between family members. Informants' voices analyzed in this chapter suggest that this is related to ideas of the self as an agent deserving and providing affection to their peers rather than fulfilling a compulsory project of relatedness. Nonetheless, while these findings lay the groundwork for understanding recurrent themes in the articulation of emic discourses of relatedness in Bhaktapur, a stronger desire for empathy does not mean that this endeavor is easy to achieve.

Furthermore, processes of moral creativity do not necessarily involve the affirmation of new ideas of family, but can also be featured by the resistance to family life itself, whether joint or nuclear, demonstrating a need to rethink one's individuality before other kin. For example, in recent scholarship on Nepal, Jeevan Sharma (2013, 2018) has demonstrated that for young men outmigration works as a rite of passage in the affirmation of one's own independence and identity away from the control of the family. In Bhaktapur, similar processes can be seen occurring across a range of ages, including younger people who are actively seeking new modes of relatedness in the pursuit of improved well-being. In an important reflection on the several dimensions of well-being, White (2010, p. 166) mentions the importance of space:

> People's understandings of and capacities to achieve well-being
> depend critically on the geography of the space they are in. For many
> this is not of course set, but variable, with daily migrations to work
> or school, or longer-term movements for employment, marriage, or
> care-based relationships. There is also an important figurative aspect
> to this. In some cultural contexts a sense of space and place is funda-
> mental to notions of moral order.

Similarly, I believe that an exploration of the spatialities of well-being is imperative in a country where house spaces and public dimensions are being restructured on a daily basis, with changing housing materials, a dramatically fast expansion of urban areas, ongoing outmigration, and the creation of new public spaces of socialization and consumption. A wealth of studies has addressed the role that space plays in shaping well-being, with some focusing on relatedness in domestic spaces in particular (e.g., Russo, Argandoña, and Peatfield 2022). My research contributes to this literature by showing that not only do spaces influence people's well-being, but that such well-being is established in the process of seeking these transformations, and that relationships themselves and the underpinning moral orders are carved and tested together with domestic spaces.

While I am far from arguing that women had no agency in the past and overall in joint households, the ongoing phenomenon of household fissions as narrated by both my male and female informants demonstrates the central role of women in initiating these processes, as well as the role of men in supporting or opposing domestic transitions. This reveals a series of combined issues, including the establishment of new desires around family dynamics (or at least of new means to achieve them) and the ways in which purposes of well-being are understood as strictly related to intimate relationships and to their spatial realization. Here, rather than being classified as a "pillow insect" that could be kicked out and sent back at any time to her parents' house, a woman can, at least ideally, feel safer in her bedroom as a place of intimacy and sharing. And her role in the domestic ecology reverts when the kitchen transitions from a place of surveillance and subordination to one of support and dialogue. Ultimately, ideals of well-being embraced by women are at the base of the initiation of these transformations.

The stories discussed in this chapter bear witness to the interconnection between ideas of family and the making of moral personhood where the family is seen as the locus of individual well-being and moral creativity. As such, established moralities are negotiated against more modern aspirations, creating a new form of dharma where family structures and relationships are tending toward smaller and more intimate groups, and through the negotiation of spatial trajectories in and out of the household. Nevertheless, negotiations can cause significant distress, and maintaining relations with extended family remains an important issue that is usually not completely abandoned, but rather reprioritized. In turn, the deterioration of the joint family system can lead to the need for additional forms of solidarity. In the next chapter, I explore the emergence of the friendship *guthi*, which becomes important in navigating logistical issues deriving from changing domestic settings, and as a strategy to respond to the direct contestation of the hierarchical social dynamics found within the *guthi* institution itself.

CHAPTER 6

Seeking "Heartfelt Help":
The Emergence of the Friendship *Guthi*

Seeking Trust

In the summer of 2018, an eleven-year-old boy from Bhaktapur named Nishan was murdered by two men who had requested a ransom of three million NPR from his parents. The kidnappers were known to dine daily at the small eatery owned by the child's mother and owed her NPR 35,000 in credit. On the day of the tragedy, they had taken Nishan with them with the pretense of buying him a mobile phone with which he would finally be able to call his father, who worked in Malaysia.[1] On the fourth day after the homicide, I heard the mother's desperate crying while I was conducting interviews on a rooftop near Taumadhi Square. She was leaning heavily on the shoulders of several women from her family, while walking along the central street of the town as part of the Newar mourning practice performed to lament the death of a family member. "That poor mother," commented the woman that I was interviewing. "Nowadays you cannot trust people; you need to know them very well to be able to trust them."

Like a modern Nepali folk tale, this was a dark story that soon entered local people's imagination. In explaining to me that "things are not going well in Nepali society these days," that "no one can be trusted," and that "people have become selfish," this crime was mentioned again during later interviews and casual encounters with local people. This was in addition to the repertoire of anecdotes about social change commonly recounted, some of which had actually been experienced by the teller, others heard from a neighbor or read on Facebook. As also seen in previous chapters, what these stories had in common was the reiteration of a motif of social transformation, the rise of conflict and struggle for people to obtain what they call "better lives," where the allusion to issues of modernity was often intertwined with notions of morality.

In previous chapters, I have discussed how modernity was portrayed by local people as a time in which conditions of life have considerably improved from the past, but also as a time characterized by strong potential for further improvement. At the same time, modernity was also discussed as a period of social and economic vulnerability due to the precarity of the Nepali economy and to rampant competition and dishonesty. Nevertheless, people stressed how new drives and needs also lead people to seek the support of others. Their voices suggest that the social world of Bhaktapurian people unfolds in a balance between perceived social vulnerability and the need for support in a daily struggle in which domestic lives and ambitions are intertwined with those of other households. In this context, trust assumes crucial importance, and aspiration leads to the need for heartfelt relations between friends as a shield against uncertainty. As a young man put it, "You need help, these days even more than before, and you need friends to give you heartfelt help to get you out of trouble when things go wrong in life." As a crucial term in the moral vocabulary of friendship in Bhaktapur, the notion of "heartfelt help" holds emotional connotations and informs the behavior of both the giver and the recipient.

Starting from these considerations, this chapter explores a particular aspect of friendship in Bhaktapur, namely its institutionalization in the form of what local people call "friendship *guthis*." These are social organizations run by friends for the provision of funerary and/or economic support to their members. My findings suggest that these groups started to appear in Bhaktapur around twenty-five years ago in the form of *dhikuti*, a type of rotating credit practice that has long been used by the Thakāli ethnic group of Mustang.[2] Additionally, friendship *guthis* have a similar structure and functions as traditional *guthis*.

I introduced the social function of the *guthi* in Chapter 2. I will briefly remind the reader here about these institutions and add some further information. There are several types of *guthis* in Bhaktapur. These are male-only groups that can have different functions. The two most important types (and to which membership is compulsory as a member of Newar society) are the *digudhya guthi*[3] (formed on the basis of a shared ancestral divinity) and the *siguthi* (a same-caste organization with the function of providing funerary services and rituals). Still today, these two types of *guthi* supervise social

relations and religious practices in Newar cities, acting as forms of social and
moral control.

When providing funerary support, the emerging friendship *guthi* substitutes the function of the traditional *siguthi*. Friendship *guthis* also adopt some
of the features of the *siguthi*, such as a hierarchical group structure headed by
an elderly leader (*takhali*), a periodic feast, the presence of a protector god,
and the performance of an annual animal sacrifice. However, a *siguthi* has
generally no financial function and in fact *guthis* with economic purposes
are rare (Gellner 1992, p. 236). This is a major difference from the friendship
guthis, which can in fact have either or both economic and funerary purposes.

This chapter addresses three main interconnected questions. First, why
are friendship *guthis* progressively fulfilling the funerary function that was
once the exclusive role of the *siguthi* in Bhaktapur? Second, why are friendship *guthis* with an economic function so widespread when there were no
financial *guthis* in the past and the *siguthi* was not known for this role? Finally,
why is it so important that the help received is "heartfelt"? In what follows, I
suggest that for the Newar middle class of Bhaktapur, these transitions are a
consequence of ongoing socioeconomic transformations at both the domestic and larger societal level. Ultimately, this chapter argues that while building
on preexisting practices of socialization (such as that of the *guthi* institution)
and on the morality of help and reciprocity, the relatively new institution of
the friendship *guthi* plays a crucial role in the networking between households in a climate of social, economic, and ideological change. This needs
to be understood within the framework of the larger societal context as a
locus of economic and social insecurity in which kinship ties are increasingly
strained. The emergence of contested love and intercaste marriages is another
reason for the need to establish friendship *guthis* when the *siguthi* and the
families of origin reject these choices and new forms of socioeconomic solidarity are needed, particularly following household fission.

Building upon the themes of aspiration and vulnerability as essential
experiential dimensions of the emerging middle class, this chapter contributes to the book's aim by exploring moralities and relationships that are in
need of being redefined and outlining how social roles are interconnected in
the pursuit of well-being.

Because of the secret nature of the *siguthi* (only members can attend the
meetings), it was not possible for me to attend their social events personally.[4] Therefore, the data provided here is based on both literature and commentaries from participants belonging to forty distinct *siguthi* institutions to

Figure 14. Traffic toward the entrance of Kathmandu.

provide an account of both ancient and modern practices. I took information about twenty-five financial friendship *guthis* (of which six also had funerary functions) and four "funerary only" friendship *guthis*. While only ten people among the one hundred households that I surveyed were part of a friendship *guthi* with funerary functions, seventy of them were either currently involved in some kind of friendship *guthi* with an economic function or had been in the past. Meanwhile, the vast majority of informants claimed that they would start a new economic or funerary friendship *guthi* with their good friends if the need arose.

I also need to add here a terminological note on the vernacular use of the term "heartily." This should be taken as the equivalent of the English word "heartfelt," possibly deriving from the local term *man-ko kurā* (lit: something that is felt). This is a form of Neplish, and as such has been maintained rather than being corrected when occurring in people's quotes to give a sense of the local appropriation of the terms; I have added the translation "heartfelt" in square brackets. Regarding the term "friendship *guthi*," this is how the vast majority of informants have described it to me. In some cases, other terms were used such as "informal" *guthi*, "financial" *guthi*, and "friends" *guthi*.

Funerary *Guthis* and Change

As introduced in Chapter 2, several scholars have pointed out the importance of the *guthi* institutions in maintaining social control on caste dynamics, controlling friends and romantic relations, and enforcing the observance
of various religious rules (see, e.g., Fürer-Haimendorf 1956, p. 30).[5] In fact,
in the past, the *siguthis* had the authority to remove the caste status and deny
funerary services to those people that did not adhere to their requirements.
As noted by Nepali (2015, p. 191), *guthi* organizations are fundamental for
understanding the maintenance of the social norms of Newar society:

> The caste and familial organization of the Newars cannot be fully
> understood without understanding their "*guthi*" institutions, which
> are of socio-religious character. While caste or sub-caste sets the
> limit to the general status-position of a person in the total society,
> his ritual and social life is regulated and controlled through these
> "*guthi*" institutions. [. . .] Further, while the manifest function of
> such *guthis* is the fulfillment of some secular or religious interest,
> they have the latent function of preserving the norms and values of
> the community.

As I start to show in the following sections, the rigidity and prerogatives of
the *siguthi* do not always suit a changing society, and people are seeking ways
to address old and new needs. As such, it is important here to further elaborate on the functions of the *siguthi* and the subsequent emergence of the
friendship *guthi* with funerary functions.

Some Notes on the *Siguthi*

The *siguthi* is a funerary and social association composed of male *fukē* people
(male members of a lineage). Customarily, membership in a *siguthi* is inherited from father to son. The *siguthi* is necessary for carrying out the appropriate funerary rituals, thus ensuring the maintenance of the cosmological
order through the reincarnation of the dead, which will need to be supported
by follow-up *śrāddha* rituals (Gutschow and Michaels 2005, p. 30). Ensuring the correct funerary practices for one's family members is one of the primary roles of the householder, alongside the matching and performing of

appropriate marriage contracts and other domestic rituals.[6] Therefore, membership in a *siguthi* is considered a moral duty of a householder.

The *siguthi* covers several funerary functions. First of all, the members have the responsibility to notify each other as quickly as possible about the death of another member or relatives living in their same household. They promptly gather wood bundles and collect and decorate the body before bringing it to the cremation site. In the past, the participants carried the body either on a bamboo carriage or on a small chariot to the cremation site (Suwal 1997, p. 6). In the past, at least five members were needed to carry the body. The members were followed in a procession to the cremation site. Some elders comment that a larger *guthi* group was better to overcome the dangers of the jungle, especially when traveling during the night. These days an ambulance service called *sab sahan* is widely used by the *siguthi* for the transportation of dead bodies.

The *siguthi* organizes annual gatherings at the house of a member on a rotating basis or else at a specific "*guthi* house" (*guthiche[n]*). During these events, a large amount of food is served by the members themselves or, which is more common these days, by a catering service. People often said that food, especially the consumption of meat, was a great motivator for attendance in the past. This motivation has now diminished due to improved livelihoods. Nevertheless, in the *siguthi* meetings, food is still a central element of socialization. *Siguthis* still perform animal sacrifices throughout the year on the occasion of the most important festivals such as Dashain, and the animal's meat is shared by the participants. While this still occurs in almost all of the forty *siguthis* from which I have taken information, some have abandoned the practice of sacrifice. As people explained, this is for several reasons, such as lack of finances to buy the animals, insufficient knowledge of the correct sacrificing process, and in some cases the outright refusal of the practice. Additional social meetings are held throughout the year to discuss economic and social matters, and food is shared in the form of *samāe baji* between the participants.[7] In recent years, the number of these meetings has been reduced in many *siguthis* to accommodate the busy lifestyles of the members.

Women are occasionally permitted to attend the events in order to help prepare the food. In some *siguthis*, the eldest woman (*naki[n]*) of the host's family is supposed to help serve the food in the meeting room. However, she cannot enter the room before having knocked at the door and received permission, otherwise it is said that she will become blind.

Here I have described some of the *siguthi* traditions in order to illustrate the social and cultural significance of these organizations. While their primary function is still to provide funerary services to their members and their households, they also are an important means of socialization and contribute to reinforcing the hierarchical system proper in the rich tapestry of Newar society. However, given the dramatic social change sweeping across Bhaktapur, the *guthi* is also now a place of tension and sometimes conflict, particularly when the younger generations refuse to adhere to the strict expectations involved within it. In fact, I suggest that one of the main causes of tension stems from the increased number of young people acquiring membership compared to the past. This is linked to domestic transitions among which household fission and migration are the most prevalent, as I will explain further in the next section.

The *Tuiga[n]*

The members of a *siguthi* must not be part of the same household and must belong to the same caste or affine caste.[8] However, since attendance is always compulsory for the oldest man of each family with a penalty fee for missing an event, when a member cannot attend, in most *guthis* his brother or son residing in the same household can act as a substitute (as people told me, this applies even when the son is a baby). A lineage membership continues even if a person wants to renounce their position, as this is transferred to his younger brother or son.

When larger households are divided into smaller nuclear families, all of the male householders living apart from one another will need to obtain *guthi* membership in order to receive the funerary service.[9] Only the eldest man (either the father or the eldest brother if the father has passed away) remains a full member, and the other independent householders become "half-members." My informants called this option *tuiga[n]*.[10] With the *tuiga[n]* membership, people can still receive the funerary services without having to attend all of the social meetings throughout the year. *Tuiga[n]* members generally only attend the annual special occasions (e.g., Dashain) and pay lower fees than the full members. While the *siguthi* is partially adjusting its rules to adapt to contemporary needs through the introduction of the *tuiga[n]* option and the reduction of fees and meeting times, this is not enough to accommodate the needs of many young middle-class householders. Additionally, these provisions appear to generate new issues, which increases resistance to attending the meetings. This occurs for at least two main reasons.

First, while in the past there would have only been one older man from each household attending the *siguthi* meetings, now several brothers and their father and uncles might have to become members of the same association if their households have been divided. From interviews with participants it emerged that in situations such as these, often people wish to avoid social events because they do not want to meet the relatives with whom they are in conflict and share *samāj baji* (which is considered a symbol of social union) due to their harsh feelings. Additionally, the combination of young and older people in the same group can create friction in terms of social practices. As some elders noted, young people do not want to be commanded, and they often refuse to accept the hierarchical structure based on seniority of the *siguthi*. As described by a schoolteacher: "The new generations don't respect the elders as they used to do in the past; they only want to give money to receive the funeral service in return, but don't care about taking part in it and respecting the social structures and dynamics internal to the *guthi*." Similarly, a *takhali* told me that young people resist attending because elders scold them if they make mistakes:

> Newer generations, if they attend at all, are generally late, arriving when the food is ready, and want to be served. Young men should serve food to the elders, but they do not want to. They must be forced to serve other members. Younger members will not even wash the vegetables, but all members should be involved in the preparations and take their responsibilities. For example, animal interiors must be fried in a certain way to cook the *degula* [lit: "meat of God"]. The new generations only want to gather, but not to cook. They prefer to use catering companies. This will probably be the future of *guthis*. However, traditional *guthis* require a specific cooking process that has been passed through the generations.

Food practices are portrayed here as an element marking a rupture between people belonging to different generations. Young members are perceived as disrespecting their duties, which involve participation and subordination within the process of preparation and consumption. Thus, it appears that the generational gap creates tensions in the group or exacerbates preexisting conflicts. Furthermore, young householders commented that they prefer to socialize with their good friends, eating out and sharing their minds freely, which is not possible within the stricter *siguthi* group. In addition, it was often mentioned that the *siguthi* fees compete with other priorities, such as children's education.

The resistance to or refusal to attend the traditional *guthi* is also linked to a lack of time and to the fact that in nuclear households adult males have nobody that can substitute for them when they cannot attend. This is because women are not allowed to substitute for their husbands, and male children are generally busy with school or other commitments. In that case, the food from the event is sent to the house, and a fee for nonattendance is charged. Having said this, I have also found that some *siguthis* are trying to overcome this issue by allowing women to attend in place of their husbands, but this is still very rare. Consequently, people who cannot attend and cannot be substituted might choose to renounce their membership altogether to avoid the fees. Due to different needs as well as a clash between generations and differing ideologies, young people might prefer to find alternatives for the funerary practices, such as creating new friendship *guthis* or joining preexisting ones, as I will explain further in the following section.

Friendship *Guthis* with Funerary Functions

All ten friendship *guthis* with funerary functions that I surveyed were composed of men from mixed backgrounds (e.g., Jyāpu, Shrestha, Kayastha, Shakya) and were no larger than twelve members. Some members came from other towns, some had conflicting relatives in their family's *siguthi* and renounced their *tuiga[n]* membership, while one had no time to attend the events and did not want to pay fees for nonattendance.

Funerary friendship *guthis* cover the same functions as the traditional *siguthi*. They decorate the body and bring bundles of wood for the fire to the cremation ground. The body is transported to the cremation spot by ambulance. After arriving, four participants help to carry the dead body from the car to the burning ground on the stretcher. They then witness the eldest son igniting the first flame and remain to watch the funerary workers tend to the fire until the body is fully converted to ashes. Furthermore, friends provide emotional support to each other on such occasions. In the case of conflicting households, or those that have resettled in new cities, seeking the heartfelt help of friends emerged as a way of ensuring one's sense of safety in a context of perceived social insecurity, something that cannot be guaranteed by the *siguthi* institution with its strict rules. Krishna Rathaur, a seventy-year-old upper-caste man, confirmed this theme when he told me that his sons created such friendship groups not only with the goal of ensuring funerary help, but also to fulfill other social, emotional, and economic functions:

> My sons believe that *siguthis* are now unnecessary because ambulances exist that can take the body to Pashupatinath.[11] However, I personally care because I want to preserve Newar culture and my friendships within the *guthi* groups. But my sons have many friends in other groups. They think cooperatively and their groups are not formed for cremation purposes but rather to go to restaurants. They can also borrow money from each other in cases of emergency and can rely on heartily [heartfelt] help. They have created these friend groups for these purposes.

Annual animal sacrifice was performed by eight of the groups, with some offering a coconut or egg instead of an animal. The sacrifice is an occasion for socialization, and there are other meetings throughout the year that include their respective families, but there are no specific rules on how many meetings there should be and when these should take place.

Friendship *guthis* with funerary purposes in Bhaktapur are often linked to economic activities, which are generally carried out in the form of the *dhikuti* practice. This could be due to the fact that, as my findings suggest, people seeking funerary support might have moved from other cities or might have had conflicts with some family members and, consequently, they would need to replenish their kinship support for both ritual and economic purposes. Nonetheless, the two types can also occur in isolation from each other. As informants explained, whether or not people want to share both funerary and economic support depends on mutual understanding between friends. The institutionalization of friendship into a friendship *guthi* is executed through a verbal or written agreement. A contract is generally needed for an economic *guthi* because not all members are necessarily good friends, and large networks are often needed to support the needs of middle-class householders.

Before moving on to explore the friendship *guthis* with economic functions in more detail, it should be noted that despite the visible issues, the *guthi* as an institution should not necessarily be seen as in decline, but rather in transformation. As I could see from my interviews, while friendship groups are often preferred because they provide heartfelt help, as well as for their absence of strict rules and for the possibility of sharing money, most people are not necessarily against the idea of traditional *guthis*. Instead, many young people say that it is right to continue the tradition, although in a revised form to suit their emerging needs.

Friendship *Guthis* with Economic Functions

Economic Functions in Preexisting Forms of Non-kin Sociability

With the exception of the *mankah guthi*, a cooperative-type volunteer association found among the Newar oil presser caste (Manandhar or Maharjan) (Toffin 1984, p. 179), there were no recorded cases of *guthis* with economic functions in the past. In fact, as noted by Gellner (1992, p. 236), "the significant fact about Newar culture is not the existence of such [economic] *guthis* but their relative rarity." As I was able to confirm, the *siguthi* only occasionally lends money to people in need to celebrate religious events. Gellner (1992, p. 236) considers this type of support as a "way of managing their capital and it is not their main, or even a normal, function." In fact, normally the *guthis* do not use "their sophisticated and powerfully binding socio-religious tradition for economic ends" (Gellner 1992, p. 236). Nonetheless, in the past there were other forms of social organization based on mutual help, such as the *bola* (Mühlich 1999, p. 84; Gellner 1992, p. 236), a form of shared work among farmers that is now practiced less and less. The *bola* groups, however, cannot be considered *guthis* because they are brief and informal (Gellner 1992, p. 236).[12]

In more recent studies, Frese (1994, p. 79, as cited in Mühlich 1999, p. 84) noted that the *mankah guthis* were starting to adopt the *dhikuti* system among the Maharjan (farmers) and Dangol (potters) in Kathmandu, while Mühlich (1999, p. 87) observed the emergence of this practice among the Shakya (upper-caste Newar) in Patan some years later. These studies demonstrate important transformations in the practices of socialization among the Newars, which follow the spread of a money-based economy and the emergence of new needs. However, these studies do not provide any information on the nature of the relationships between members. While there was "solidarity, shared task responsibility, status parity in commensal and other contexts, and membership seniority was based on generation and age" between the associates of *guthi* and *bola* groups (Allen 1987, p. 101), the members were always associated by either lineage or locality. That is to say, while they might have been friends, these associations were not based on friendship. Differently, the concept of "heartfelt help" was at the base of the "ritual friendship" practice among the Newars known as *twae chinegu* (lit: "connecting threads") (Okada 1957) and of the *dhikuti* practice among the Gurungs (Messerschmidt 1982).

Ritual friendship (also known in Nepali as *mit lagaunu*, lit: "wearing a new bond")[13] was a practice sanctioned by a religious ritual, formalizing "existing warm interpersonal relationships" (Okada 1957, p. 212) between two boys or two girls and encouraging "the mutual exchange of practical aid in times of stress" (Okada 1957, p. 212). Following the ritual, the two friends were considered to be linked by blood and, in fact, the relationship has also been defined as "artificial brotherhood" or "ritual brotherhood" (Adam 1936, p. 541). In both *mit lagaunu* and *twae chinegu*, the ritual siblings could belong to a different macrostatus. This means that people who cannot intermarry with each other and cannot share boiled rice are exceptionally allowed to establish such a relationship. As noted by Levy (1990, p. 142), this practice was somewhat in opposition to the strict Brāhmanical rules that organize society in a hierarchical order in Bhaktapur. In fact, in the past, if two children were friends and belonged to different caste groups, they had to renounce their relationship from the day on which they performed *kayta pujā* (the ritual of initiation that marks the moment when boys are expected to start formally respecting appropriate social rules). Instead, through the *mit* ritual they were permitted to continue being friends. Having said this, however, ritual bonds could not be created between clean and unclean statuses, that is to say, the two extreme poles of the caste system (Levy 1990, p. 142).

As noted by Messerschmidt (1982, p. 5), ritual friendship was established for both "functional and affective reasons." The most important responsibility of *mit* siblings was to perform funerary rites and to observe death-related pollution restrictions of each other's partner or collateral fictive relatives (Messerschmidt 1982, p. 23). Furthermore, ritual friendship had an important economic function. While ritual siblings had no inheritance rights (Adam 1936, p. 541), there was indeed a moral obligation to help a *mit* in financial need (Okada 1957, p. 217). In fact, there was prestige involved in taking a *mit* who was considerably poorer or "lower caste," because the doer could become known for his good deeds (Okada 1957, p. 215). According to Hindu morality, being wealthy is not condemned as a sin. However, only through generosity can a better future life be achieved (Okada 1957, p. 214). Similarly, Levy (1990, p. 142) stressed the economic function of these relationships in Bhaktapur, stating that ritual friendship "allowed men to further cement a friendship [. . .] or, for men in business, to put a business relationship on a kin-like basis." From Levy's (1990, p. 142) insights and the personal experiences of my informants, I suggest that the bond was progressively becoming more related to the provision of mutual economic support in a historical phase in which social capital was needed by people to start their businesses in the context of an emerging money-based economy. Moreover, Levy (1990, p. 142) suggests that such ritual friendships were increasingly becoming the result of personal choice among men at the time of his research. While this practice is in disuse these days for both boys and girls, friendship as a social practice built on a foundation of trust and on the provision of reciprocal support in times of difficulty has become increasingly important among younger generations.

Similar to the case of ritual friendship among the Newar, one feature of the *dhikuti* practice across several other ethnic groups was its interconnection between socializing practices and economic functions. Scholars of Nepal have stressed the sense of trust and reliance that the *dhikuti* associates had for one another in case of need. For example, Messerschmidt (1979, p. 156) commented that the *dhikuti* is "formed in a spirit of cooperation among friends and if a member comes into hard times he can appeal to his *Dhikur* 'brothers for help.'"[14] The emerging practice of the friendship *guthi* shares several aspects with both the *dhikuti* and ritual friendship from which Newars can draw cultural resources. This includes the provision of mutual and heartfelt help in times of crisis and the possibility of interconnecting economic and funerary support. Additionally, much like the *dhikuti*, financial support in the friendship *guthi* organizations with economic functions is provided through the form of rotating credit. This is articulated in several variants, as I elaborate further in the next section.

Friendship *Guthis* with Economic Function: Formation and Composition

The number of members in a friendship *guthi* with economic function may vary greatly. Having collected detailed information from twenty-five groups, I have seen membership numbers as small as four and as large as fifty-five. The age of the participants also varied, but the majority were aged between forty and fifty. These associations existed in both single and mixed-gender formats. In all groups, people were strictly Newar from the locality and there were no formal caste restrictions, with people from a Jyāpu background establishing groups with upper-caste people, such as Shrestha, Shakya, and Kayastha. The association of members from different castes is a considerable difference from the *siguthi*. However, I did not find a single friendship *guthi* that included what people call "very low-caste" members, that is those castes who traditionally performed the activities of butchers, sweepers, death specialists, musicians, painters, and so on. "They have their own groups," several people said, explaining that regardless of their economic possibilities there is still stigma attached to visiting each other's houses even when they are good friends. This shows once again that while caste discrimination is less common than in the past, it still plays a role in the articulation of relatedness among the middle class. These limitations lessen when people are "very good friends," but this is more likely to occur in small groups in which relationships are more intimate. Further studies will be needed to investigate social practices among people from lower-caste backgrounds.

Among members of friendship *guthis*, there is a shared belief that it is better to have a few good friends than a larger group of friends that cannot be trusted. Nevertheless, while cultivating only a few well-established friendships, people might still become part of larger networks. When one person brings their good friends into other groups of trusted people to which they are already linked, a new chain of trust is created. After joining, members get to know each other better, depending on the stability and length of the *dhikuti* system chosen, through recurrent attendance of social events. In this way, mutual understanding is maintained and heartfelt help is ensured.

Participants in the groups collect and share money, which serves as a base for each or some of the members' needs. They generally take it in turns to collect the sums and deposit it in a bank from which they earn interest. The fees vary largely in friendship groups, spanning from NPR 1,000 to NPR 30,000 per month. The leader is generally the eldest, as per *guthi* tradition, and the title of this leader is *takhali* (meaning elder or leader), like the traditional *guthi* leaders. In women's groups the leader is also the eldest member, and in mixed-gender groups women can also be leaders based on seniority. The emergence of women-only or mixed-gender groups and the presence of female leaders reveal specific prerogatives of a middle class characterized by gender equality. I suggest that this is related to women's empowerment following education, access to the job market, and their increased role in decision-making in domestic settings.

A portion of the money gathered is used to organize social events or parties (also referred to as *bhoj*) throughout the year with the goal of bringing together whole family units. These are held at the house of one of the members or at what people locally call a "party palace," which is a venue for hire. They might also be held at picnic spots or near religious shrines where sacrifices are performed (e.g., the Suryabinayak picnic ground in Bhaktapur municipality or Dakshinkali, near Kathmandu). In some cases, monthly events are held at local bakeries and cafes. The goal of monthly events is to discuss economic matters, to collect money, to share food, and to organize annual events, but also to have fun and support each other in case of need. The fact that family members (including spouses and children) are allowed to attend such events is a considerable difference from the traditional *siguthi*.

Money-Sharing Typologies

In terms of how the money is shared, groups can adopt several different methods based on the needs of the participants. Sometimes, those who join a group may need some start-up funding for a new business or for some incumbent household expenditure, such as college fees or medical expenses. Alternatively, they may just want a safety net in case something goes wrong in their life. I have classified the different typologies into short-term, long-term, and potential systems. Each system adopts different *dhikuti* variants.

The sharing dynamic of the short-term type can come in three main forms. In the first and most common form, the length in months of the system is based on the number of participants and it is dissolved at its conclusion. In this system, one member takes their share each month. For example, if there are twenty members, each month all members deposit the same amount of money in the fund (for example, NPR 2,000) for twenty months, and each month one member takes the whole sum (in this case NPR 40,000). Alternatively, the short-term system can be based on immediate needs and funds are only given to one or more members. This is purely based on trust, and it is expected that the same would be done for the other members in the future if needed. This system can also be based on a lottery system, known as "*dhikuti khelaunu*" (lit: "play the *dhikuti*"). In the latter, the first person picked randomly gets everything and leaves the group. The other members put money in again, and the next person chosen takes the amount. This continues until the last person, who only receives the bank interest (if the money was deposited in a bank). In this way, each member has access to some capital, and those who are drawn earlier can have access to a large sum in a short time.

Figure 15. A shop selling decorations for Diwali.

In the case of the long-term systems, the money-sharing can continue indefinitely, with members depositing regularly to the funds and only withdrawing in case of need. These long-term groups can come in the form of "interest-type" groups in which only wealthier members deposit regularly, and any of the members can take and pay back the sum with additional interest. In contrast to the type of economic support entailed in the *twae chinegu* practice, this modality shows that the members of a friendship *guthi* acknowledge the need to improve the condition of all friends involved. The short-term system is more common than the long-term one, as it better suits the needs of people starting small businesses. Finally, in the potential system, members of a friendship *guthi* meet regularly and maintain close relationships even though there is not a *dhikuti* currently active. Within these groups, there is the idea that a new *dhikuti* system can be initiated at any time by a member in need through the discussion of their situation with friends and through mutual understanding. This often occurs in the context of preexisting friendship relations or of friendships already institutionalized within a friendship *guthi* with funerary functions.

The decision about the type of group, the sharing dynamics, the duration, the interests involved, and the designation of the senior leader occur during an initial meeting. At the beginning of the *dhikuti,* there is often a written contract in which people agree on the system, the interest to be repaid in case of loans, and so on. After establishing the type of system, members continue to meet regularly to foster trusting bonds and to receive support from their peers on issues they might have. In the next sections, I will explore four selected case studies of financial *guthis* to show how the groups are formed and composed and their underlying motivations. By providing ethnographic evidence of those elements that are common to both the traditional *siguthi* and the friendship *guthi,* I start to outline how cultural continuities intertwine with new middle-class needs and prerogatives. Furthermore, by unveiling the intersections between the economic and social functions of these groups, I demonstrate that social interactions are needed to foster trust in the provision of heartfelt help.

Case Studies

Ganesh Khoteja

One of my key informants, Ganesh Khoteja, a forty-nine-year-old construction worker and the son of a farmer, is a member of a long-term friendship *guthi* composed of nineteen members that started thirteen years ago. Every member deposits NPR 3,000 per month, and they gather once per year, sharing traditional food and drinks and performing sacrifices to Ganesh. The members of this friendship *guthi* are men in their forties (with some members in their thirties). "I am now the leader even though I am only forty-nine!," Ganesh noted with a large smile, alluding to the fact that in the traditional *guthi* the leaders are generally much older. The members belong to ten different castes, but they are all Newar from the locality and they were friends from school. According to Ganesh: "Friends are necessary in case of emergency and for economic and funerary reasons. They give heartily [heartfelt] help and can share family and business problems and discuss what to do and can give important advice, share knowledge on politics, news, family matters, and share family events. In the past only relatives came to food events and ceremonies, but now also friends are invited to attend rice feeding ceremonies, weddings, and funerals." This group acts as a fund for

safety, from which anyone can take money in case of need. Ganesh personally took money only once to fund his son's education, but he continues to
put his share in regularly.

Lal Kayastha

Another informant, Lal Kayastha, is a sixty-year-old hotel owner. He is a
member of several groups, including an official cooperative (Siddhi Ganesh)[15]
and the traditional *siguthi*. Lal also belongs to two long-term friendship
groups of fifteen and fourteen members respectively. Both of these groups
gather monthly. Lal explained: "These groups started twenty years ago with
the purpose of helping each other financially, discussing business and family
issues, and sharing *samāe baji*." The first group also has a funerary function.
It is composed of fifteen people and they regularly gather in one of the members' houses. They put NPR 1,450 per person per month into the fund, and
this fund also covers the cost of food. The member that receives money from
the group works in rotation and must pay interest on the loan. Lal joined the
first group after hearing about it from some good friends. He was invited to
drink with them one day after work so that he could be introduced to the
group and formally become a member and sign the contract: "I knew that
I could trust the people because they were well known to my good friends.
Now many years have passed, and they are all good friends of mine. Also
our wives and children have become friends. It has been important for me
to have their support to be able to buy the hotel. Once I started the business it was easier for me to support my children's education, but we need
money all the time and the groups provide security if the business goes bad."
There are fourteen members in the second group, consisting of work friends
who have relocated to Bhaktapur or are unwilling to attend their *siguthi* and
therefore need help with funerary services. The members belong to various
caste groups (such as Jyāpu, Shrestha, Shakya), although there are no members from very low-caste backgrounds. While anyone is welcome to participate, "they may only participate if they are very good friends of some of the
members," Lal says. He then added that to foster trust the groups need to be
established by good friends, and members need to meet regularly. While all
of this group's members are male, wives may attend food events if they wish.
They put in NPR 1,000 per month, and members meet monthly in cafes
and once per year in the house of the member who gets the annual share.

The hosting member uses some of the money to buy food, and "it is trusted that he will do the right thing," Lal explains. "He may keep some money for himself from the fund or even use his own money to buy extra food. The members do not check." Part of the money can also be used to buy animals to be sacrificed, but they have only made animal sacrifices four times in the last fifteen years. In both of the groups to which Lal belongs, there is a practice of resetting the funds after each member has had his chance to use and replace the money. Any leftover funds are then shared out, and members are asked whether they want to renew their membership. New members may join at this time.

Sumeet Chitrakar

Sumeet Chitrakar, a fifty-seven-year-old retired construction worker and current owner of a tea shop, joined a friendship group fifteen years ago with the goal of sharing money and starting a business. He started this short-term financial group with people who were already his good friends and who were members of the same *siguthi* association to which he belonged. At first, he needed money to buy a bus. From renting the bus to transportation companies, he eventually saved enough money to buy his own tea shop two years ago. In this group, there were twenty male members and the group lasted only twenty months. The members were old school friends and people from the community. As he commented, the management of this group was based on reciprocal trust, and friendship was fostered through social gatherings at local restaurants (*patis*) on both a monthly and annual basis (where the latter are larger events including the members' families). Sumeet believes that the *siguthi* and the friendship *guthi* are both necessary:

> *Siguthi* is important for death management, and friends are important for help with money and family problems, but nowadays friends can help with death management too. The difference is that friends also provide emotional support. Say, you might have an issue, and friends would have your back. You don't expect help if friends cannot do it, but they still try to make an effort to help. To know that you have your back covered is very important when you have so much happening in your life, so many thoughts and daily life issues, from the small to the big expenditures and family problems.

Here Sumeet raises another important theme, namely the need for "peace of mind." A friend can provide that sense of security in a context of increased uncertainty.

Sushila Shrestha

Sushila Shrestha, a fifty-two-year-old businesswoman and the owner of a clothing factory, is a member of three groups of friends, including women-only and mixed-gender forms. The first group belongs to the long-term typology and is composed of fifty-four members including men and women, and they are all friends from school. In this group, ten members deposit NPR 2,000 in a bank every month. If the others need to take some money, then they will have to repay it with added interest. The interest was decided in advance when the group was formed and the contract written. They have a monthly meeting at a local bakery where they share their problems, such as economic and business issues.

The second group belongs to the typology that I have called "potential" and is composed of only three women who are very close friends from college and "can share any problem." Sushila included this group in her list of friendship *guthis* even if they have never shared money. However, she said that they would in case of need. As she explained: "We are very close and trust each other and care for each other as family members. We can talk about family issues, economic worries, important decisions to make, children's education and how to make them grow up well. We would start a *dhikuti* system if we needed to. Some of us are wealthier so we might start a system in which some members put in more and the others repay later on with a small interest."

The third group is composed of twelve members who share NPR 1,500 per month. She personally took from the funds only once for her children's education. The members first met when they were all visiting the same hospital in Kathmandu to stay with their sick relatives (mothers, fathers, children). Sushila was in the hospital to assist her mother for two months. I asked her to explain how their relationship developed. She said: "During those two months, I had the time to get to know these people very well. We were all in the same hospital room and during that time we all shared similar worries and understood each other's problems and gave support by chatting and gathering together for the lunch breaks. One day one of us proposed starting a *dhikuti* system. I already knew what it was and I agreed straight away."

Sushila's reflection reveals how similar shared existential conditions and time spent together can contribute to foster trust. Later in our conversation she reflected on the importance of having good friends not only to overcome issues in life, but also to avoid betrayal. She mentioned the story of a woman in Bhaktapur who stole the money from a group that she was part of and flew to the United States. Another story that has been circulating is that of a member who was robbed and killed while on his way to deposit the money in the bank. These were the only incidents of this type that I encountered throughout my research in Bhaktapur. The relative absence of crimes surrounding these practices confirms the concomitant solidarity among members and the effectiveness of selective bonds in encouraging reliability. Additionally, accountability might derive from fear of the social condemnation that would follow such a crime. In fact, one of the two incidents involved someone who was leaving the country, possibly to avoid repercussions in terms of social ostracism. During follow-up interviews, the same interviewees and other informants provided their views on the formation of friendship, on the spread of socioeconomic vulnerability, and on the importance of trusted friends among an emerging middle class to foster social security and accountability. I examine these aspects in the next section.

Vulnerability and the Importance of Friends

Friendships often start at school, where children of mixed genders and caste backgrounds spend a large amount of time together. "It is the fact that we spent a lot of time together that made us very good friends, because we know each other well and can trust each other," says a young man about his friends. People refer to close friends as *mile juma pāsā* (which they translate as a "very good," "close," and "understanding" friend) and as *du nugale nise mile juma pāsā* (lit: "a friend who is close to your heart").[16] Friendship is seen locally as something that grows in the understanding of each other's personality and life problems, especially when people grow up. In fact, important changes in the value and function of friendship bonds occur in the transition from youth to adulthood. As commented by an old farmer: "When people are young, they do not feel any responsibility and only want to have fun, but as soon as they get married and have children, all the problems start, and they suddenly need help. They will need the help of God and of trusted people, such as their friends." While it is not wholly accurate to say that young people do not feel any responsibility before getting married, it is true that their responsibilities change and expand when they start a family. It is then that they do not only have to take care of their parents, but also of their own family. In adulthood, problems arise relating to household management and the associated internal and external conflicts. In this phase, friends provide material and emotional support, and these two aspects are strictly intertwined.

When adult friends are very close to each other, they are said to have a mutual understanding, which in this context means that they can trust each other and establish reciprocal expectations. This is considered particularly important with the increasing need for support in a climate of socioeconomic insecurity. In fact, among the people I talked to, there was the perception that the spirit of economic development, while creating more possibilities, also causes more pressures and vulnerabilities. For example, Sumeet commented: "These days people want commodities and enjoyment like never before, and in order to obtain them, as much money as possible needs to be made, even if this means sacrificing honesty. People care more about money than relationships. In the past, shopkeepers would give credit to everyone, but this is no longer possible because people will not pay back their debts unless they are forced to. The same is for me with my new coffee shop, I cannot give credit to anyone unless I know them very well." Alongside this idea of a broken social contract, interviewees provided various perspectives about how the new needs and drives can lead people to dishonesty. An explanation that was often given is that people no longer believe in God, as a direct consequence of education, and as such they do not fear God's punishment for their immoral behavior. This was observed by Lal: "In the past people were afraid of God and of future punishments to come after death. They thought that the gods were always watching them. Now people are educated and know that the gods are not real, so they have no fear." With these words, Lal echoed a reflection by Sushila, who stressed that social rules are less often observed these days compared to the past: "In the past, 99 percent of people trusted each other. They would always do what they said they would do and followed all of the social rules. Now 90 percent of people are selfish and don't fear God, and therefore there is no longer mutual understanding between people in society."

At the same time, the perceived decline in religious beliefs also means that many people no longer believe in a stable and predestined karma. As such, they do not consider poor conditions of life as a punishment for sins of previous lives, and they can now actively work to improve their current position. This aspect was discussed by a *guthi* leader:

> New generations do not care about religion or believe in any gods. They do not fear punishment and are very materialistic. They only want material things, before and after. They believe that we simply are born and die. They only want to enjoy themselves and they need to make money, in one way or another. They lie to obtain their goals, which is to have an easy life, with enough money for heaters and air conditioners, cars to go wherever they want, and to have every possible facility. In the past, people believed that the difficulty of life was a punishment for the sins of previous lives. This is no longer believed so everybody wants to improve their life situation.

From these voices, social mobility emerges as an explanation of why it is becoming harder to trust people. In the past, honesty was based on the knowledge of one's position in society and was strictly linked to family and *guthi* backgrounds, a net that is now progressively falling apart. Furthermore, in discussing social mobility, several informants stressed the fact that the locality has now extended and opened up to new members, including people coming from village areas. Such newcomers are not well known by the community and therefore less trusted. Sumeet added that competition, as a side effect of social mobility, has also entered kin relations: "In the past, money was less important to people than it is now. Now money is everything, especially for younger generations. People will do anything to obtain it. This is at the expense of honesty, not just towards strangers, but even to one's own relatives." Similarly, Ganesh commented that friends are progressively substituting for old kinship relations: "There have been big changes in Nepal. People are more educated and have broadened their minds. The consequence, however, is that people are now more selfish. This is causing changing family structures and responsibilities. Now people rely more on their friends and their heartily [heartfelt] help to get them out of trouble. They have mutual understanding with their friends and know what to expect from them." The idea of a broken social order, which according to people follows social mobility, is used here as an explanation for rampant dishonesty. That is to say, people no longer have that mutual understanding of each other's position in society, thus reducing social reliability, and therefore new forms of social solidarity are needed.[17] Friendship *guthis* address the growing need for different dynamics of socialization

Figure 16. A *purohit* performing a *śrāddha* ritual.

by supporting social mobility and at the same time acting as a shield against the socioeconomic vulnerability that is engendered by both the structural conditions of the middle class in Nepal and by accelerated social change, through the creation of personal bonds of trust.

Pursuing Aspirations and Mitigating Vulnerabilities

I started this chapter by addressing several interconnected questions: why the newly emerging form of non-kin sociability found in the friendship *guthi* is progressively taking the funerary function that was once performed by the *siguthi*; why a *guthi* with economic functions is emerging in a society in which this was previously absent; and finally, why it is so important to people that the help received through such associations is heartfelt. I first argued that friendship *guthis* with funerary functions are created when traditional kinship ties have fallen apart due to either household conflict or migration. Furthermore, the *siguthi* often appears to be too inflexible to suit the needs of middle-class families. While there is evidence of some ongoing adjustments, such as the emergence of the *tuiga[n]* option, there are still considerable areas of resistance regarding the fees, time commitment, and the social practices involved. Additionally, the assembling of members from different ages through the *tuiga[n]* option itself (as a consequence of changing household settings and needs) causes internal conflict, creating further resistance to attendance.

In friendship *guthis*, by contrast, even if the age of members can vary, the majority share similar life problems that are common to middle-class people. Nevertheless, various aspects of the *siguthi* are maintained in both economic and funerary friendship *guthis*, such as the presence of tutelary deities, annual feasts with occasional animal sacrifice, monthly meetings, hierarchical structures with designated leaders, and rotating duties in the organization of events. Yet, while there are some evident continuities, there are also some important points of difference. The main changes include the addition of economic functions and the type of relationship between the members, which is not based on caste but rather on personal choice. At the same time, these findings not only reveal new middle-class prerogatives, but also the perduring importance of death rituals. The emergence of these groups also shows that to address old and new needs, people articulate solutions in the form of both modern social practices and old social structures, such as that of the traditional *guthi* and the ancient practice of the *dhikuti* system.

Clifford Geertz (1962, p. 260) observed that forms of rotating credit generally emerge in societies that are transitioning from an agrarian to a commercial economy. This can be seen in Bhaktapur, where monetization and tertiarization have transformed social relations dramatically. Furthermore, stressing the aspect of social change, Geertz (1962, p. 263) commented:

> It seems likely, too, that the rotating credit association is merely one
> of a whole family of such intermediate "socializing" institutions
> which spring up in societies undergoing social and cultural change,
> not only in the economic, but in the political, religious, stratificatory,
> familial, and other aspects of the social system as well. The building
> of "middle rungs" between traditional society and more modern
> forms of social organization seems to be a characteristic activity
> of people caught up in the processes of social transformation. As a
> group, this family of institutions should be, consequently, of particular interest for students of social and cultural development, highlighting, as they do, some of the central tensions involved in such

development and the sorts of mechanisms by means of which those tensions are resolved.

The transitions mentioned by Geertz can be seen in Bhaktapurian society at both the economic and social levels. Nevertheless, as Shirley Ardener (1964, p. 221) asked, "Why do these associations flourish in some societies which have made this transition, while they are less important in others which have also done so?" For the people in the case studies discussed here, the answer seems to be in the specific existential dimensions of aspiration and vulnerability of the middle class and in the preexisting norms of socialization from which they take and refuse selected aspects to fulfill old and new needs. In this context, help in the areas of economic and funerary needs is expected from friends in a heartfelt manner. This is due to perceived social insecurity but also because of a need for emotional support in a context of increased stress. While relatively large networks are also often created (in which case a formal contract is usually required to ensure reliability), enduring and intimate ties are nonetheless established with very good friends.

These aspects are combined with ideas of moral friendship that, as I have suggested, may derive from preexisting ideas of mutual help as it existed within ritual friendship, which entailed a moral imperative for help and reciprocity. Within the bond of ritual friendship, ritual friends were expected to support each other in times of difficulty, providing economic aid and emotional support in life-crisis events, as well as performing funerary rites for each other in case of death as if they were a direct relative. This bond was based on the notion of heartfelt feelings and made exceptions to caste restrictions. The same notion of "heartfelt help" was used by my informants to discuss the mutual help provided by friendship through the *dhikuti* practice.

Mark Liechty (2008, p. 88) observed that rotating credit clubs foster middle-class practices in Kathmandu, allowing consumers to buy "everything from gold and real estate to motorcycles and furniture." Similarly, in a study of *ganye* and *kidu*, which are two systems of mutual aid among Tibetans, Beatrice Miller (1956) suggested that the groups should be seen as features of an emerging middle class, though she did not explain exactly why. In proposing a similar reflection among a Bhaktapurian middle class, I suggest that this is because they can fulfil their economic interests, which are often family-oriented, and receive support in case of difficulties in the context of the weakening of the joint family that predominated in the past. Noticeably, the more recent studies conducted by Liechty (2008, p. 88) in Kathmandu and Katharine Rankin (2004, p. 111) in Sankhu show widespread dishonesty surrounding informal rotating credit activities.[18] This demonstrates that the practice of the *dhikuti*, which has been so widely studied among several ethnic groups of Nepal, is carried out in very different ways in varying social contexts, even when similar needs are present. My findings show that in Bhaktapur these practices follow a peculiar morality of friendship, which is codified locally under the vocabulary of "heartfelt" help.

In this context, friends assume crucial importance, considered by some to be at the level of family relations, although with the added benefit of "understanding" each other due to similar experiences of domestic and economic issues. United by a similar existential condition that is projected toward life improvement, members of friendship *guthis* work collaboratively for the accumulation of capital in each household to support their needs and aspirations. These might include ambitious life projects, such as starting a business, funding children's education, or building a new house.[19] Both economic and social aspects revolve around the needs of middle-class nuclear families, materializing in immediate expenditures and in long-term investments, which are made possible by the affirmation of a money-based economy and an ideology of social mobility. Here, frequent socializing in what in Chapter 3 I defined as "public spaces of intimacy" allows for trust to be established through the sharing of food during social events involving whole family units, and for economic capital to be shared and increased. In turn, this contributes to the shaping of a middle-class culture with its shifting moralities, which expand to inform both the dominion of intrahousehold socialization and non-kin relatedness.

In summary, this book has so far argued that an emerging middle class in Bhaktapur influenced by changing ideologies and the pursuit of increased well-being has been forced to rethink and renegotiate kinship relationships in line with shifting moral discourses. This can be seen through changing parenting dynamics (Chapter 3), marriage choices and practices (Chapter 4), and household structures (Chapter 5). The result of these changes is that there has been a lessening of kinship safety nets, and people are searching for moral, social, and economic support elsewhere. Here we have seen the emergence of friendship *guthis* through which people can pursue their aspirations and mitigate vulnerabilities. These structures contain established cultural elements deriving from *guthi* institutions as well as new forms of solidarity, equality, and trust, reflecting the ongoing moral shifts in the wider society.

CHAPTER 7

To Expect or Not to Expect:
Making "Modern" Elders Between
Anxiety and Well-Being

A Sense of Precarity

Walking down the narrow streets of Bhaktapur on a summer day, I could feel the cool humidity of the old houses falling heavily on my skin. Every now and then, a broken building on the edge of the road or a small descending path let the sun's rays pass through, revealing the green foliage of the forests and fields surrounding the city. The landscape was changing at a fast pace, with newly built houses progressively eating away the land. Buddha was still sleeping in peace, in the form of a green hill at the edge of the valley, while around him columns of smoke rose high in the blue sky. Beyond them, only visible on a clear day such as this, the white edges of the Himalayan chain peeked over the horizon. Ram was waiting for me at his house's doorstep at the end of the road. I followed him inside, and the darkness of the first two floors soon gave space to the warm sun as we walked up to the rooftop terrace. "This is *bikās*," he commented while looking at the valley and shaking his head in a sign of disapproval. As we sat at the plastic table on the terrace, his wife, Beti, brought us some tea with her usual sweet smile.

Ram and Beti Khoteja are an elderly Newar couple who worked on their small farm for most of their life with the help of their sons, during a time when farming was still one of the main economic activities of the town. Everyone has now left them. "This is one of the consequences of *bikās*," Ram said. They both then revealed to me their worries for the future. Beti explained: "Our economic situation is very difficult. Ram has injured his hand and can no longer work like he did in the past as a farmer and carpenter. He now only gets small commissions, while we both still work, despite the difficulties, on our tiny farm. However, this farm doesn't produce much anymore. In this very hard financial situation, we do not have the support of the government, which only helps people older than seventy."[1] Forty years ago, a Chinese company rented their land for two years and extracted the fertile soil from the ground to use in a brick factory. As a result, their land now produces less than half the amount of rice than before. After having sold part of their property and given the profit to their sons to help them move and live independently, they are now anxious about their future prospects. Ram explained:

> Even after they moved away from us, our sons take care of us as
> best they can, even if their lives are so busy. Of the three, the eldest
> occasionally gives us some money. The second still works in farming
> and gives us rice, while we still have to buy products such as oil, salt,
> and clothes. The third one never helps. He is the only one who has
> completed a bachelor and now he is working in Kathmandu. We are
> afraid [ḍarāunu] of what could happen to us in the future, and we
> have to deal with daily problems, such as how to pay the *guthi* fees.
> The *guthi* has lent us some money, but now we have to give it back.

The sense of precarity that permeates the lives of older adults such as Ram and Beti is a common scenario in Nepali middle-class families as a consequence of transitions in domestic arrangements and relations and economic transformations. Following the fall of the Rana regime, measures of development, such as the institution of health care systems, the decrease of infectious and parasitic diseases, drinking water improvement, and better access to food have led to significant demographic transitions in Nepal. Alongside the reduction in infant and maternal mortality, average life expectancy has increased dramatically from 62.5 years in 2000 to 69.2 years in 2015 (WHO 2017). However, medical literature focused on research among Newar people has pointed out the emergence of a sense of loneliness and overall perceived low quality of life among the elderly citizens, and a concurrent rise in noncommunicable diseases and chronic conditions (Manandhar and Joshi 2019).[2] A similar trend can be seen worldwide, particularly in countries where demographic and economic transitions are most evident (Croll 2006; WHO 2017; Coe 2021; Aboderin 2004). Recent literature on Nepal has linked the condition of vulnerability experienced by older adults with changing household structures and relationships in which grown-up children prioritize the interests of their nuclear households over those of their elderly parents (e.g., Goldstein, Schuler, and Ross 1983, p. 721; Goldstein and Beall 1986; Zharkevich 2019, p. 890), particularly in the context of middle-class needs and vulnerabilities, and in some cases because of outmigration (Speck 2017; Khanal, Rai, and Chalise 2018).[3] Despite the contribution of these studies in conceptualizing aging in relation to domestic transitions, we still know very little of the daily life realities occurring within families and about the perspectives of the elders themselves. As I suggest in this chapter, distress among the elderly in Bhaktapur needs to be understood in the framework of a revision of dharma. Thus, understanding kinship relationships and well-being requires looking at the intertwining of old and new domestic moralities that guide and are guided by ideas of family and self.

Alongside discourses of distress, when talking with Ram, Beti, and other older adults in Bhaktapur, another perspective emerged, namely the conscious effort to rethink one's expectations in the domestic sphere by weighing old and new ideals and needs. Similar to informants from other age groups, the elderly people that I interviewed articulated their experience through discourses of modernity as a contradictory time, where life improvement and new ills overlap. As I discussed in previous chapters, this difficult period thus becomes both a moment of moral self-making and of revision of the dharma system. It is the analysis of how this self-reflexive process of adjustment is carried out by senior people that guides this chapter. In the first sections, I discuss two concurring discourses that were used locally to conceptualize the phenomenon of generational breakdown among middle-class households in the city of Bhaktapur. These I have called the "discourse of danger" (using a term by Kleinman 1999, p. 362) and the "narrative of hardship." While the discourse of danger reveals generalized anxiety among the local elderly population about their future conditions, the discourse of hardship revealed an effort to empathize with one's children and to rethink one's moral self as "modern." In the second part of the chapter, I will move on to explore two selected case studies of senior citizens who actively negotiate reciprocity and rethink expectations in different ways, ultimately shaping their own moral identities as "modern."

Weaving together the intimate lives of people with larger socioeconomic and demographic transitions, I demonstrate that traditional dynamics of reciprocity entailed in domestic relations are being reshaped based on new needs and moral premises. In so doing, I embrace the call from several anthropologists to explore emic perspectives on modernity and development (Liechty 2008; Pigg 1996), an endeavor that becomes especially crucial when such concepts become part of local moral narratives.

For this chapter, I have included data collected with older adults who have passed the official retirement age (fifty-eight years) and who have children that are married and belong to a middle-class group. Further in-depth studies will be needed to explore other dimensions of social exclusion, looking, for example, at the case of people living in retirement homes or who have been forced into homelessness.[4]

The Generational Breakdown

In her study of American society and Western Europe, historian Tamara Hareven (1982, p. 3) noted that "the isolation older people are facing now is the result of the breakdown of the three-generational extended family under the impact of industrialization." Evidence suggests that this is also true for Nepal, where young adults are caught between two generations that they need to take care of.[5] Intergenerational contracts are problematic in societies in which there are "few institutional alternatives to the family as a source of security in old age and a dearth of economic opportunities that would allow the family the basis for long-term accumulation" (Kabeer 2000, p. 478).

In Nepal, the government gives full responsibility to the family to care for the elderly. Under the Senior Citizens Act (SCA 2006, article 4/1), "it shall be the duty of each family member to maintain and care for the senior citizen, according to the economic status and prestige of the member" (Sharma Bhattarai 2013, p. 355).[6] The contents of such provisions of care and the sanctions that nonconforming people risk incurring are left very unclear in this recent legislation. Yet, despite the evident difficulties experienced by both elders and their carers, Croll (2006) suggests that in contexts of crisis such as this, the intergenerational contract is often actively revised rather than broken.

In the next sections, I shall introduce ongoing discourses that make up an intersubjective ground within which elders rethink their roles in the framework of a domestic dharma. These ideas are shaped based on personal experiences, word of mouth, and the media. I believe with Kleinman (1999, p. 362) that discourses of danger can also be promoters of action, and I suggest that in the studied context these enable processes of moral revision of one's own rights and duties entailed in kinship bonds.

A poem by Nepali poet Indra Bahadur Rai (in Hutt 2012, p. 118) goes: "'The mountains are we who remain, the rivers are those who are leaving,' said the youth. 'The rivers are always going somewhere, but they always remain,' said the old man, 'we hills are always washed along by change.'" Similarly, the older people whom I met are constantly revising their own moral views and behaviors to embrace, adjust to, and actively negotiate change. To discuss these themes, I will first return to my conversation with Ram and Beti, and then examine some commentaries from other informants.

Discourses of Danger

Ram and Beti had a lot to do that morning, and after having our tea on the rooftop we moved downstairs to the little garden at the back of their house. While I was helping them to clean up dry soybeans to extract their seeds, Ram continued our conversation, making his point by telling a story:

> I am very sad [dukhī] in my heart [man] that there is not much
> respect for the elders anymore. Children no longer respect [adar]
> the elders due to a lack of moral education. Moral education was a
> subject that used to be taught at school. They taught the children
> to respect their elders as gods, including fathers, mothers, and
> teachers. This subject is now gone, and they are instead taught that
> they should make as much money as possible and the ways to do
> it. When I was a child, there was a story that they used to teach us.
> It was about two blind parents and their respectful son. He carried
> them one at the time to the temples every day to worship the gods.
> This was an example of how children should behave. This is a big
> change from the past.[7] We [elders] treated our own elders in differ-
> ent ways and took care of them. I took care of my own parents, and
> so did my wife.

Ram's impressions and relative sadness are not an isolated case. New stories circulate among the elders of the town regarding rampant immorality. These are often related to inheritance issues, and some local people talk about elderly men being killed by their own children to obtain their inheritance. A story that I heard more than once, and that had been discussed by local people on Facebook, was that of a young man who tricked his old mother into leaving her house and going with him for a trip around the valley. He brought her to a retirement home instead and left her there until she died. Her postmortem photo was shared on Facebook to strengthen the imagery of her lonely death and the sin (*pāp*) of her uncaring son. The ensuing comments stressed the unfairness of the son's behavior. As a retired carpenter noted, he was in fact expected to reciprocate his mother's sacrifices: "He had studied medicine, his mother had spent all her savings to send him to good schools, and then he abandoned her."[8] The idea of immorality being linked to a lack of reciprocity was a recurrent theme in people's comments, especially in opposition to the care given to nuclear families. All of these accounts are based on an ongoing discourse of modernity as opposed to tradition, which articulates a transition of the social position of the elders from that of "gods" (*dēvatāharū*) to that of "burdens" (*bōjha*).

In traditional Hindu Newar households, parents are responsible for teaching their children the appropriate dharma and getting them married according to specific astrological and caste conditions (Levy 1990, p. 188; Nepali 2015, p. 199).[9] In turn, it is expected that the elders will be served as gods in old age by their grown-up children (see Subedi 2003, p. 3, p. 10; Goldstein, Schuler, and Ross 1983, p. 718). The oldest man (New. *nayā* or *thakali*) has the most authority in the family and makes decisions that connect the household to the wider society, including economic and marriage alliances (Levy 1990, p. 112). The *nayā* holds his position until his death, when he is ritually prepared to pass to a new state of existence. However, some scholars have questioned the assumption that being considered akin to gods meant happiness for the elderly and instead argued that an idealized idea of old age does not actually correspond to historical reality (Michaels 2020; Subedi 2003, p. 8).[10] On the one hand, what the experience of old age meant in the past for its actors in Bhaktapur can only be subject to speculation due to an absence of ethnography on the topic. On the other hand, local people and scholars of Nepal generally agree that there was "a tacit intergenerational agreement" (Speck and Müller-Böker 2020, p. 7) between parents and children, an unspoken contract of reciprocity, which was fostered by both socialization practices and economic interests (Goldstein, Schuler, and Ross 1983, p. 719). In a modern context, new concomitant needs and ideologies have impacted domestic authority and household flows toward new moralities of exchange. This is explained by some with the decline in the fear of god's punishment for the inobservance of *dharma*.

For many families, economic factors are not the only reasons for incapability, as competing interests are also understood in terms of a rupture of existential trajectories. Take, for example, this story, which I was told by a retired bank officer, of a rich father and his educated son, which combines both the commentary on the preference for his own new family and a sense of incapability in a context of migration:

> A man spent 60 *lakhs*[11] so that his son could study in the United
> Kingdom. His son got a job as a police inspector. The father asked
> him, "Why don't you come back and take care of us now?" He said
> that he couldn't because he and his new family lived in the United
> Kingdom as citizens. The children had started school and he and his
> wife had good jobs there. Consequently, he abandoned his family
> and his inheritance. His father was very rich and had three houses,
> one of which had sixty-four rooms. But they remained empty. One
> of these houses was taken by the Maoists who told the old man that
> he already had enough houses and if he wanted it back, he needed to
> join the revolution.

While this older man was not poor and his son had a good job abroad and had settled comfortably with his family, their life trajectories diverged. This story demonstrates that discussions about parental care are not necessarily confined to economic matters. Instead, care encompasses other emotional aspects, including spending time together. This often cannot be done as is exemplified here. The son had finally achieved that better life that his parents had been building for him at the expense of permanently leaving the family unit. This situation of generational breakdown means that the lives and trajectories of parents and children can become fundamentally diverted from one another, creating crucial care dysfunctions.

Even if the preference for one's own nuclear family can be seen from both men's and women's perspectives, the blame for children neglecting their parents is often put on the wives, who are said to drag husbands away from their elderly parents. For example, an elderly man told me the story of how his own son, who moved to the United States with his wife, was forced away from his family of origin due to her pressure. According to him, his son and his wife moved to the United States to escape the rules of the family:

> They had a love marriage and moved together to the USA. Since he
> got married and left, he stopped caring about us. He only cares about
> the family of his wife, who also moved to live in the USA with them.

When he wants to call us, he can only do it in secret from his wife, so he usually goes to the toilet to call us. She gets angry if she finds out; she is very dominating. The conflict started a few years ago, after their first year of marriage, when they were still living together with us. My son was working in the family business and my daughter-in-law was working and helping in the house. Inside and outside the household many people joked about her personality and attitudes. For example, my son did not ride a motorcycle and she did. She eventually got sick and she accused the mother-in-law of being the cause of that, saying that she had beaten her, but this was not true. The real reason is that they did not like the joint family.

While I could not verify that this woman had been beaten by her mother-in-law, evidence from my findings suggests that this was a likely possibility given that I found that this did occur in many other families. This same informant commented later in the interview that "if the children were not educated, they would have been more respectful." While education is generally discussed by local people as a positive aspect of Westernization, it is also believed to provide a perspective from which the children no longer feel obligated to follow the expected familial responsibilities, as they see the world in a new light. This can create social tensions, especially when the families of origin do not reconsider their conservative perspectives.

The Narrative of Hardship

What I have shown so far is that ongoing discourses of danger and moral decline are built upon an idealized past through themes of betrayal and abandonment. Unwillingness is attributed to immorality, as a direct consequence of ideational factors such as education. These reflections often made people feel sadness for something that is perceived as lost. Overall, people's stories revealed several major stressors in modern families, including migration and competition for care with spouses and children. Yet, I found that there is another discourse prevalent among local people, that of hardship and suffering as a distinct feature of modernity, in which one's children are described as incapable of providing support to their parents, rather than unwilling to do so. It is building on this notion that people rethink their moralities of expectation and embrace an active role in relieving their children from sufferance (*dukkha*) itself. The narrative of hardship can be clearly observed in the comment of Sita, a middle-aged farmer:

Nowadays, parents invest lots of money in their children and care about their future [*bhabiṣya*]. They want to give them good lives [*rāmro jīvanī*]. In the past, children were needed to work in the fields and in the house and were only expected to obey [*jabarjasti*] their parents in a submissive way. Now this has changed. By giving their children a good education, parents believe that they will not have to suffer [*kaṣṭa*] like they did in the past and be able to stand on their own feet [*bachaharu atma nirvar huna sikna parcha*]. But by giving more love now, they also expect more care in the future. The truth is, however, that the children will not be able to care for them.

Sita's perspective resonates with a broader theme in the data that I gathered, which is not only a reason for anxiety, but also the very basis for building resilience. In other words, an acknowledgment of hardship for many local people can eventually foster empathy and a willingness to actively revise the intergenerational contract from the perspective of parents themselves. As Csordas (1990) and other cultural anthropologists have postulated, individual agency is crucial in conditioning and reshaping the world of experience. This is done in Bhaktapur through a reconsideration of the moral frameworks within which people rethink themselves as modern. As Ram Khoteja told me:

To be healthy you need to have peace of mind; this means to do the things that are your responsibility to do as a modern father. For example, helping your children. Also, you need to accept that things are different from the past, and act as a consequence. This means not expecting anything in return from your children.

Ram's perspective on not expecting, as a distinctive quality of a "modern" father or mother, was shared by several other people whom I interviewed. For others, one should expect care from one's children based on an ideal of mutual support, rather than on ideals of respect and submission. Both of these perspectives reveal the efforts of older adults to empathize with their children's middle-class condition as one marked by vulnerability and aspiration. In practice, this was enacted by the people that I talked to through the performing of small lucrative activities (such as selling vegetables in the central market or handmade products to tourists) in order to contribute to the household's expenditures when living with their children or to support themselves when living on their own. When they were still economically and physically self-sufficient, people often reflected on what their future condition would be like. Yet, while they all hoped to be close to their children and grandchildren and to be part of their lives, they had different ideas among themselves about what was appropriate to expect. In the next sections, I explore how two local elders (Lakshmi and Ram) rethink expectations in individual ways by building their own moral narratives on notions of modernity, in order to shape their own moral selves within revised kinship dynamics and moral frameworks.

To Expect or Not to Expect

Lakshmi

Fifty-eight-year-old Lakshmi lives in a very small apartment in a modern-style building just outside of the old city, while her sons and daughters-in-law live in a building nearby. Her house consists of a small room with one bed that she shares with her elderly mother, and a small kitchen area in the corner. This small space is generally packed with children (her own grandchildren left by her sons on their way to work for the afternoon shifts, and the children of the neighbors who come to play). During one of my visits, Lakshmi recounted a story:

> There was a couple with two children who lived in Bhaktapur. The son studied in the United States and the daughter got married and moved to live in Kathmandu. Eventually, the elderly father developed an illness and became blind. His wife asked their children for help. The son never returned from America to see his father. The daughter saw him once after leaving her children at school. She only stayed for a short while because she had to stay with her own children, which she said were more important. This is a bad aspect of modernity; in the past the elders were treated as gods, now they are treated as burdens.

Lakshmi's story sounds like a variation of Ram's tale that was taught in the curriculum of moral education. In both stories, the aspect of blindness recurs as a narrative element to demonstrate the absolute needs of the elderly parent.

While the good son carried the parents to the temples every day, the bad son never returned from America to see his father. The daughter, still living in Nepal, only had time for her own children. "But our situation is different from this story," Lakshmi commented, "because I am a different mother-in-law, and my daughters will care for me. I trust them more than my own sons."

While pretending to protect myself from the gunshots of seven-year-old Shuvam who, hidden behind the half-open door, was laughing while playing with his new toy, I further discussed with Lakshmi what it means to be a good mother. She mentioned the importance of making the people that one loves happy, even at the cost of sacrificing one's own needs. "A good mother," according to Lakshmi, "should also be a good mother-in-law." In this respect, she believes she is, in her own words, "atypical" and "modern":

> In the future, my own daughters-in-law will take care of me. They love me more than my sons. I am a different mother-in-law, because usually the mother-in-law is not nice to her daughters-in-law. But I am different, I am a modern person, I do everything I can for them, and I don't make their life difficult. I am respectful [àdaraniya], I don't say "yuck!" when I see something that I do not like. So I am a good mother [rāmro āmā] because I take care of my daughters-in-law and they will take care of me. I help them with the house chores, sometimes I stay in the evening and cook dinner for them.

Here, Lakshmi stresses that the reciprocity of care with her daughters-in-law is stronger than that with her sons, suggesting that it is not necessarily in the blood ties that a morality of relatedness is built, but rather in the mutuality of care, through empathizing with each other's existential conditions. Rethinking the archetypal relationship of the mother-in-law, Lakshmi affirms her modern self and expects care in return.

The relationship of the mother-in-law with the daughter-in-law has been of central interest among scholars of Nepal in the exploration of household socialization (see Bennett 1983; Des Chene 1998; Gray 2008; Nepali 2015). A daughter-in-law is expected to be submissive to her mother-in-law and to serve her respectfully. From the emergence of new domestic needs and the entrance of many women into the workforce, it follows that the relationship between the mother-in-law and the daughter-in-law is also undergoing significant transformations. Women often no longer have the time to take care of the house, while children go to school, and everyone lives their lives in different rhythms. Additionally, the education of women can bring them to resist subordination to their in-laws and husbands, an aspect that often leads to household fission (see Chapter 5). From her perspective, Lakshmi understands this and is determined to help her daughters-in-law. She believes that being a modern mother-in-law means reshaping this relationship inter-subjectively in terms of mutual help, an approach that substitutes old ideas of hierarchical submission.

Further reflecting on whether she is a good mother, Lakshmi stressed her own role as a daughter, showing that a good parent (both mother and father) is understood locally as one who also takes care of their elderly parents and not only of their children. Despite this ideal, taking care of the elders is considered by some such as Lakshmi to be a rare moral act, a social role that most people are believed not to fulfill:

> I am a good mother because I also take care of my own mother, while other mothers simply bring their old parents to aged care houses. I did not trust my brothers and sisters-in-law to take care of my old mother, so I kept her here with me, in my small house. Since my mother is sick, the doctor has said to give her food every two hours, but in very small amounts. I give her small pieces of boiled potatoes, dried fruits, such as raisins, and tea. I do what I think is right [*uchit*] because I care and love her.

Lakshmi does what she thinks is right for both her own mother and her daughters-in-law. In taking care of her own mother, she follows her heart, and in a way also a traditional idea of respect for one's elders, which, as she says, is disregarded by most people in contemporary times. Having acknowledged this breakdown, Lakshmi trusts that her own daughters-in-law will take care of her. Here, trust is the result of the conjoint effort of her mind and heart working toward an understanding of her daughter-in-law's daily life stresses, which in turn (as she expects) will generate empathy for her own condition in the future.

Ram

At the beginning of this chapter, I introduced Ram and Beti's anxiety about the future. However, Ram has a firm belief that a "good father" should not expect anything in return from his children for the sacrifices that he has made for them. This is what in his opinion makes a "modern father." By using the notions of mind and heart, he commented:

> You might feel sad because you don't see respect for the elders around you and sometimes for yourself. This makes you full of worry [cintā] for the future. But you also have the love for your children, and you know that they love you. One needs to pacify these dwelling feelings in one's heart. In this way, a modern father has relief [rahat aram] in his heart.

To help his children, Ram has given them most of his family land. As I introduced earlier in the book, this is considered a rather new practice, since in the past sons were expected to obtain their inheritance at the death of their father. But despite having provided help to his sons, Ram does not consider it appropriate to expect something in return. For him, this would be somewhat immoral, and care should only be accepted under revised moral conditions that enable a modern dharma. Similar to Lakshmi's case, Ram's attitude seems to be a way to embrace change, empathizing with his children in this new social milieu in which the old respect is no longer practiced. Nonetheless, they have different ideas on what to expect in return.

Ram and his wife Beti have conflictual discussions on this topic, showing how different narratives are put in place to respond to this revision of reciprocity even within the same families. Beti said: "Nowadays, we only eat together with our sons on special occasions. Sometimes I want to call them to ask them to fix things in the house, but my husband does not want me to annoy [risāunu] them and always tries to stop me from calling them." Ram further explained: "I do so because I know that they have their own problems and responsibilities toward their children, and also their wives don't like it if we call them all the time. Maybe I am an atypical parent, but I don't want them to perceive us as a burden." While Beti described herself as having "a more traditional perspective," like Lakshmi, Ram considers himself "atypical" and "modern." He is, in his own words, "modern." While Ram's comments at the beginning of this chapter reveal that he experiences suffering for the way he is treated by his children, at the same time he commits himself not to have expectations from them, in this way avoiding additional sufferance.

The Hindu value of dependence of aged people on their children has been observed by several scholars in the explanation of the attitudes of the elderly

toward their changing social status. For example, Vatuk (1990, p. 66) eluci-
dated that in an Indian context reciprocity is generally understood as a lifelong
cycle of mutual obligations in which dependency of the elders on their children is regarded as a repayment for what they had given in earlier years, and
that there is no guilt associated with pressuring one's children to provide care
in return. Similarly, in a Chinese context, Davis-Friedmann (1983, p. 13) noted
that "acceptance of dependency in a society that observes the norm of reciprocity creates the most decisive support for the favourable attitudes toward
the elderly," meaning that parents do not feel like burdens to their children.

However, dependency can also create suffering in the elderly when occurring under certain conditions. In fact, the same study by Vatuk (1990) also
demonstrates that this can happen when they perceive that their children
see them as burdens, often in those situations when they become physically
incapacitated, or are perceived as a weight on the household's resources. In
Bhaktapur, this leads aging parents themselves to reflect on the morality of
expecting or not expecting anything in return from their children. Ram's situation confirms these sentiments: "I am a modern person, and I am different
from other parents. I am very proud [garba] of my children, and I do not
expect anything in return for all that I have done for them. Most other parents say 'We have done a lot for you. Now what will you do in return?' Other
parents have sold their land to be able to educate their children, so when
they get older, they expect [apēkṣā] that the children take care of them. But
this is not the right question to ask your children." Ram suggests here that a
modern parent should only receive when the children wish to give, based on
their love and capabilities.

According to this perspective, a parent's effort becomes something akin
to a "pure gift" (using a term by Mauss 2002). Derrida (1992, p. 128) argued
that a pure gift is in fact impossible, and that even when the doer refuses to
think in terms of reciprocity, they will still weigh and judge the behavior of the
recipient. Nevertheless, Noonan (1984, p. 695) reaffirms the possibility that
the gift is conceptualized, at least ideally, as a pure form of exchange: "[The
idea] that the gift should operate coercively is indeed repugnant and painful
to the donor, destructive of the liberality that is intended." It follows that the
notion of the pure gift, albeit unattainable, could for some be the ideal condition of exchange. As Ram's case demonstrates, this is achieved through an
effort to pacify one's emotions and thoughts, to attune the heart-mind, in this
way allowing for a sense of well-being. This is achieved through an understanding of modernity as a time of hardship and the consequent reshaping of

one's role through the management of expectations, ultimately transforming a domestic dharma itself through a revision of the moralities of expectation.

For their part, most of the adult children interviewed expressed their sense of duty toward their parents, and their guilt deriving from the difficult and paradoxical situation of living abroad, studying or working full time, which often leads them to not be able to reciprocate their parents' sacrifice due to time and/or economic restrictions, in this way not fulfilling their dharma. This was evident in an interview with Ayush, one of the sons of Ram and Beti Khoteja, who is a schoolteacher and lives in Kathmandu:

> I feel guilty [*dōṣī*] whenever I think of my elderly parents left alone. But it is very hard. They complain that my brothers give them more than what I do, but they have not had any children yet and do not have the same expenses that we have. It is not just the school, there are daily things to do and to buy for them, and when other children get those things then we have to do too. It all starts in the early morning, to support this whole house, to take care of them all. My wife too helps, otherwise we would not be able to make any savings. It is all the fruit of daily sweat (Nep. *pasinā*) to give our children a better life. Hopefully also to enjoy some time off together one day, but there is not much time left each day. And I have to take care of my parents too, leave some money aside for them, and it is difficult to please everyone.

How can adult children take care of both elder parents and their own children when financial possibilities and pressures make this process more and more difficult? As Ayush suggests, the daily economic struggles might make money itself gain an added emotional charge.[12] The perspective of a better life to be achieved in the future through the sacrifice of the present animates most of the reflections of the younger people that I interviewed, but they very often also problematized their moral responsibility toward the elders.

Making Modern Elders

Empirical and theoretical explorations of changing domestic arrangements and relationships in connection to the life satisfaction of older people are becoming urgent as aging populations increase dramatically in developing countries such as Nepal. In the previous pages, I discussed how ideas of modernity are used to rethink expectations and moral self-making by local elders themselves in Bhaktapur. Bringing together local people's narratives, I first examined one of the most painful paradoxes of modernity for older adults in Nepal, which is the breakdown of intergenerational expectations of reciprocity, wherein children do not reciprocate their parents' sacrifices. Posing a challenge to established cultural frameworks, the generational breakdown requires individual intervention to bring back order in an otherwise unintelligible nomos. In contemporary Nepal, older adults are in a peculiar position, having faced accelerated social transformations during the course of their lives. While Liechty (2008) has extensively explored the processes that define moral selves among a wide range of choices and messages, particularly among the youth in Kathmandu, there is still a gap in understanding how older people define their moral selves in the context of social change.

The people that I interviewed articulated their experience through discourses of modernity as a contradictory time when life improvement and new ills overlap. A common element that could be seen across these stories is the constant tension in achieving an understanding of one's adult children's life perspectives through the rethinking of one's role and expectations. While "discourses of danger" reveal generalized anxiety among the local elderly population about their future conditions, the "discourse of hardship" point to an effort to empathize with one's children and rethink one's moral self as "modern." While each person had their individual perspective, two main broad reflections emerged that are well exemplified by the case studies of Lakshmi and Ram. For some, such as Ram, giving is a selfless act and nothing should be expected in return even when giving involves sacrifice. For others, such as Lakshmi, expectations are not in opposition to love. Lakshmi's position stresses an ideal reciprocity of care, which is based on a different emotional basis of exchange, opposing traditional ideals of care based on respect. For Lakshmi, this means establishing a "modern" relationship with her daughters-in-law, expecting heartfelt care rather than compulsory respect in return. In a way, this means that she continues to give, even after her sons got married, because it is now that they need her the most. Calling themselves "modern," both Lakshmi and Ram added notions of independence and selfless sacrifice to the shaping of their own selves as moral in a fast-changing social world.

Whereas studies of the status of older adults in Nepal mainly focus on the negative sides of their life condition my findings show what it means to become modern and find a sense of moral purpose from the perspective of aging people. There is no doubt that aging is a phase of life that holds culture-specific connotations across different societies. At the same time, it is now established among scholars that individual personality is never completely formed in adults, and it is plastic in nature, meaning that people keep shaping and revising their individuality and morality into old age. The most prominent scholar advancing this approach to aging is Margaret Clark (1967, p. 63), who noted:

> Personality is rather an ongoing process of interaction between the sociocultural world and the internal life of the individual—a process that continues throughout the life cycle. As anthropologists, we have learned little about the last half of that process and the diverse ways in which different cultures may pattern it. [. . .] A person not only must learn how his culture defines the "proper" manner of growing up; he must learn the "proper" manner of growing old—and failures to perceive or conform to these cultural dicta may bring him into serious conflict with society.

Clark builds her argument on the legacy of the school of culture and personality and the evolution of the anthropological discipline, an approach that shapes psychological discourse based on the belief that personality is constantly revised and readjusted. In confirming Clark's argument, the findings discussed in the previous pages show that the making of moral personhood among aging people in Bhaktapur is intertwined with ideas of modernity in a self-reflexive process. Furthermore, the case studies discussed here not only unveil how perspectives of the future might generate social suffering, but also how this is articulated according to the potential to rethink one's own role in the kinship network, which in turn establishes an intimate experience of social change. Despite the diversity of these experiences, a process of domestic adjustment involves an intersubjective conversation that weighs both pre-existing moral frameworks (such as the Hindu ideal of domestic reciprocity) and new ideologies (such as the modern mantra of providing one's children with better lives). It seems to me that the idea of modernity as an ideal of life improvement pushes toward the establishment of mutual understanding as a way to ensure the well-being of one's children. At the same time, in this way older adults also ensure their own well-being by establishing a moral self that is attuned to a new order of things.

This chapter contributes to this book's aim by exploring changing relationships and the development of moral selves in a context of accelerated change. It shows how the elderly revise dharma by rethinking their own position toward their children, mediating between old expectations and new needs, demonstrating this negotiation (which is personal and also economically restrained) to achieve their own and their children's well-being. In conclusion, through an analysis of the selected case studies, in this chapter I demonstrated not only that "moral experiences are [...] sentiment-based affairs" (Throop 2012, p. 158), but also substantially relational. Navigating their identities through a revision of old and new narratives, the people of these stories work toward the establishment of emotional nuances of kinship with their adult children, shortening the gap between their existential trajectories. At the same time, while "endurance makes the reality of hanging on appear dynamic and virtuous" (Weiss 2022, p. 65), in other words making it possible to go through hardship, these findings corroborate the literature that problematizes the circulation of care and support within families. Therefore, new policies will need to be implemented to account for the struggle of the elders and their adult children in the context of socioeconomic development.

Moral Selves, Social Change, and Hierarchies of Values

Making a Modern Dharma

This book has investigated how domestic relations and individual moralities are being revised in Bhaktapur in the pursuit of idealized well-being, and how dialogic processes between kin contribute to shaping social change from within. Throughout the chapters of this book, I have explored selected stories that show how people make sense of their moral selves in a context of a societal-wide moral disruption by navigating conflicts and seeking adjustments. Among family members, different perspectives were brought into conversation through the revision of a preexisting ethos that is conceptualized emically as "traditional" and through the negotiation of foreign ideas that are understood as "modern." This confirms Liechty's (2008) stance that the making of moral modernities involves much more than the assimilation of Western ideas and practices, taking instead the form of a dialogic process through which a modern dharma can be defined. In fact, the people that I interviewed and spent time with were shaping their social roles in a domestic cosmos, revising themselves simultaneously as modern, moral, and Newar.

In Chapter 2, I introduced the emergence of a middle class in Bhaktapur and started to argue that the experience of middle-classness unfolds largely within the framework of domestic relatedness and in the envisaging of a shared life plan for the betterment of one's life condition. In the remaining ethnographic chapters, I discussed selected cases of moral dilemmas and explored the emotions involved as well as the considerations made by people in revamping the moral basis of kinship. In Chapter 3, I examined parental ideas on how children should be educated to become moral adults. Episodes of moral breakdown often lead to situations of avoidance between parents and children, and I suggested that this might be a stratagem to both preserve kinship and to continue following problematic norms or divisive worldviews. This situation was exemplified by the story of Dor Bahadur's children, who celebrated a birthday during a mourning period. This celebration defied "traditional" cultural norms and yet this issue was avoided by Dor Bahadur and his wife to maintain harmonious relations. The celebration of Vishnu's birthday became a moral laboratory, particularly when Dor Bahadur's daughter tried to explain the precautions that she and her brother were taking to avoid transgressing the rules. While kinship preservation and the ideal of harmony run like a golden thread in most stories, the accounts discussed also demonstrate that fractures, fissions, and alternative kin relationships are very common. I also outlined how maturing children develop alternative forms of interaction with their peers to affirm their moral identities through practices that would otherwise be sanctioned by their parents. As I will further elaborate in a moment, kinship ruptures and alliances have much to do with moral negotiations and with the values that come into play each time. If in some cases norms are revised to enable the persistence of a kin relationship, in other cases bonds are broken. In this conclusive chapter, I suggest that this generally occurs when other values or even other relationships are deemed more important.

Experimenting with concrete rules, subterranean moralities eventually emerge and become dominant. This becomes evident in the case of marriage choices, which, as I showed in Chapter 4, are still experienced as an individual as much as a collective affair and yet can function as a turning point in the making of one's independent identity as a young adult. I demonstrated that an ideal of well-being shapes both marriage choices and expectations. At the same time, while there is space for an individual's and a couple's well-being to eventually prevail over other priorities, the institution of marriage is still very much embedded in social constructions and constrictions. In fact, spousal relationships themselves are shaped in the search for "balance," "well-being," and "happiness," and are strictly intertwined with negotiations of moralities between cultural conformity and change. This is carried out through the enactment of a dimension of mutual understanding between the partners conceptualized as "companionship." This demonstrates an ongoing preoccupation with relational continuity in a spousal relationship, rather than a compulsion for change and promiscuity as postulated by Giddens (1992) in other contexts as a feature of "modern" relationships.

The emerging ideal of companionship substitutes old notions of marriage as an enforcer of social order through the reproduction of domestic hierarchy. As such, strengthening spousal bonds often exacerbates tensions with the families of origin. I unpacked this topic in Chapter 5, where I discussed conflicting interests over household flows, which required a revision of value hierarchies and the division of domestic spaces. Further, I suggested that the willingness to live in a nuclear setting was an added factor in the decision to separate. In fact, the choice to separate is itself seen locally as a moral transgression, and it was therefore justified by means of other factors such as the wrongdoing of others in the household. The dynamic of seeking justifications to affirm a new moral basis for one's "deviant" behavior from sociocultural expectations recurred in several other stories. It was "because these are the new generations" that the family of Dewa accepted his intercaste marriage with Tika, and only because "love is stronger than society" was his family eventually able to overcome their initial resistance to accepting an otherwise impermissible deviance. This shows that changing understandings of marriage and family responsibilities still need to be mediated with prescribed social roles and duties. At the same time, external social structures of support, such as the emerging friendship *guthis*, which I examined in Chapter 6, create the possibility to go against sociocultural norms without incurring "social death." Finally, conflict between one's family of origin and of creation becomes dramatic later in life, when the elderly parents often have to deal with conditions of abandonment while also struggling to reshape their own position within the moral framework that keeps them connected with their children, as discussed in Chapter 7.

These findings support my argument that the quest for well-being in Bhaktapur is intersubjective in a Husserlian sense, insofar as it involves actions through which social actors actively work to coordinate with one another to attune their existential dimensions while making sense of, and by revising, their lived reality. A loosely drafted script seems to repeat itself across the many stories analyzed, unfolding as an oscillating balance of power between parents and children, which dialogically shapes moral selves from generation to generation. Thus, while each individual and each family face different issues and resolve them in personal ways, these stories have recurrent traits. A common element that could be seen across the selected narratives is the constant preoccupation with achieving mutual understanding, as a state of things in which both parties are comfortable with their own moral behavior, and in which "society" is deemed acquiescent. When this is not possible, and stronger values push for change, then "society" itself is transformed. Thus, the value of well-being appears to be sought in relation to kinship continuity, and constant tensions do not encompass, at least in most cases, terminal ruptures.

The theory of attunement-entanglement by Zigon (2014) works well to explain what I found among the Newars of Bhaktapur. According to Zigon (2014, p. 22), attunement is not an action "done by an individual who psychologically adjusts; rather, attunement in the ontological sense is that foundational capacity that allows relationships to assemble." In other words, the process of attunement-entanglement is an inherent part of any given relationship, and it is constructed on the basis of specific Newar domestic cosmologies. These span ritual and economic dimensions, as well as emotional and ideological planes, to which each individual contributes through the fulfillment of their assigned *samskāra* steps, that is, following their own prescribed dharma. The ontological condition that guides individuals toward the reproduction of a moral ideal in order to maintain a relationship is what Zigon (2014, p. 24) calls "fidelity." Contrasting moral ideals involve a negotiation of the directions of fidelity toward specific social actors who might be in competition with one another, working under disparate ideals of individual and common well-being for the establishment of a modern dharma. The latter can thus be seen as an intersubjective ground on which relationships are harmonized and moral selves are shaped.

An exploration of attunement and fidelity as ontological conditions for morally being-in-the-world allows us to go beyond a discussion of notions of good, evil, responsibility, and freedom as universal constructs, instead approaching them emically. If being-in-the-world is "always already entangled in a multiplicity of relationality" (Zigon 2014, p. 21), the type of relationships that underpin how each human existential condition is rooted into specific relations with their world need to be examined in each context. For example, for the Urapmin people studied by Robbins (2004), moral self-reflection and confession are the strategies used to repristinate individual moral selves in a context of recurrent ethical dilemmas. For middle-class Newar people in Bhaktapur, a modern moral ethos involves constant tension between fracture and connection in the net of *māyā*, and a sense of insecurity about social bonds is experienced in alternating moments of understanding and rupture, in other words through a redefinition of mutuality of being itself. These concurring values of life betterment and ideals of attunement to a net of relatedness are the basis on which micro-dimensions of social change unfold.

I believe that an "assemblage" approach, as discussed by authors such as Zigon (2010, 2013), Ong and Collier (2005), and DeLanda (2006), can be useful to give a sense of the fragmentation of local moral realities. At the same time, trying to bring together all the stories under recurring themes, I have so far attempted a "moderatum generalisation" (Williams 2002), which is an interpretation "explicitly formulated within a context of supporting evidence" (Payne and Williams 2005). That is, assuming an intimate perspective on people's everyday lives does not exclude a broader understanding of the social worlds in which these experiences unfold. Far from being taken as typical cases, the selected stories show instead how different people's experiences are from one another, and yet how common ideas are spread across a changing society. In the next section, I shall attempt an interpretation of the intimate making of modern moral personhood in the context of Nepal as a developing country, with a focus on the middle-class existential condition for how it intertwines with material conditions of life. I then move to discuss them through the lens of a hierarchy of values by Robbins (2007, p. 296).

Sketching a Middle-Class Experience

Theoretically, in this book I approached the middle class in Nepal as a cultural practice whose existential dimensions are shaped by conditions of aspiration and uncertainty. Similar to the Muscovite man described by Zigon (2009) whose moral experience is centered around the repetition of moments of suffering, the accounts of local people outlined in this study reveal the "tensions, contradictions and struggles of living through" an "existentially disruptive period" (Zigon 2009, p. 97). The tensions between aspiration and uncertainty are experienced actively in terms of self-discovery, through which notions of modernity and tradition are questioned.

Arguably, even the lives of the farmers during and after the Rana regime were marked by uncertainty, being constrained by unpredictable weather conditions and by dramatic socioeconomic marginalization, as I discussed in Chapter 2. Yet, they were involved in a more stable context of social norms, which, while possibly producing considerable stress, must have generated a different type of anxiety from what their descendants are experiencing in Nepal as a developing country ambivalently marked by enhanced possibility for change as well as different layers of social and economic vulnerability. As

Canclini (1995) postulated, uncertainty and anxiety are features of modern times due to material and social precariousness. As suggested by Bauman (2013, p. 82), this has much to do with an experience of "becoming" in the context of "liquid modernity": "Living under liquid modern conditions can be compared to walking in a minefield: everyone knows an explosion might happen at any moment and in any place, but no one knows when the moment will come and where the place will be." While economic precarity is certainly a reality affecting domestic relationships in many ways, what interested me to demonstrate and discuss in this book has been the relational doubts and conflicts emerging in a time of increased possibilities and diversified interests rather than examining change through an economic lens. Social and financial vulnerability is experienced from a domestic perspective in terms of precariousness of those very webs of relatedness on which local people depend in a condition of "ontological dependence." This follows from the fragmentariness of individual interests that characterize the domestic sphere as each person pushes for their own life plan, in turn revealing the problematization of individual roles in the household, as well as conditions of exchange, reciprocity, and care. If diverging interests and ideals are not a totally new feature in Newar families, these are intensified by both modern views and material conditions of life, where the two things are, I suggest, inseparable.

At the same time, change is intertwined with continuities, and notions of modernity and tradition are filled with contextual meanings in each situation, providing a moral ground for individual choices. For example, while the friendship *guthis* are a product of middle-class prerogatives, they are shaped significantly by local sensitivities that draw from relational values and moralities that are inextricable from those very needs. In fact, a middle-class imaginary that rotates around the betterment of living conditions generates a new existential perspective that is projected toward the future and that at the same time intertwines with local cosmologies. This existential, time-based dimension is accompanied by another perception of time that perdures from the traditional system of Bhaktapurian Hindu tantric beliefs, that is, the maintenance of the old cyclic process of dead and ancestor support through funerary rites and ritual feeding ceremonies. These concurring ideas and their negotiation reveal the construction of a lifeworld that involves intersubjective actions through which "people both create social reality and are constrained by the pre-existing social and cultural structures created by their predecessors" (Ritzer 2011, p. 219). Dharma here plays the role of a nomos in transition. In this context, *māyā* itself is the motivator to both follow and revise dharma. In fact, in the process of seeking balance, people appear to be particularly worried about preserving their kinship relationships, although usually through modified and negotiated moral premises, because it is only within solid webs of relatedness that an intelligible nomos can be affirmed and that moral selves can be conceptualized and be able to find fulfillment and purpose in the social system.

The fear of loneliness and social death among Newar people in Bhaktapur was also noted by Parish (1994, p. 83). For example, consider this comment from one of his informants: "If a person does things that are not in the liking of the twa:, then suffering (I) will come to that person. [. . .] He could get sick. He would need help. But people won't help. The twa: gives help to those who are liked—will help them when they suffer. Or this person might have to go frequently to Kathmandu. There would be no one at home. A thief might steal [from his home]." This quote reflects very well the preoccupation of local people with being involved in a social net of relations, be these domestic or extradomestic. This is possibly enhanced in a society that has for centuries relied (and still does to a large degree) on kinship ties for all life cycle–related issues and daily needs in the absence of a welfare government. And yet, social death does not only entail the loss of receiving practical help. If being liked, as this informant observed, is the condition for receiving help, not being liked is itself experienced as a moral failure, not only causing material hardship and the impossibility of fulfilling necessary ritual duties, but also one's inner suffering deriving from the rejection of others. Why would anyone risk falling into such social anomie? Despite this risk, rule contestation and deviance occur because new meaningful relationships can be formed through this process of moral creativity. The strengthening of social ties that do not only rely on reciprocal likability but rather on an indissoluble relationship becomes a further guarantee of relatedness in the fragile net of *māyā*. *Māyā* is needed to fulfill both old and new priorities, as a mediation between individual and familial interests, and to maintain kinship roles entangled in their *saṃsāra* duties. For example, the importance of the cult of the dead, which is crucial in Hindu society and in the Newar society of Bhaktapur and a constitutive part of the integrated metaphysics and social world of the mesocosm, is based on family continuities, while new concerns around *māyā* itself generate tensions, fractures, and new relational desires.

In practice, the processes of norms negotiation from a bottom-up perspective discussed in the chapters of this book reveal a contestation of recurring themes that are central to dharma as a moral system in transition, including gender aspects, power dynamics in the household, age-appropriate behaviors, and so on. In negotiating social norms and roles, people are debating and experimenting with the ground of mutual understanding, through which personal goals of life betterment are mediated with ideals of domestic well-being. The generalization attempted so far is essential to start theorizing on how micro and macro dimensions of meaning intertwine to shape a Bhaktapurian modern lifeworld through a reconfiguration of hierarchies of values.

Moral Selves, Social Change, and Hierarchies of Values

To understand social change, we need to consider the topics of contestation and the existential predispositions involved in each context. As Mattingly (2014, chap. 1) postulated, "to recognize the mysteries of the everyday one must look with detailed care at how social conditions become dialectical for people living with them." Similarly, I believe that a discussion on social change demands a reflection on the notion of agency for how this unfolds as a dialogic experience. In his theory of interactionism, George Herbert Mead (1934) advanced the argument that social norms of interaction function not only as the ground rules for social interaction, but also that these norms are revised in the context of human interaction. In fact, as noted by Mines (in Sökefeld 1999, p. 438): "Much of self-awareness is brought into consciousness precisely because it takes the form of both internal and actual arguments with others about how to behave and how behaviour should be estimated." In Bhaktapur, this largely takes place within the household. Here, affection is not in opposition to self-interests, and the project of life improvement is thought of as a matter of reciprocal care and expectations. The chapters of this book have provided a window into how people in Bhaktapur dialogically negotiate their lifeworlds through the shaping of broader "ideoscapes" (using a term by Appadurai 1990, p. 296) within which they are immersed, and into how they adjust to the socioeconomic contexts in which their lives are entangled.

I agree with Robbins (2007, p. 296) that an exploration of local hierarchies of values can be a useful approach for understanding how established sociocultural norms interact and collide with ideas of freedom and individual choice. Similar to Dumont (1980, 1986), Robbins (2007, 2012) argues that elements of a culture are organized within hierarchies of more or less valued elements. Nonetheless, within local moral worlds there are always conflicting views that can derive from different perspectives and social positions (Kleinman 1999, p. 361), where different social roles hold different values. Furthermore, as observed by Sahlins (1992, p. 24), "to 'modernize' the people must first learn to hate what they already have, what they have always considered their well-being." In this tension, moral freedom depends on how strong a value is and whether one is willing to affirm it at the cost of going against society, against kin, or even colliding with one's own private morality.

The stories discussed reveal an ongoing negotiation of a hierarchy of values, whose creative power is proportioned to one's motivation to affirm oneself as a moral individual who is pursuing a life plan and doing so while nested in a secure net of relationships. Through their interactions, Bhaktapurian parents and children, spouses, and peers actively seek their way through well-being as an ideal that is carried out by local and foreign bodies, the government, the media, and other local people in order to define goals and priorities and their own individual positions toward the achievement of intersubjective wellness. All of these dimensions are related with an idealized notion of well-being, which was conceptualized in personal ways by different actors. An understanding of what values are in play in each context and what interests prevail is crucial for understanding the unfolding of these processes seen through conflicts and adjustments. In Bhaktapur, conceptualizing the family as a nexus between self and society through a negotiation of hierarchies of values also requires that we rethink the dichotomy between individualism and collectivism for how it has generally been addressed in the study of Hindu social worlds.

The role of individual choice in Hindu families has often been analyzed within the framework of a dichotomy between individualism and collectivism, where the latter has also been defined as "sociocentrism" (see Shweder & Bourne 1984) or "holism" (Dumont 1980, p. 272). Through the concept of holism, Louis Dumont (1980, 1986; also Dumont & Béteille 1987) described a sociocentric shared value common to South Asian societies that "neglects or subordinates the human individual" (Parish 1994, p. 186) in favor of the interests of the social group. Along these lines, some scholars of Hindu society have affirmed that among Hindu people "the social environment never provided an opportunity to the individual to feel that he had interests apart from those of the family" (Kapadia 1958, p. 246). Other scholars have harshly criticized this viewpoint, rejecting the dichotomy. Among them, some have argued that this approach obfuscates the reality of individual mental and emotional processes, and they have stressed instead the centrality of individual experience in Hindu social worlds (Mines 1988; Béteille et al. 1986).

Despite the important contribution of these criticisms in stressing the role of individual agency in all social contexts, the normative power of social values and institutions (be that the civic society, family, and so on) as outlined by Dumont should not be overlooked, even when people "depict themselves as active agents, pursuing private goals and making personal decisions that affect the outcome of their lives" (Mines 1988, p. 568). In fact, in the Newar context, Toffin (1984, p. 123) has observed that private and public lives are so strictly intertwined that the pressures that society exercises on the family are peculiar to Newars among other Nepali ethnic groups. Yet, as my findings demonstrate, a close permeability between self and others does not necessarily lead to cultural conformity. Indeed, I suggest that the very fact that the "self" is entangled in a living "net of relationships" (Parish 1994, p. 187) is the reason why conflict and negotiations are also so predominant in the domestic sphere, largely due to the necessary adjustments between individual desires, perceptions of moral behavior, and the expectations of others. It is in this balance that Newar people form their moral selves. Thus, despite the discordances, being part of a family is as fundamental for the shaping of Newars' selves as much as it is "a process of becoming" (Parish 1994, p. 126), since "family love and empathy, family duty and necessity, family conflict and tension make them what they are" (Parish 1994, p. 126). In concurring with Parish that relatedness should be seen as a process of becoming, in this book I stressed moral creativity rather than conformity. In the case studies examined, the concept of mutual understanding was used by the people themselves to explain how ideas of relatedness are changing alongside and through a reconsideration of individual selves.

In rejecting the dichotomy between individualism and collectivism, and embracing the notion of relatedness as a process of becoming, I suggest that attunement needs to be conceptualized within a spectrum of positions in the context of a domestic hierarchy. In this perspective, the family becomes a nexus between self and society and a moral laboratory *par excellence*. While in the past there was certainly agency and possibly willingness to deviate from family interests, today ideals of well-being that challenge a preexisting ethos are stronger, more widespread, and more economically viable. The very idea of mutual understanding is thus being redefined within a framework of new moral values and possibilities, involving notions of empathy and intimacy. Practices of personhood in Bhaktapur are therefore at the same time intimate and social. While similar issues experienced by the people of the stories in this book might have always existed, these would have had to be largely subterranean due to a socialized need to conform to a collective order, and they are now becoming dominant, leading to the alteration and subversion of preexisting hierarchies of values.

As noted by Robbins (2007, p. 301), stable conflicts are important elements in cultures in the affirmation of values through the enactment of dialectics. Differently, conflicts that arise in phases of sociocultural change are due to the introduction of new values or to transformation occurring in the hierarchy of preexisting values, where these processes become motors of social change. In fact, factors of "stress" leading to kinship fractures should not necessarily be seen as something completely new and "hence creating problems that cannot be solved by applying routine or traditional devices" (Beals and Siegel 1966, p. 91). Instead, old strains might become stresses when people want to and can afford to disagree. In this sense, while forceful mutual understanding was a "traditional device" (Beals and Siegel 1966, p. 91) to solve problems based on generalized ideas of moral behavior, in contemporary times these devices might not work due to people's unwillingness to compromise. The grounds and the rules of negotiation between individual and group have thus changed. Strains become stresses as they become catalysts for social change, unfolding in a continuity of relatedness rather than rupture, generating moments of moral breakdown through which people have to negotiate their views to repristinate a collective nomos, the shared ground of values that makes being-in-the-world possible.

Final Considerations

Offering new insights on middle-classness and family in contemporary Nepal, this book lays the groundwork for further investigation. In particular, future studies could make comparisons with other Newar cities and other ethnic groups. The findings discussed can also provide a valuable contribution for the implementation of family-sensitive policies and governmental and nongovernmental initiatives targeting Nepali families. This might take into account the need to take care of the elders, the frustrations of the youth, and the increase in domestic conflict engendered by socioeconomic ambitions and perils.

More broadly, by examining the interrelated and mutually influencing ways in which people revise relationships, shape their moral selves, and ultimately negotiate social change through the making of a modern dharma, this book sheds new light on the processes through which moral ideas and behaviors are negotiated for the purposes of attaining well-being from a domestic perspective. By looking at the domestic as the locus of the negotiations between social change and continuity, and at conflict as a dialogic process of cultural revision, this work contributes to recent debates in the fields of kinship studies, anthropology of conflict, and moral anthropology, providing a new perspective on the making of moral modernities in Nepal. As White (2010, 164) noted, personal values and goals are "located within broader normative frameworks and ideologies, understandings . . . of the sacred, what the moral order is and should be, and what it means to live a meaningful life." And Christopher (1999, 147) reminds us, any discussions on well-being raise crucial questions on the very nature of the "human": "What is the self that is in relation to others? Is it the individualistic self who has relationships to get certain psychological needs, such as intimacy, met? Or is it the self experienced as metaphysically connected to others such that identity already incorporates others?" In providing ethnographic evidence of these processes, the broader significance of *Modern Dharma* is located in the analysis of the interconnection between relationships and well-being, which is significant across virtually all human societies.

I shall now conclude this work with a final sketch that assists me in painting a more concise picture of the findings discussed:

Talking to André Beteille who was a student at the time, and who was praising the work of well-known social scholars such as Parsons and Lévi-Strauss, his teacher Mysore Srinivas (1976, p. xv) once said: "Yes, but do you think they really understand the messiness of social life?" In this book, I have attempted to address this messiness, which, while we might never fully grasp it, nonetheless reveals people's efforts to make sense of their lifeworlds through never-ending clashes and adjustments. Ultimately a social space very much worth being explored, the domestic is the venue in which the articulation of moral behaviors takes shape, where ideas and practices are filtered and go back out into the world.

GLOSSARY

Ajur ajur: to be in harmony
Āpasī samājdari: mutual understanding
Āśrama: stages of Hindu life
Bhatache[n]: from the perspective of a woman, the husband's home (New.)
Bikāś: modernity, development
Brāhman: highest priestly Hindu caste responsible for leading prayers and religious
    functions
Buhāri: daughter-in-law
Che[n]: house
Chhetri(ya): second highest caste of rulers, warriors, and administrators
Chulō: cooking area
Cinā: certificate containing horoscopic information provided at birth by a *purohit*
Cintā: anxiety
Dāl bhāt: a dish composed of rice and lentils
Dashain: Hindu festival signifying the victory of good over evil, celebrated both in
    Nepal and India. It is an occasion for the whole family to gather together and
    share food, and animal sacrifices are performed to worship the goddess Durga
    who defeated the demon Mahisasur.
Dharma: religious duty associated with a person's caste or stage of life
Dhikuti: a system of rotating credit
Digudhya guthi: ancestor *guthi* with the role of worshipping the ancestral deity of the
    family. The duty to worship is passed turn by turn by agnatic members of the
    extended family network.
Dimāg: brain-mind
Dukkha: sufferance, hardship
Fukē: agnatic members of a *digudhya guthi*
Ghar: house
Grihastha: householder
Guthi: Newar social and religious association
Ijjat: honor, reputation
Jabarjasti ko bujhai: forceful understanding
Janko: Newari ritual of first rice feeding ceremony of an infant; also called *pasni*

Jata tu: good match

Jyāpu: Newar caste of the farmers (when not capitalized: farmer)

Karma: fate, spiritual principle of cause and effect where actions and intentions of individuals influence their future. It can also be seen as one's destiny to be owned and shaped.

Kathina jīvana: difficult life

Kisān: farmer

Kul: lineage

Lajjā: shame

Lamē: marriage mediator, matchmaker

Man: heart-mind

Man ko shanti: peace of mind (also *biśrānti*)

Mane-khanlhagu: lonely heart talk (New.)

Māyā: love, attachment, terrain illusion

Moksa: release from the cycle of rebirth

Najur najur: to not be in harmony

Nepal Sambat: Nepali New Year, started in 879 CE in the name of philanthropist Sankhadhar Sākhwā who freed local people from their debts (see Pradhananga 2012)

Pāp: sin, violation of dharma

Pāsā: friend

Phuki: Newar lineage group

Pujā: worship

Purohit: Hindu priest

Rāksī: local alcohol obtained from the distillation of rice (also known as *ailā*)

Rāmro jīvanī: good life

Rāmro mānche: good person

Samāe baji: traditional Newari dish prepared during festivals, family celebrations, and get-togethers consisting of *baji* (beaten rice), fried black soybeans, fresh ginger pieces, broiled/marinated meat, dried fishes, savory lentil *pattis*, and *rāksī*

Samāj: society

Samsāra: the cycle of death and rebirth to which life in the material world is bound

Samskāra: rites of passage marking the life cycles from birth to death

Sannyasi: ascetic

Siguthi: Newar funerary association

Śrāddha: ritual ceremony to commemorate deceased people of the household and ancestors

Takhali: elder man, also a *guthi* leader

Thache[n]: a married woman's natal home

Thakāli: ethnic group of Mustang

Thar: clan of people sharing the same surname

Ṭikā: mark of blessing put on the forehead

Tuiga[n]: a modality of *guthi* membership, also known as "half membership"

Twa: neighborhood in a Newar city. It is thought to have human-like qualities, embodying the judgment of others. A neighborhood is known as *tole* when referring to its spatial dimensions.

Vanaprastha: going to the forest to retire; forest retirement

NOTES

Chapter 1

1. Bhaktapur means "the city of devotees" (from the words *bhakta*, which means "devotee," and *pur*, which means "city").

2. These are clan-like units that have a role in determining the occupation of people in the city, as well as their role at festival events. The *thars* are subdivided in what Levy has defined as "macrostatus" levels, ranking from the Brāhmans to the untouchables (see Levy 1990, p. 17).

3. For a discussion of the Newar caste system, the reader will find useful information in Levy (1990), Owens (1989), and Gellner (1986).

4. The notion of "Western" is generally used in Nepal to refer to Indian culture (M. Liechty 2022, pers. comm., Dec. 29).

5. Poverty is defined in the same study as the condition in which people live on less than USD$1.90 a day.

6. Similar approaches to the study of the notion of middle class can be seen in other contexts, particularly in studies produced in the 1960s and 1970s, for example in the United States (Sennett and Cobb 1972) and in India (Ross 1961).

7. According to Hausner and Sharma (2013), there are more than two million Nepali workers just in India.

8. On the link between well-being and relationships, see Camfield, Choudhury, and Devine (2009), Gough and McGregor (2009), and Sointu (2005).

9. Sociologists too have consistently underlined the need to study relationships and intimacy as they are impacted by and in turn shape social change around the world (see, e.g., Illouz 2007; Jamieson 1997; Giddens 1992; Bauman 2013), and also how they influence well-being (McKie 2005).

10. For further discussion of this notion of vulnerability, see the recent work *Political Economy of Social Change and Development in Nepal* by Jeevan Sharma (2021).

11. I discuss my findings on eating habits and ideas of health elsewhere (Tiné 2020).

12. See Trawick (1990) for a similar approach to notions of love in a Tamil family.

Chapter 2

1. The term *jyāpu* (lit: peasant) is considered somewhat derogatory by some local people, particularly by those belonging to activist communist groups, who suggested

using *kisān* (lit: worker in the fields) instead. However, people from a *jyāpu* background were in some cases proud of the original term because of its historical significance as it highlights their past of struggle and resilience; I have therefore used the term *jyāpu* in this chapter to discuss the evolution of farming activities in a historical perspective.

2. Or *jhara* in Newari.

3. They provided medical services while trying to convert the population to Christianity (see Liechty 1997, p. 19).

4. See also Höfer (1979) for the social implications of the caste system. See also the recently published English translation of the Muluki Ain by Khatiwoda, Cubelic, and Michaels (2021).

5. Lewis (1986) criticized the Bhaktapur Development Project for not making use of the ethnographic knowledge provided by several anthropologists during their activities, including himself. While I agree with Lewis, I also believe that the report by Haaland (1982) can be considered a useful document on the events of the time because it contains quotes (even if only a few) from local people.

6. The caste strata are further complicated in other internal hierarchical divisions in the macrostatus, which also regulates marriage practices. The macrostatus includes several *thars*, or households with the same surnames. Finally, the Newar caste system is located in a larger caste system including other ethnic groups. The discussion on the functioning of the caste system found its most prominent theorization in Dumont's work (1980), according to which hierarchy is framed by the concepts of purity and impurity. These concepts are expressed through several aspects of daily life, such as food practices and spatial distributions (Parish 1998). The concepts of purity and impurity define which people can accept water and cooked food from whom, as water is believed to absorb the impurity of the person that it is in contact with. As a consequence, food practices, such as cooking rice, will absorb all the impurities of the cook through the medium of water. Within the Newar caste system, Brāhmans have a fundamental role in religious rituals that mark the major milestones in each cosmological year and provide a ritual means for the maintenance of the social hierarchy. In complete contrast to the highly respected role of Brāhmans, untouchable sweepers, who lie outside of the Varnas, perform a very different role within society, which is to absorb the impurities of the city, in this way guaranteeing its purity (Parish 1998).

7. This data is according to the 1971 census (in Levy 1990, p. 62). This included both Hindu and Buddhist Newar farmers. The farmer group is known as Maharjan in the Buddhist community of Bhaktapur.

8. Or *jhara* in Newari.

9. The Gorkhas were originally a tribe of Brāhmans and warriors that had settled in the village of Gorkha in the hills of Nepal to escape from the Muslim invasion of Rajasthan (India) in the 1600s (Anderson 2016, p. 36; also Wright 1877, and Hasrat 1970).

10. See Wright (1877, pp. 57–67).

11. From that day, the members of the king's family were kept in a state of obscurity and only held symbolic power, as they were still considered by the local people to be an

incarnation of Vishnu (Anderson 2016, p. 38). The king and his family went to live in a mansion called at the time the "Happy Cottage," located in the Narayanhiti palace in Kathmandu. This is now known as Tribhuvan Sadan.

12. Historians have provided several interpretations as to why the British Empire never colonized Nepal, including the lack of roads (which made movement difficult and would have increased the costs of war), the diplomacy of Jung Bahadur, and the need to maintain a delicate balance with other countries in Asia including China. In his paper "Selective exclusion: Foreigners, foreign goods, and foreignness in modern Nepali history," Liechty (2008, p. 9) explains how through a process of "selective exclusion" the British and the Gorkha empire exploited one another to their advantage through economic relationships, protection, exchange of commodities, and provision of soldiers. Following defeat in the Anglo-Nepalese War (1814–1816), also known as the Gurkha War, Nepal was forced to accept a permanent British Resident in the Kathmandu Valley.

13. For a discussion of the Newari language movement, see Gellner (1986, pp. 128–34).

14. They are now remembered as the four martyrs of Nepal.

15. At the time, he was a member of the Youth League and he is now the chairperson of NWPP.

16. A *ropani* corresponds to 0.126 acres of land.

17. The BDP was initiated by the West German Development Agency and His Majesty's Government of Nepal.

18. For example, in the years following the BDP activities, under the idea of *safa sahar* (lit: "clean city"), the BM employed the local sweepers to perform cleaning activities, but also soon involved numerous *jyāpu* (Dhakal and Pokharel 2005, p. 192). It was not easy to convince the local people to perform activities that were traditionally associated with low-caste status, such as cleaning the streets and collecting garbage. To transform the negative connotation of the activity, the BM portrayed them as an essential and valuable social service, publishing photographs of the people who collected garbage in a popular local magazine. Among these, there were some personalities of high status, such as politicians. In fact, the BM made the cleaning of the streets a compulsory activity for the chairmen of the wards and encouraged highly respected citizens, such as Brāhmans and professionals, to sweep the streets publicly and on public occasions (Dhakal and Pokharel 2005, p. 192).

19. The NWPP was founded by Comrade Rohit, whose political views were aligned with North Korea and soon entered into conflict with ANKS.

20. The NWPP has had a constant majority in the Bhaktapur Municipality (BM) political scene, with a striking *jyāpu* representation over the last thirty years (Hachhethu 2004, p. 62).

21. Staple produce included rice, wheat, maize, potatoes, pulses, peas, barley, sugarcane, ginger, tomatoes, onions, and soybeans.

22. A new influx of workers from the hills to the valley was made possible by the new bus line that took advantage of the road connecting Pokhara to Kathmandu, built in 1973 (Ishii 1980, p. 171).

23. These usually remove important parts of the soil, making the land less fertile.

24. This is a Nepali traditional painting style.

25. Nowadays, the literacy rate in Bhaktapur is 81.68 percent. Across the local population of Bhaktapur, 90.48 percent of men and 72.65 percent of women are literate (CBS 2012, p. 4). Among the various ethnic groups, Newars present the highest intergenerational change with significant increase in upward mobility in education and access to jobs, surpassing their father's education level (WB 2016, p. 13).

26. Following students' and intellectuals' protests, in 1980 King Birendra Bir Bikram Shah Dev (1972–2001) was forced to launch a referendum to decide whether or not to keep the Panchayat system. In the election results the Panchayat won against the multiparty system.

27. According to some scholars, this movement would have been inspired by Zulfikar Ali Bhutto's execution in Pakistan and the fall of the Berlin Wall in 1989 (Einsiedel, Malone, and Pradhan 2012, p. 7).

28. This shows that the foreign influence that the Ranas had so much feared had been crucial in forming those new ideologies that were at the base of the pro-democracy movement of 1990.

29. The empowerment of women and the dynamics of social change were only about to begin and would be observed elsewhere across several Nepali ethnic groups (see, e.g., Rankin 2004).

30. This included the CPN-UML and the CPN-M.

31. The 2015 constitution established Nepal as a secular state.

32. Nowadays agriculture in Nepal is prevalently led by corporations with very low paid workers.

33. Education was made free and compulsory since Nepal adopted its first constitution in 1948. In terms of health care, the Health System was introduced as the General Health Plan in 1956, generating new practical possibilities for well-being.

Chapter 3

1. During a mourning period, all the direct men of a family (*fukẽ*) have to wear white clothes. This does not include the family of the married daughters, who become part of their husbands' families.

2. This is also done with English words that have entered the local vocabulary. For example, when I showed people a portrait that I made of them, they would often smile and say "same-same!"

3. This is also known as an "impurity period" (*asuddhata awadhi*).

4. See, for example, the work by Margaret Mead (1954). Her studies flourished in the same period in which European historians such as Philippe Ariès (1962) were further developing the pioneering work on childhood in historical perspectives by Karl Mannheim (1970).

5. Children are called *bacchā* in Nepali and *macchā* in Newari until they are seven or eight (Onta-Bhatta 2001, p. 246) or otherwise until the onset of puberty, at which

point they start being called *yuva* (specifically *yuva vyakti* for males and *yuva nari* for females). The Newar terms are *lyahma* for males and *lyase* for females until the age of thirty, regardless of their marital status (Gutschow and Michaels 2008, p. 190). Another common term has emerged in recent years to refer to the youth: the English word "teenager."

6. Children are given a name by the astrologer (*joshi*) at birth, but this is kept secret until the *janko* ritual, which is celebrated at six months of age for a girl and seven months for a boy (Toffin 1975, p. 50). Janko is also known as the "name-giving ceremony" (coinciding for some families with the first ingestion of solid food by the baby). After *janko*, children are considered an official part of the family and for most families still to this day, this is the time when they can be cremated, rather than buried, in case of premature death. Toffin (1975) considers *janko* a family ceremony, the first *samskāra* of a child to officially enter the family as a member.

7. I have discussed elsewhere how willingness to spoil the children might be a cause of the spread of unhealthy diet in Bhaktapur (Tiné 2020).

8. Generally the boys would help in the fields and the girls would take care of younger children in the house (Onta-Bhatta 2001, p. 246).

9. See also Levy's (1996) comparative discussion on parenting styles in Bhaktapur and Piri.

10. On the importance of education among Newar people see Shakya (2010).

11. This notion of maturation resonates with the metaphor of a fruit that ripens, as reported in Skinner (1990, p. 101).

12. This confirms the findings by Kohrt and Maharjan (2009, p. 111).

13. This is a Newar ritual consisting of taking a bite from a piece of ginger, then buffalo meat, and then dried fish, alternating with sips of alcohol (*rāksī*). After each sip, the officiant of the ritual refills the glass to the top. The person receiving it should have their hands crossed, palms upward. These days alcohol is often substituted with curd, especially when served to children. This ceremony is now confined to birthdays, initiation rituals, and other special occasions (for example, our going away ceremony when we left Bhaktapur). People recount that in the past, this type of offering would be provided to visitors to the house, a tradition that has now been replaced by the offering of tea.

14. Short for "video logs."

15. There are also food shops specializing in one food item only, such as *bara* (lentil patties) and *chatamari* (rice bread with toppings, also known as "Nepali pizza").

16. This is a fashionable practice but also a way to strengthen emotional bonds between friends through interaction in a different environment from that of the household. This follows from the relatively recent opening and establishment of restaurants and cinemas. These started to emerge gradually some fifty years ago and increased in the last decade on the wave of the tourism boom and the emergence of an affluent Nepalese middle class. The official abolishment of the caste restrictions made it possible for people from different caste groups to dine together. Another new phenomenon is that

of nuclear families dining in restaurants together (generally with very young children and in some cases with friends). Family members in the past would have seldom dined together or shared food from the same plate, as distancing among members and the observance of hierarchical rules around food consumption would not have allowed such practices (Löwdin 1998). Also, the introduction of Western-style celebrations such as for birthdays and anniversaries is a new thing from the past.

17. Poletti (2021, p. 16) has pointed out the emergence of new dimensions of empathy between parents and children in Nepal, which would challenge traditional attitudes of subordination.

Chapter 4

1. They hide because interactions and public displays of affection are strongly condemned by traditional standards of behavior that consider them inappropriate.

2. See Quigley (1986) on the norm of isogamy among the Newars, and Bajracharya (1959) on traditional marriage practices.

3. The term most often used in Bhaktapur is the Newar version *bhaumacha* or *bhamcha*.

4. A red mark placed on the forehead as a sign of blessing.

5. Further investigations might also explore the relationship between notions of companionship and the theme of the commodification of sexuality in Kathmandu as discussed by Liechty (2008).

6. For example, two more mature couples told me that they sometimes resort to what they called the "fight rooms," as places where a spouse might go and unwind or sleep after a quarrel.

Chapter 5

1. I discuss Maya's case elsewhere (Tiné 2021b).

2. The living contribute through food offerings and little balls made of flour and water (*pinda*), which during annual *śrāddha* provide the dead with a new body.

3. A similar approach was adopted by Gray (2006) in his study of the architecture of lifeworlds among the Baum-Chhetri.

4. The *pujā kothā* is often shared between nuclear households as it was in the past.

5. This is in order to purify the body.

6. A woman's rights in her husband's house (*bhatache[n]*) are protected by custom by her ties within her own house of origin (*thache[n]*) (Shepard 1985, p. 205). After the birth of the first child and with growing ritual responsibilities, the relationship of a young wife with her husband's household becomes even stronger and the contact with her family of origin becomes looser. Nonetheless, an important link with the *thache[n]* remains to guarantee support to her in case of mistreatment in the *bhatache[n]* (see Shepard 1985, p. 205).

7. Similar findings are reported by Parry (2001, p. 816) in the study of social change and marriage among middle-class families in India.

8. These percentages are calculated based on data extracted from CBS (2012).

9. See also Acharya and Ansari (1980, as cited in Parish 1994, p. 299). For a definition of household types based on locality, in this chapter I use a schematization of definitions developed by Pauline Kolenda (1968) in her study of Indian family structures. According to this scheme, families are distinguished as "nuclear" (composed of husband, wife, and children), "subnuclear" (a nuclear family plus one member of a previous nucleus, such as a widowed elder parent), and "joint" (two or more nuclei together). The latter can be "lineal" (parents and married children) or "collateral" (brothers and their wives and children).

10. Spaces might also be rented out or converted into hotel rooms. In this way, a householder can fulfill both their traditional duty to build a house for their sons and the modern mantra to provide them with an easier life. The traditional duty is not necessarily opposed to the ideal of a joint unit, since it was expected to be fulfilled after the death of their own father. In any case, this ideal might have rarely been an actualized reality due to the relative staticity of the living spaces within the city walls.

11. Renting was not commonly practiced in Bhaktapur at the time of Niels Gutschow's survey in 1982 (N. Gutschow 2021, personal communication, June 7).

12. Further studies could assess the occurrence, or lack thereof, of similar aspects among groups of other socioeconomic statuses and ethnic backgrounds.

13. For example, this was said to include the "complete dish" called locally *samāe baji* and various meat-based dishes.

14. In Nepal, rice holds a strong symbolic power in defining a household (Levy 1990, p. 111). For an extensive discussion of the social and symbolic role of food in Newar society see Löwdin (1998).

15. I have explored this case study in more detail in the paper "Two kitchens and other modern stories: Rethinking the family in contemporary Nepal through household conflict and fission" (Tiné 2022b).

16. This was also used interchangeably with "my house" (*mero ghar*).

17. Similarly, outside of the valley people do not need to respect the mourning dress code (which prescribes white, beige, or gray clothes) to attend to business or leisure activities.

Chapter 6

1. See Satyal (2018).

2. The term *dhikuti* derives from the Thakāli language, from the word *dhu-khor* (lit: "grain rotating turn by turn") (Messerschmidt 1979, p. 155), while in Nepali it means "storehouse" (Chhetri 1995, p. 453).

3. Also called locally Dewali *guthi* (see Nepali 2015, p. 194).

4. The reader will find useful information on other *guthis* (e.g., Widdess 2013) and more detailed descriptions on the *siguthi* itself in Gellner (1992), Quigley (1985b), Toffin (1984, 2005), Nepali (2015), Sharma (2015), Sakya (2000), Shrestha (2012), Pickett (2014), and Owens (1989).

5. See also Nepali (2015), Levy (1990), and Toffin (2005, p. 11).

6. See Nepali (2015, p. 125), and Gutschow and Michaels (2005).

7. *Samāe baji* is a complete meal consisting of rice, lentils, a fried egg, a fried fish, ginger, meat, and soybeans.

8. For example, I have found that the castes Dhukwa, Paila, Wainju, and Duwal are generally associated. Nevertheless, there are other *guthi* types which include members of different caste groups, such as the *Taleju guthi* (see Toffin 2005, p. 6). The function of this was to include multiple strata of the population at their public festivals (see Nepali 2015, p. 197). Through their participation, they represented and reiterated the asymmetrical relationship between the king and the people (Toffin 2005, p. 9).

9. This applies even in cases in which they have only separated their kitchen facilities from one another, which marks the household's symbolic boundaries.

10. I have not found any reference to the *tuiga[n]* option in previous studies of the Newar *guthi*. Therefore, while I cannot confirm that this is a completely new phenomenon, it is surely becoming more common. For example, I encountered a *guthi* composed of fifty-five regular members and one hundred *tuiga[n]* members. This new practice involves a necessary revision of the rule of nonrelatedness between members.

11. This is the largest cremation ground in Kathmandu. The main cremation spot in Bhaktapur is Masanghat.

12. There was also a similar practice among the Chhetris called *parma* (Gray 2008, p. 179; Mühlich 1999, p. 91).

13. This is what local people told me. Adam (1936, p. 541) refers to *mit* as meaning both "brother" and "friend."

14. See also Pignède (1966), Miller (1956), and Haugen (2005, p. 54).

15. Siddhi Ganesh is one the largest cooperatives in Bhaktapur. It is composed of 16,000 members and they meet annually.

16. The Nepali term for friendship is *mitratā*.

17. Ian Gibson (2017a, 2017b) has discussed how trust and solidarity are sought in Bhaktapur by some people through conversion to Christianity.

18. In fact, these groups might not be seen positively by upper-class and upper-caste groups (N. Gutschow 2021, personal communication, August 8), but more research is needed to confirm this.

19. Similar findings were discussed by James (2012) in her study of an emerging middle class in Africa. These findings contribute to preexisting work conducted by Osella and Osella (1998) on kinship and friendship and new forms of sociality in India. More recently, Saavala (2012, pp. 74–75) found similar ideas among local middle-class people in India: her informants considered friendship as a source of economic and moral support.

Chapter 7

1. This is NPR 1,000 per month, and they are currently sixty-four and sixty-seven.

2. Some studies have linked poor life satisfaction with malnutrition (Ghimire et al. 2018).

3. Similarly, Browne, Danely, and Rosenow (2021) have stressed the link between elderly vulnerability and dimensions of economic precarity in several countries including Japan, Uganda, Micronesia, Iraq, Mexico, the United Kingdom, and the United States.

4. For some preliminary studies on this topic, see Michaels (2020) on the system of the *āśrama* and Rai, Khanal, and Chalise (2018) on abuse endured by the elderly before going to retirement homes. For an account of more positive experiences see Acharya (2008). On similar topics see also Baral, Chhetri, and Bhandari (2021), Shah et al. (2021), and Singh, Upadhyay, and Chalise (2021).

5. See also Kumar (1995).

6. The senior citizen allowance of NPR 1,000 per month introduced in 1995 is not sufficient to cover basic needs (Sharma Bhattarai 2013, p. 362) and in some cases is difficult to access (Speck 2021). There is an additional NPR 1,000 monthly support for the widows of those who served in the public sector. This is still not sufficient when families are poorer, struggling, or when elders are left alone.

7. This is a variation of the popular story of Shrawan Kumara. For a longer version of this story see Michaels (2020, p. 298). Moral education is still taught in some schools. A study by Shrestha and Parajuli (2019) shows that while moral education is taught in both private and public schools, teachers at public schools instill more moral values (in their leisure time) than in private schools, and that yoga and meditation are taught more in public schools with the support of outside agencies in some schools. However, this study is based only on responses of teachers and students but not on the actual practices of teachers. New research will be needed to unpack the actual teaching practices inside the classroom as well as the daily behavior of students to understand if these impact their moral conduct.

8. There is at present only one day care center for the elderly in Nepal at Cupin Ghat, Pashupatinath.

9. The social status of authority of the elders was based on Hindu scripts, such as the Sanskrit Vedas (e.g., Manu II.121), the Grihya Sutras, and the Dharmashastra.

10. For example, Cohen (1998) suggests that the concept of declined provision of care for the elderly in modern times is a myth spread in gerontological studies and that the condition of the elderly was in fact not any better in the past.

11. One *lakh* corresponds to one hundred thousand NPR.

12. This resonates with the findings by Zharkevich (2019, p. 889).

BIBLIOGRAPHY

Abeyasekera, A. L. 2021. *Making the right choice: Narratives of marriage in Sri Lanka*, Rutgers University Press, New Brunswick.

Aboderin, I. 2004. "Modernisation and ageing theory revisited: Current explanations of recent developing world and historical Western shifts in material family support for older people." *Ageing and Society* 24, no. 1, pp. 29–50.

Acharya, P. 2008. "Senior citizens and the elderly homes: A survey from Kathmandu." *Dhaulagiri Journal of Sociology and Anthropology* 2, pp. 211–26.

Adam, L. 1936. "The social organization and customary law of the Nepalese tribes." *American Anthropologist* 38, no. 4, pp. 533–47.

Aengst, J. 2014. "Adolescent movements: Dating, elopements, and youth policing in Ladakh, India." *Ethnos* 7, no. 5, pp. 630–49.

Ahearn, L. M. 1999. "'A twisted rope binds my waist': Locating constraints on meaning in a Tij songfest." *Journal of Linguistic Anthropology* 8, no. 1, pp. 60–86.

———. 2003. "Writing desire in Nepali love letters." *Language and Communication*, no. 23, pp. 107–22.

———. 2012[2001]. *Invitations to love: Literacy, love letters and social change in Nepal*, 8th ed. University of Michigan, Ann Arbor.

Allen, M. 1982. "Girls' pre-puberty rites among the Newars of Kathmandu Valley." In M. Allen and S. N. Mukherjee, eds., *Women in India and Nepal*, Australian National University, Canberra, pp. 211–51.

———. 1987. "Hierarchy and complementarity in Newar caste, marriage and labour relations." *Mankind* 17, no. 2, pp. 92–103.

Anderson, M. 2016. *The Festivals of Nepal*, Rupa Publications, New Delhi.

Appadurai, A. 1990. "Disjuncture and difference in the global cultural economy." *Theory, Culture and Society* 7, pp. 295–310.

———. 1996. *Modernity at large: Cultural dimensions of globalization*, University of Minnesota Press, Minneapolis.

———. 2004. "The capacity to aspire: Culture and the terms of recognition." In V. Rao and M. Walton, eds., *Culture and public action: A cross-disciplinary dialogue on development policy*, Stanford University Press, Stanford, pp. 59–84.

Ardener, S. 1964. "The comparative study of rotating credit associations." *Journal of the Royal Anthropological Institute of Great Britain and Ireland* 94, no. 2, pp. 201–29.

Ariès, P. 1962. *Centuries of childhood*, Penguin, Harmondsworth.

Bajracharya, P. H. 1959. "Newar marriage customs and festivals." *Southwestern Journal of Anthropology* 15, no. 4, pp. 418–28.

Baral, M. A., Chhetri, A. and Bhandari, P. 2021. "Abuse of older adults before moving to old age homes in Pokhara Lekhnath Metropolitan City, Nepal: A cross-sectional study." *Plos One* 16, no. 5, pp. 1–15.

Barré, V., Berger, P., Feveile, L., Toffin, G. and Fouque, R. 1981. *Panauti: Une ville au Nepal*, Berger-Levrault, Paris.

Bauman, Z. 2013. *Liquid modernity*, Kindle version, Polity Press.

Beals, A. R. and Siegel, B. J. 1966. *Divisiveness and social conflict: An anthropological approach*, Stanford University Press, Stanford.

Becker, M. 2021. "'It's all about education': Middle-class, high-caste women's aspirations of choice, freedom and modernity in urban Nepal." *The Asia Pacific Journal of Anthropology* 2, no. 5, pp. 434–53.

Bennett, L. 1983. *Dangerous wives and sacred sisters: Social and symbolic roles of high-caste women in Nepal*, Columbia University Press, New York.

Bennett, R. and Zaidi, A. 2016. "Ageing and development: Putting gender back on the agenda." *International Journal of Ageing in Developing Countries* 1, no. 1, pp. 5–19.

Berger, P. L. and Kellner, H. 1964. "Marriage and the construction of reality: An exercise in the microsociology of knowledge." *Diogenes* 12, no. 46, pp. 1–25.

Berger, P. L. and Luckmann, T. 1966. *The social construction of reality: A treatise in the sociology of knowledge*, Doubleday and Company, New York.

Betancourt, T. S. and Khan, K. T. 2008. "The mental health of children affected by armed conflict: Protective processes and pathways to resilience." *International Review of Psychiatry* 20, no. 3, pp. 317–28.

Béteille, A., Ahmed, A. S., Allen, N. J., Carter, A. T., Ingold, T., Lock, G., Srinivas, M. N. and Varenne, H. 1986. "Individualism and equality [and comments and replies]." *Current Anthropology* 27, no. 2, pp. 121–34.

Bhandari, P. 2021. *Matchmaking in middle class India: Beyond arranged and love marriage*, Springer, Singapore.

Bhandari, P. and Titzmann, F. 2017. "Changing family realities in South Asia." *South Asian Multidisciplinary Academic Journal*, no. 16, pp. 1–13.

Bhattarai-Upadhyay, V. and Sengupta, U. 2016. "Unsettling modernity: Shifting values and changing housing styles in the Kathmandu Valley." *Open House International* 41, no. 2, pp. 87–94.

Bista, D. B. 2020[1991]. *Fatalism and development: Nepal's struggle for modernization*, 6th ed., Orient BlackSwan, Kolkata.

Brauner-Otto, S. R. 2009. "Schools, schooling and children's support of their ageing parents in rural Nepal." *Ageing and Society* 29, no. 7, pp. 1015–39.

Browne, V., Danely, J. and Rosenow, D. 2021. *Fragile resonance: Caring for older family members in Japan and England*, Cornell University Press, New York.

Brunson, J. 2014. "'Scooty girls': Mobility and intimacy at the margins of Kathmandu." *Ethnos* 79, no. 5, pp. 610–29.

———. 2016. *Planning families in Nepal: Global and local projects of reproduction*, Rutgers University Press, New Brunswick.

Burghart, R. 1984. "The formation of the concept of nation-state in Nepal." *Journal of Asian Studies* 44, no. 1, pp. 101–25.

Caldwell, J. C., Reddy, P. H. and Caldwell, P. 1984. "The determinants of family structure in rural South India." *Journal of Marriage and Family* 46, no. 1, pp. 215–29.

Cameron, M. M. 1998. *On the edge of auspicious: Gender and caste in Nepal*, University of Illinois Press, Urbana.

Camfield, L., Choudhury, K. and Devine, J. 2009. "Wellbeing, happiness, and why relationships matter: Evidence from Bangladesh." *Journal of Happiness Studies* 10, no. 1, pp. 71–91.

Canclini, N. 1995. *Hybrid cultures: Strategies for entering and leaving modernity*, University of Minnesota Press, Minneapolis.

Carsten, J. 2000. *Cultures of relatedness: New approaches to the study of kinship*, Cambridge University Press, Cambridge.

———. 2004. *After kinship*, Cambridge University Press, Cambridge.

Central Bureau of Statistics. 2012. *National population and housing census 2011 (national report)*, Government of Nepal, National Planning Commission Secretariat, Kathmandu.

Chhetri, R. B. 1995. "Rotating credit associations in Nepal: Dhikuri as capital, credit, saving, and investment." *Human Organization* 54, no. 4, pp. 449–54.

Christopher, J. 1999. "Situating psychological well-being: Exploring the cultural roots of its theory and research." *Journal of Counseling and Development* 77, no. 2, pp. 141–52.

Chua, J. L. 2014. *In pursuit of the good life: Aspiration and suicide in globalizing South India*, University of California Press, Berkeley.

Clark, M. 1967. "The anthropology of aging, a new area for studies of culture and personality." *The Gerontologist* 7, no. 1, pp. 55–64.

Coe, C. 2021. *Changes in care: Aging, migration, and social class in West Africa*, Rutgers University Press, New Jersey.

Cohen, L. 1998. "No aging in India: The uses of gerontology." *Culture, Medicine and Psychiatry* 16, no. 2, pp. 123–61.

Collier, J. 1997. *From duty to desire: Remaking families in a Spanish village*, Princeton University Press, New Jersey.

Croll, E. J. 2006. "The intergenerational contract in the changing Asian family." *Oxford Development Studies* 34, no. 4, pp. 473–91.

Csordas, T. J. 1990. "Embodiment as a paradigm for anthropology." *Ethos* 18, no. 1, pp. 5–47.

Davis-Friedmann, D. 1983. *Long lives*, Stanford University Press, Stanford.

DeLanda, M. 2006. *A new philosophy of society: Assemblage theory and social complexity*, Continuum International, London.

De la Sablonnière, R. 2017. "Towards a psychology of social change: A typology of change." *Frontiers in Psychology* 8, no. 397, pp. 1–20.

De la Sablonnière, R., French Bourgeois, L. and Najihb, M. 2013. "Dramatic social change: A social psychological perspective." *Journal of Social and Political Psychology* 1, no. 1, pp. 253–72.

Derné, S. 1991. "Beyond institutional and impulsive conceptions of the self: Family structure and the socially anchored real self." *Ethos* 20, no. 3, pp. 259–88.

———. 1994. "Violating the Hindu norm of husband-wife avoidance." *Journal of Comparative Family Studies* 25, no. 2, pp. 249–67.

———. 2000. "Culture, family structure and psyche in Hindu India: The 'fit' and the 'inconsistencies.'" *International Journal of Group Tensions* 29, no. 3, pp. 323–48.

———. 2005. "The (limited) effect of cultural globalization in India: Implications for culture theory." *Poetics* 33, no. 1, pp. 33–47.

———. 2009. "Well-being: Lessons from India." In G. Mathews and C. Izquierdo, eds., *Pursuits of happiness: Well-being in anthropological perspective*, Berghahn Books, New York, pp. 127–46.

Derrida, J. 1992. *Given time*, The University of Chicago Press, Chicago.

Des Chene, M. K. 1998. "Fate, domestic authority, and women's wills." In D. Skinner, A. Pach III and D. Holland, eds., *Selves in time and place: Identities, experience, and history in Nepal*, Rowman and Littlefield, Lanham, pp. 19–50.

Dhakal, S. and Pokharel, S. 2005. "Local movements, political processes and transformation: A case study of Bhaktapur Municipality." *Occasional Papers*, no. 11, pp. 178–201.

Doebele, W. A. 1987. "Land policy." In L. Rodwin, ed., *Shelter, settlement and development*, Allen and Unwin, Boston, pp. 110–32.

Doherty, V. S. 1978. "Notes on the origins of the Newars of the Kathmandu Valley of Nepal." In J. F. Fisher, ed., *Himalayan anthropology: The Indo-Tibetan interface*, De Gruyter Mouton, The Hague, pp. 433–46.

Donner, H. 2008. *Domestic goddesses: Maternity, globalization, and middle-class identity in contemporary India*, Ashgate, Aldershot.

———. 2016. "Doing it our way: Love and marriage in Kolkata middle-class families." *Modern Asian Studies* 50, no. 4, pp. 1147–89.

Douglas, E. 2005. "Inside Nepal's revolution." *National Geographic Magazine*, no. 51, pp. 46–65.

Dumont, L. 1980. *Homo hierarchicus: The caste system and its implications*, The University of Chicago Press, Chicago.

———. 1986. *Essays on individualism: Modern ideology in anthropological perspective*, The University of Chicago Press, Chicago.

Dumont, L. and Béteille, A. 1987. "On individualism and equality." *Current Anthropology* 28, no. 5, pp. 669–77.

Duranti, A. 2010. "Husserl, intersubjectivity and anthropology." *Anthropological Theory* 10, no. 1–2, pp. 16–35.

Einsiedel, S., Malone, D. M. and Pradhan, S. 2012. *Nepal in transition: From People's War to fragile peace*, Cambridge University Press, New York.

Elias, N. 2001. *Society of individuals*, Bloomsbury Publishing, London.

Emmrich, C. 2014. "Ritual period: A comparative study of three Newar Buddhist menarche manuals." *South Asia: Journal of South Asian Studies* 37, no. 1, pp. 80–103.

Fassin, D. 2012. "Towards a critical moral anthropology." In D. Fassin, ed., *Moral anthropology*, Wiley-Blackwell, Malden, pp. 1–17.

Feinberg, R. 2011. "Do Anutans empathize? Morality, compassion, and opacity of other minds." In D. W. Holland and C. J. Throop, eds., *The anthropology of empathy: Experiencing the lives of others in Pacific societies*, Berghahn Books, New York, pp. 151–68.

Foucault, M. 1988. *Technologies of the self: A seminar with Michel Foucault*, Tavistock Publications, London.

Fricke, T. E. 1986. *Himalayan households: Tamang demography and domestic processes*, Umi Research Press, Ann Arbor.

Fujikura, T. 1996. "Technologies of improvement, locations of culture: American discourses of democracy and 'community development' in Nepal." *Studies in Nepali History and Society* 1, no. 2, pp. 271–311.

———. 2013. *Discourses of awareness: Development, social movements and the practices of freedom in Nepal*, Martin Chautari, Kathmandu.

Fuller, C. J. and Narasimhan, H. 2008. "Companionate marriage in India: The changing marriage system in a middle-class Brāhman subcaste." *Journal of the Royal Anthropological Institute* 14, no. 4, pp. 736–54.

Fürer-Haimendorf, C. 1956. "Elements of Newar social structure." *Journal of the Royal Anthropological Institute of Great Britain and Ireland* 86, no. 2, pp. 15–38.

Gammeltoft, T. M. and Oosterhoff, P. 2018. "Mental health in domestic worlds." *Medical Anthropology* 37, no. 7, pp. 533–37.

Geertz, C. 1962. "The rotating credit association: A 'middle rung' in development." *Economic Development and Cultural Change* 10, no. 3, pp. 241–63.

———. 1973. *The interpretation of cultures*, Basic Books, New York.

Gellner, D. N. 1986. "Language, caste, religion and territory: Newar identity ancient and modern." *Archives Européennes de Sociologie* 27, no. 1, pp. 102–48.

———. 1991. "Hinduism, tribalism and the position of women: The problem of Newar identity." *Man* 26, no. 1, pp. 105–25.

———. 1992. *Monk, householder, and tantric priest: Newar Buddhism and its hierarchy of ritual*, Cambridge University Press, Cambridge.

———. 1997. "Caste, communalism, and communism: Newars and the Nepalese state." In D. N. Gellner, J. Pfaff-Czarnkela and J. Whelpton, eds., *Nationalism and ethnicity in a Hindu kingdom: The politics of culture in contemporary Nepal*, Routledge, Abingdon, pp. 151–84.

Gellner, D. N. and Quigley, D. 1995. *Contested hierarchies: A collaborative ethnography of caste among the Newars of the Kathmandu Valley, Nepal*, Clarendon Press, Oxford.

Ghimire, D. J. and Axinn, W. G. 2013. "Marital processes, arranged marriage, and contraception to limit fertility." *Demography* 50, no. 5, pp. 1663–86.

Ghimire, S., Baral, B. K., Karmacharya, I., Callahan, K. and Mishra, S. R. 2018. "Life satisfaction among elderly patients in Nepal: Associations with nutritional and mental well-being." *Health and Quality of Life Outcomes* 16, no. 118, pp. 1–10.

Gibson, I. 2013. "Book review: Yogesh Raj, History as mindscapes: A memory of the peasants' movement of Nepal." *South Asia Research* 33, no. 1, pp. 97–99.

———. 2017a. "Pentecostal peacefulness: Virtue ethics and the reception of theology in Nepal." *Journal of the Royal Anthropological Institute* 23, no. 4, pp. 765–82.

———. 2017b. *Suffering and hope: Christianity and ethics among the Newars of Bhaktapur*, Ekta Books, Kathmandu.

Giddens, A. 1992. *The transformation of intimacy: Sexuality, love and eroticism in modern societies*, Polity Press, Cambridge.

Gilbert, K. 1992. "Women and family law in modern Nepal: Statutory rights and social implications." *New York University Journal of International Law and Politics* 24, no. 2, pp. 729–58.

Gilbertson, A. 2014. "From respect to friendship? Companionate marriage and conjugal power negotiation in middle-class Hyderabad." *South Asia: Journal of South Asian Studies* 37, no. 2, pp. 225–38.

Goldstein, M. C. and Beall, C. M. 1981. "Modernization and aging in the Third and Fourth World: Views from the rural hinterland in Nepal." *Human Organization* 4, no. 1, pp. 48–55.

———. 1986. "Family change, caste, and the elderly in a rural locale in Nepal." *Journal of Cross-Cultural Gerontology* 1, no. 3, pp. 305–16.

Goldstein, M. C., Schuler, S. and Ross, J. L. 1983. "Social and economic forces affecting intergenerational relations in extended families in a Third World country: A cautionary tale from South Asia." *Journal of Gerontology* 38, no. 6, pp. 716–24.

Gough, I. and McGregor, A. 2009. *Wellbeing in developing countries: From theory to research*, Cambridge University Press, Cambridge.

Gray, J. N. 2006. *Domestic mandala: Architecture of lifeworlds in Nepal*, Ashgate Publishing, Hampshire.

———. 2008[1995]. *The householder's world: Purity, power and dominance in a Nepali village*, 2nd ed., Oxford University Press, New Delhi.

Greene, P. D. and Henderson, D. R. 2000. "At the crossroads of languages, musics, and emotions in Kathmandu." *Popular Music and Society* 24, no. 3, pp. 95–116.

Grieve, G. 2003. "Signs of tradition: Compiling a history of development, politics, and tourism in Bhaktapur, Nepal." *Studies in Nepali History and Society*, no. 7, pp. 281–307.

———. 2006. *Retheorizing religion in Nepal*, Springer, New York.

Grossman-Thompson, B. 2017. "'My honor will be erased': Working-class women, purchasing power, and the perils of modernity in urban Nepal." *Journal of Women in Culture and Society* 42, no. 2, pp. 485–507.

Gutschow, N. 1980. "The urban context of the stupa in Bhaktapur/Nepal." In A. L. Dallapiccola and S. Z. Lallemant, eds., *The stūpa: Its religious, historical and architectural significance*, Franz Steiner Verlag, Wiesbaden, pp. 137–46.

———. 2017. *Bhaktapur—Nepal: Urban space and ritual*, DOM Publishers, Berlin.

Gutschow, N. and Kreutzmann, H. 2013. *Mapping the Kathmandu Valley: With aerial photographs by Erwin Schneider*, Himal Books, Kathmandu.

Gutschow, N. and Michaels, A. 2005. *Handling death: The dynamics of death and ancestor rituals among the Newars of Bhaktapur, Nepal*, Harrassowitz Verlag, Wiesbaden.

———. 2008. *Growing up: Hindu and Buddhist initiation rituals among Newar children in Bhaktapur, Nepal*, Harrassowitz Verlag, Wiesbaden.

———. 2012. *Getting married: Hindu and Buddhist marriage rituals among the Newars of Bhaktapur and Patan, Nepal*, Harrassowitz Verlag, Wiesbaden.

Haaland, A. 1982. *Bhaktapur, a town changing: Process influenced by Bhaktapur Development Project*, Craftsman Press, Bangkok.

Hachhethu, K. 2004. "Municipality leadership and governance: A case study of Bhaktapur." In L. R. Baral, K. Hachhethu, H. Sharma, K. P. Khanal and D. Kumar, eds., *Nepal: Local leadership and governance*, Adroit Publisher, New Delhi, pp. 33–72.

———. 2007. "Social change and leadership: A case study of Bhaktapur city." In H. Ishii, D. N. Gellner and K. Nawa, eds., *Political and social transformations in North India and Nepal*, Manohar, New Delhi, pp. 63–89.

Hagen, T. 1980. *Nepal: The kingdom of Himalaya*, Oxford and IBH Publishing Co., New Delhi.

Halpern, J. 2001. *From detached concern to empathy: Humanizing medical practice*, Oxford University Press, New York.

Hareven, T. 1982. *Family time and industrial time*, University Press of America, Lanham.

Hasrat, B. J. 1970. *History of Nepal as told by its own and contemporary chroniclers*, VV Research Institute Book Agency, Hoshiarpur.

Haugen, N. 2005. "The informal credit market: A study of default and informal lending in Nepal." MA book, University of Bergen.

Hausner, S. and Sharma, J. 2013. "On the way to India: Nepali rituals of border-crossing." In D. N. Gellner, ed., *Borderland and lives in Northern South Asia*, Duke University Press, Durham, pp. 94–116.

Hodgson, B. H. 1874. *Essays on the languages, literature and religion of Nepal and Tibet*, Trubner and Co., London.

Höfer, A. 1979. *The caste hierarchy and the state in Nepal: A study of the Muluki Ain of 1854*, Universitätsverlag Wagner, Innsbruck.

Hollan, D. 1997. "The relevance of person-centered ethnography to cross-cultural psychiatry." *Transcultural Psychiatry* 34, no. 2, pp. 219–34.

———. 2005. "Setting a new standard: The person-centered interviewing and observation of Robert I. Levy." *Ethos* 33, no. 4, pp. 459–66.

———. 2009. "Selfscapes of well-being in a rural Indonesian village." In G. Mathews and C. Izquierdo, eds., *Pursuits of happiness: Well-being in anthropological perspective*, Berghahn Books, New York, pp. 211–27.

Husserl, E. 1970a. *The crisis of European sciences and transcendental phenomenology: An introduction to phenomenological philosophy*, Northwestern University Press, Evanston.

———. 1970b. *Logical investigations*, Humanities Press, New Jersey.

Hutt, M. 2012. *Eloquent hills: Essays on Nepali literature*, Martin Chautari, Kathmandu.

Illouz, E. 2007. *Cold intimacies: The making of emotional capitalism*, Polity, Cambridge.

International Organisation for Migration. 2016. *Legislative provisions regulating women's access and ownership of land and property in Nepal*, International Organisation for Migration, Geneva.

Ishii, H. 1980. "Recent economic changes in a Newar village." *Contributions to Nepalese Studies* 8, no. 1, pp. 157–80.

James, D. 2012. "Money-go-round: Personal economies of wealth, aspiration and indebtedness." *Africa: The Journal of Interdisciplinary African Institute* 82, no. 1, pp. 20–40.

Jamieson, L. 1997. *Personal relationships in modern societies*, Polity, Cambridge.

Jankowiak, W. 2009. "Well-being, cultural pathology, and personal rejuvenation in a Chinese city, 1981–2005." In G. Mathews and C. Izquierdo, eds., *Pursuits of happiness: Well-being in anthropological perspective*, Berghahn Books, New York, pp. 147–66.

Kabeer, N. 2000. "Inter-generational contracts, demographic transitions and the 'quantity-quality' tradeoff: Parents, children and investing in the future." *Journal of International Development* 12, no. 4, pp. 463–82.

Kakar, S. 1978. *The inner world: A psycho-analytic study of childhood and society in India*, Oxford University Press, Delhi.

———. 1990. *Intimate relations: Exploring Indian sexuality*, The University of Chicago Press, Chicago.

Kaldate, S. 1962. "Urbanization and disintegration of rural joint family." *Sociological Bulletin* 11, no. 2, pp. 103–11.

Kantor, P. 2003. "Women's empowerment through home-based work: Evidence from India." *Development and Change* 34, no. 3, pp. 425–45.

Kapadia, K. M. 1958. *Marriage and family in India*, Oxford University Press, Oxford.

———. 1959. "The family in transition." *Sociological Bulletin* 8, no. 2, pp. 68–99.

Kaspar, H. 2005. *"I am the household head now": Gender aspects of out-migration for labour in Nepal*, Nepal Institute of Development Studies (NIDS), Kathmandu.

Kavedžija, I. 2019. *Making meaningful lives: Tales from an aging Japan*, University of Pennsylvania Press, Philadelphia.

Khanal, P., Rai, S. and Hom Chalise, N. 2018. "Children's migration and its effect on elderly people: A study at old age homes in Kathmandu." *American Journal of Gerontology and Geriatrics* 1, no. 1, pp. 1–6.

Khatiwoda, R., Cubelic, S. and Michaels, A. 2021. *"Mulukī Ain" of 1854: Nepal's First Legal Code*, Heidelberg University Publishing, Heidelberg.

Khokhar, T. 2019. *Is the term "developing world" outdated?*, World Economic Forum, viewed 1 December 2021, https://www.weforum.org/agenda/2015/11/is-the-term -developing-world-outdated/.

Kleinman, A. 1999. "Experience and its moral modes: Culture, human conditions, and disorder." In G. B. Peterson, ed., *The Tanner Lectures on Human Values* 20, University of Utah Press, Salt Lake City, pp. 355–420.

Kleinman, A., Das, V. and Lock, M., eds. 1997. *Social suffering*, University of California Press, Berkeley.

Kohrt, B. A. and Harper, I. 2008. "Navigating diagnoses: Understanding mind-body relations, mental health, and stigma in Nepal." *Culture, Medicine and Psychiatry* 32, no. 4, pp. 462–91.

Kohrt, B. A. and Maharjan, S. M. 2009. "When a child is no longer a child: Nepali ethnopsychology of child development and violence." *Studies in Nepali History and Society* 14, no. 1, pp. 107–42.

Kolenda, P. M. 1968. "Region, caste, and family structure: A comparative study of the Indian 'joint' family." In R. I. Crane, ed., *Regions and regionalism in South Asian studies: An exploratory study*, Duke University, Durham, pp. 147–226.

Kumar, S. V. 1995. *Challenges before the elderly: An Indian scenario*, MD Publications, New Delhi.

Kunreuther, L. 2018[2014]. *Voicing subjects: Public intimacy and mediation in Kathmandu*, Martin Chautari, Kathmandu.

Lamb, S. 1997a. "The beggared mother: Older women's narratives in West Bengal." *Oral Tradition* 12, no. 1, pp. 54–75.

———. 1997b. "The making and unmaking of persons: Notes on aging and gender in North India." *Ethos* 25, no. 3, pp. 279–302.

Lefebvre, H. 1991. *The production of space*, Blackwell Publishers, Oxford.

Leuchtag, E. 1958. *With a king in the clouds*, Hutchison, London.

Lévi, S. 1899. "Rapport sur sa mission dans l'Inde et le Japon." *Comptes rendus des séances de l'Académie des Inscriptions et Belles-Lettres* 43, no. 1, pp. 71–92.

LeVine, R. A. 1982. *Culture, behavior, and personality: An introduction to the comparative study of psycho-social adaptation*, Aldine, New York.

Levy, R. I. 1975. *Tahitians: Mind and experience in the Society Islands*, The University of Chicago Press, Chicago.

———. 1983. "Introduction: Self and emotion." *Ethos* 11, no. 3, pp. 128 –34.

———. 1990. *Mesocosm: Hinduism and the organization of a traditional Newar city in Nepal*, University of California Press, Berkeley.

———. 1994. "Person-centered anthropology." In R. Borofsky, ed., *Assessing cultural anthropology*, McGraw-Hill, New York, pp. 180–87.

———. 1996. "Essential contrasts: Differences in parental ideas about learners and teaching in Tahiti and Nepal." In C. M. Super and S. Harkness, eds., *Parents' cultural belief systems: Their origins, expressions and consequences*, Guilford Press, New York, pp. 123–42.

———. 1998. "Selves in motion." In D. Skinner, A. Pach III and D. Holland, eds., *Selves in time and place: Identities, experience, and history in Nepal*, Rowman and Littlefield, Lanham, pp. 321–29.

Levy, R. I. and Hollan, D. H. 1998. "Person-centered interviewing and observation in anthropology." In R. Bernard, ed., *Handbook of methods in cultural anthropology*, Altamira Press, Walnut Creek, pp. 333–64.

Lewis, T. T. 1984. "The Tuladhars of Kathmandu: A study of Buddhist tradition in a Newar merchant community." PhD book, Columbia University.

———. 1986. "The anthropology of development in Nepal: A review article of foreign aid projects in the Kathmandu Valley." *Contributions to Nepalese Studies* 13, no. 2, pp. 167–80.

———. 1989. "Childhood and Newar tradition: Chittadhar Hridaya's 'Jhī Macā.'" *Asian Folklore Studies* 48, no. 2, pp. 195–210.

———. 1994. "Book review of 'Mesocosm: Hinduism and the Organization of a Traditional Newar City in Nepal' by Robert I. Levy (with Kedar Raj Rajopadhyaya)." *HIMALAYA: The Journal of the Association for Nepal Himalayan Studies* 14, no. 1, pp. 53–55.

Liechty, M. 1997. "Selective exclusion: Foreigners, foreign goods, and foreignness in modern Nepali history." *Studies in Nepali History and Society* 2, no. 1, pp. 5–68.

———. 2005. "Carnal economies: The commodification of food and sex in Kathmandu." *Cultural Anthropology* 20, no. 1, pp. 1–38.

———. 2008[2003]. *Suitably modern: Making middle-class culture in a new consumer society*, Martin Chautari, Kathmandu.

———. 2009. "Youth problems: An introduction." *Studies in Nepali History Society* 14, no. 1, pp. 35–38.

———. 2010. *Out here in Kathmandu: Modernity on the global periphery*, Martin Chautari, Kathmandu.

———. 2017. *Far out: Countercultural seekers and the tourist encounter in Nepal*, University of Chicago Press, Chicago.

Lienhard, S. 1984. *Songs of Nepal: An anthology of Nevar folksongs and hymns*, Center for Asian and Pacific Studies, Honolulu.

Lim, F. K. 2008. *Imagining the good life: Negotiating culture and development in Nepal Himalaya*, Brill, Leiden.

Löwdin, P. 1998. *Food, ritual and society among the Newars: A study of social structure and food symbolism among the Newars*, Mandala Book Point, Kathmandu.

Lynch, C. 2007. *Juki girls juki girls, good girls: Gender and cultural politics in Sri Lanka's global garment industry*, Cornell University Press, Ithaca.

Lyotard, J. F. 1984. *The postmodern condition: A report on knowledge*, University of Minnesota Press, Minneapolis.

Luckmann, T. 1983. *Life-world and social realities*, Heinemann Educational Publishers, Portsmouth.

Maharjan, S. M. 2013. "Attitudes towards love among the Newars in Kathmandu." MA book, Tribhuvan University.

Manandhar, N. and Joshi, S. K. 2019. "Morbidity pattern among elderly population of Changu Narayan municipality, Bhaktapur." *Journal of Nepal Health Research Council* 17, no. 44, pp. 408–12.

Mannheim, K. 1970. "The problem of generations." In P. Kecskemeti, ed., *Essays on the sociology of knowledge*, Routledge and Kegan Paul, London, pp. 276–320.

Maqsood, A. 2017. *The new Pakistani middle class*, Harvard University Press, Cambridge.

March, K. S. 2002. *"If each comes halfway": Meeting Tamang women in Nepal*, Cornell University Press, New York.

Marriott, M. 1976. *Hindu transactions: Diversity without dualism*, Committee on Southern Asian Studies, University of Chicago, Chicago.

Marx, K. 2005[1973]. *Grundrisse: Foundations of the critique of political economy*, Kindle edition, Penguin.

Mattingly, C. 2014. *Moral laboratories: Family peril and the struggle for a good life*, University of California Press, Oakland.

Mauss, M. 2002[1954]. *The gift: The form and reason for exchange in archaic societies*, Routledge, London.

McAdams, D. P. 2019. "'First we invented stories, then they changed us': The evolution of narrative identity." *Evolutionary Studies in Imaginative Culture* 3, no. 1, pp. 1–18.

McKie, L. 2005. *Families, violence and social change*, Open University Press, London.

Mead, G. H. 1934. *Mind, self and society*, The University of Chicago Press, Chicago.

Mead, M. 1954. *Coming of age in Samoa: A study of adolescence and sex in primitive societies*, Pelican Books, London.

Messerschmidt, D. A. 1979. "Dhikurs: Rotating credit associations in Nepal." In J. F. Fisher, ed., *Himalayan anthropology: The Indo-Tibetan interface*, Mouton, Paris, pp. 141–65.

———. 1982. "Miteri in Nepal: Fictive kin ties that bind." *Kailash: A Journal of Himalayan Studies* 9, no. 1, pp. 5–43.

Michaels, A. 2020. "The 'holy joint family' in South Asian ageing theories." In C. Brosius and R. Mandoki, eds., *Caring for old age: Perspectives from South Asia*, Heidelberg University Publishing, Heidelberg, pp. 285–304.

Mikesell, S. L. 1993. "A critique of Levy's theory of the urban mesocosm." *Contributions to Nepalese Studies* 20, no. 2, pp. 231–54.

Miller, B. D. 1956. "Ganye and Kidu: Two formalized systems of mutual aid among the Tibetans." *Southwestern Journal of Anthropology* 12, no. 2, pp. 157–70.

Mines, M. 1981. "Indian transitions: A comparative analysis of adult stages of development." *Ethos* 9, no. 2, pp. 95–121.

———. 1988. "Conceptualizing the person: Hierarchical society and individual autonomy in India." *American Anthropologist* 90, no. 3, pp. 568–79.

———. 1994. *Public faces, private voices: Community and individuality in South India*, University of California Press, Berkeley.

Mühlich, M. 1999. "Credit relations in Nepal: Social embeddedness and sacred money." *European Bulletin of Himalayan Research*, no. 17, pp. 69–100.

Nepali, G. S. 2015[1965]. *The Newars: An ethno-sociological study of a Himalayan community*, 2nd ed., Mandala Book Point, Kathmandu.

Noonan, J. T. 1984. *Bribes: The intellectual history of a moral idea*, The University of California Press and Macmillan Publishing Company, Berkeley.

Okada, F. E. 1957. "Ritual brotherhood: A cohesive factor in Nepalese society." *Southwestern Journal of Anthropology* 13, no. 3, pp. 212–22.

Oldenburg, R. 2001. *Celebrating the third place: Inspiring stories about the great good places at the heart of our communities*, Da Capo Press, Boston.

Oliphant, L. 1852. *A Journey to Katmandu (the capital of Nepaul), with the camp of Jung Bahadoor*, Appleton and Company, New York.

Ong, A. and Collier, S. J. 2005. *Global assemblages: Technologies, politics, and ethics as anthropological problems*, Wiley-Blackwell, Malden.

Onta, P. 1994. "Rich possibilities: Notes on social history in Nepal." *Contributions to Nepalese Studies* 21, no. 1, pp. 1–43.

Onta-Bhatta, L. 2001. "Childhood constructed, childhood lived: Law and social history in Nepal." *Studies in Nepali History and Society* 6, no. 2, pp. 231–69.

Orenstein, H. and Micklin, M. 1966. "The Hindu joint family: The norms and the numbers." *Pacific Affairs* 39, no. 3–4, pp. 314–25.

Osella, C. and Osella, F. 1998. "Friendship and flirting: Micro-politics in Kerala, South India." *Journal of the Royal Anthropological Institute* 4, no. 2, pp. 189–206.

Osella, F. and Osella, C. 2000. *Social mobility in Kerala: Modernity and identity in conflict*, Pluto Press, London.

Owens, B. M. 1989. "The politics of divinity in the Kathmandu Valley: The festival of Bungadya/Rato Matsyendranath." PhD book, Columbia University.

Palriwala, R. 1994. *Changing kinship, family, and gender relations in South Asia: Processes, trends, and issues*, Women and Autonomy Centre, Leiden University, Den Haag.

Parish, S. M. 1994. *Moral knowing in a Hindu sacred city: An exploration of mind, emotion, and self*, Columbia University Press, New York.

———. 1998. "Narrative subversions of hierarchy." In D. Skinner, A. Pach III and D. Holland, eds., *Selves in time and place: Identities, experience and history in Nepal*, Rowman and Littlefield Publishers, Maryland, pp. 51–85.

Parry, J. P. 2001. "Ankalu's errant wife: Sex, marriage and industry in contemporary Chhattisgarh." *Modern Asian Studies* 35, no. 4, pp. 783–820.

Payne, G. and Williams, M. 2005. "Generalization in qualitative research." *Sociology* 39, no. 2, pp. 295–314.

Peacock, J. L. and Holland, D. C. 1993. "The narrated self: Life stories in process." *Ethos* 21, no. 4, pp. 367–83.

Pickett, M. 2014. *Caste and kinship in a modern Hindu society: The Newar city of Lalitpur*, Orchid, Bangkok.

Pieper, J. 1975. "Three cities of Nepal." In P. Oliver, ed., *Shelter, sign and symbol*, Barrie and Jenkins, London, pp. 52–69.

Pigg, S. L. 1992. "Inventing social categories through place: Social representations and development in Nepal." *Society for Comparative Studies in Society and History* 34, no. 3, pp. 491–513.

———. 1996. "The credible and the credulous: The question of 'villagers' beliefs' in Nepal." *Cultural Anthropology* 11, no. 2, pp. 160–201.

Pignède, B. 1966. *Les Gurungs: Une population Himalayenne du Népal*, Mouton, Paris.

Poletti, S. 2021. "Loving fathers and deferential sons: Hermeneutic respect and the controversies of empathy in Nepal." *Ethnos*, pp. 1–22.

Pradhan, B. 1981. *The Newar women of Bulu*, Centre for Economic Development and Administration, Kathmandu.

Pradhananga, G. D. 2012. "The sands of time." *The Kathmandu Post*, 29 January 2012, pp. 1–2.

Prasain, K. 2021. "Restaurants say they will open dine-in service from next week." *The Kathmandu Post*, viewed 1 March 2022, https://kathmandupost.com/money/2021 /06/28/restaurants-say-they-will-open-dine-in-service-from-next-week.

Prus, R. 1997. *Subcultural mosaics and intersubjective realities: An ethnographic research agenda for pragmatizing the social sciences*, SUNY Press, Albany, NY.

Quigley, D. 1985a. "Household organization among Newar traders." *Contributions to Nepalese Studies* 12, no. 2, pp. 13–44.

———. 1985b. "The guthi organizations of Dhulikhel Shresthas." *Kailash: A Journal of Himalayan Studies* 12, no. 1–2, pp. 5–62.

———. 1986. "Introversion and isogamy: Marriage patterns of the Newars of Nepal." *Contributions to Indian Sociology* 20, no. 1, pp. 75–95.

Raeper, W. and Hoftun, M. 1992. *Spring awakening: An account of the 1990 revolution in Nepal*, Viking Press, New York.

Rai, B. 2014. "Not so happily ever after: The number of Nepali women filing for divorce is rising." *Nepali Times*, viewed 1 January 2022, https://archive.nepalitimes.com /article/nation/%20number-of-nepali-women-filing-for-divorce-rises,1513.

Rai, S., Khanal, P. and Chalise, H. N. 2018. "Elderly abuse experienced by older adults prior to living in old age homes in Kathmandu." *Journal of Gerontolology and Geriatric Research* 7, no. 1, pp. 1–5.

Raj, Y., ed. 2008. *Bhaktapurko Kisan Andolan: Krsnabhakta Caguthiko Katha: Unkai Mukhbata (Bhaktapur's peasant movement: The story of Krishna Bhakta Caguthi in his own words)*, Published by Krishna Bhakta Caguthi.

———. 2010. *History as mindscapes: A memory of the peasants' movement of Nepal*, Martin Chautari, Kathmandu.

Rankin, K. N. 2001. "Governing development: Neoliberalism, microcredit, and rational economic woman." *Economy and Society* 30, no. 1, pp. 18–37.

———. 2004. *The cultural politics of markets: Economic liberalization and social change in Nepal*, University of Toronto Press, Toronto.

Regmi, P. R., Teijlingen, E. R., Simkhada, P. and Acharya, D. R. 2011. "Dating and sex among emerging adults in Nepal." *Journal of Adolescent Research* 26, no. 6, pp. 675–700.

Ritzer, G. 2011. *Sociological theory*, McGraw-Hill, New York.

Robbins, J. 2004. *Becoming sinners: Christianity and moral torment in a Papua New Guinea society*, University of California Press, Berkeley.

———. 2007. "Between reproduction and freedom: Morality, value, and radical cultural change." *Ethnos* 72, no. 3, pp. 293–314.

———. 2012. "Cultural values." In D. Fassin, ed., *A companion to moral anthropology*, John Wiley and Sons, New York, pp. 115–32.

Robbins, J. and Rumsey, A. 2008. "Introduction: Cultural and linguistic anthropology and the opacity of other minds." *Anthropological Quarterly* 81, no. 2, pp. 407–20.

Ross, A. D. 1961. *The Hindu family in its urban setting*, University of Toronto Press, Toronto.

Rosser, C. 1966. "Social mobility in the Newar caste system." In C. Fürer-Haimendorf, ed., *Caste and kin in Nepal, India and Ceylon: Anthropological studies in Hindu-Buddhist contact zones*, Asia Publishing House, New York, pp. 68–139.

Russo, M., Argandoña, A. and Peatfield, R. 2022. *Happiness and domestic life: The influence of the home on subjective and social well-being*, Routledge, London.

Saavala, M. 2012. *Middle class moralities: Everyday struggle over belonging and prestige in India*, Orient BlackSwan, New Delhi.

Sahlins, M. 1992. "The economics of develop-man in the Pacific." *RES: Anthropology and Aesthetics* 21, pp. 12–25.

———. 2013. *What kinship is—and is not*, The University of Chicago Press, Chicago.

Sakya, A. M. 2000. "Newar marriage and kinship in Kathmandu, Nepal." PhD book, Brunel University.

Sakya, K. and Griffith, L. 1980. *Tales of Kathmandu: Folktales from the Himalayan kingdom of Nepal*, House of Kathmandu, Brisbane.

Salagame, K. K. 2013. "Well-being from the Hindu/Sanātana Dharma Perspective." In I. Boniwell, S. A. David and A. Conley Ayers, eds., *Oxford Handbook of Happiness*, online edition.

Satyal, U. 2018. "Eleven-year-old kidnapped boy found dead." *The Himalayan Times*, viewed 10 May 2021, https://thehimalayantimes.com/kathmandu/eleven-year-old -kidnapped-boy-found-dead.

Sawyer, R. K. 2003. *Group creativity: Music, theater, collaboration*, Lawrence Erlbaum Associates, Mahwah.

Schegloff, E. A. 2006. "Interaction: The infrastructure for social institutions, the natural ecological niche for language, and the arena in which culture is enacted." In N. J. Enfield and S. C. Levinson, eds., *Roots of human sociality: Culture, cognition and interaction*, Berg, Oxford, pp. 70–96.

Scheper-Hughes, N. 1982. *Saints, scholars and schizophrenics: Mental illness in rural Ireland*, University of California Press, Berkeley.

Schutz, A. 1970. *On phenomenology and social relations*, The University of Chicago Press, Chicago.

Schutz, A. and Luckmann, T. 1973. *The structures of the life-world*, Northwestern University Press, Evanston.

Sennett, R. and Cobb, J. 1972. *The hidden injuries of class*, Cambridge University Press, Cambridge.

Seymour, S. C. 1999. *Women, family, and child care in India: A world in transition*, Cambridge University Press, Cambridge.

Shah, A. M. 1988. "The phase of dispersal in the Indian family process." *Sociological Bulletin* 37, no. 1-2, pp. 33-47.

Shah, R., Carandang, R. R., Shibanuma, A., Ong, K. I., Kiriya, J. and Jimba, M. 2021. "Understanding frailty among older people living in old age homes and the community in Nepal: A cross-sectional study." *Plos One* 16, no. 4, pp. 1-15.

Shakya, D. 2010. "Education, economic and cultural modernization, and the Newars of Nepal." In D. Kapoor and E. Shizha, eds., *Indigenous knowledge and learning in Asia/Pacific and Africa: Perspectives on development, education and culture*, Palgrave Macmillan, New York, pp. 131-44.

Sharma, G. N. 1990. "The impact of education during the Rana period in Nepal." *Himalayan Research Bulletin* 10, no. 2-3, pp. 1-7.

Sharma, J. R. 2008. "Practices of male labor migration from the hills of Nepal to India in development discourses: Which pathology?." *Gender, Technology and Development* 12, no. 3, pp. 303-23.

———. 2013. "Marginal but modern: Young Nepali labour migrants in India." *Young* 21, no. 4, pp. 347-62.

———. 2018. *Crossing the border to India: Youth, migration, and masculinities in Nepal*, Temple University Press, Philadelphia.

———. 2021. *Political economy of social change and development in Nepal*, Bloomsbury, New Delhi.

Sharma, P. R. 2015. *Land, lineage and state: A study of Newar society in mediaeval Nepal*, Social Science Baha, Kathmandu.

Sharma Bhattarai, L. P. 2013. "A new genre of social protection policy for older people: A critical analysis of legislative development in Nepal." *Journal of Aging and Social Policy* 25, no. 4, pp. 353-70.

Sharma Rawal, D. and Agrawal, K. 2016. *Barriers to women's land and property access and ownership in Nepal*, International Organization for Migration, Kathmandu.

Shepard, J. W. 1985. "Symbolic space in Newar culture." PhD book, The University of Michigan.

Shrestha, B. G. 1999. "The Newars: The indigenous population of the Kathmandu Valley in the modern state of Nepal." *Contributions to Nepalese Studies* 26, no. 1, pp. 83-117.

———. 2012. *The sacred town of Sankhu: The anthropology of Newar ritual, religion and society in Nepal*, Cambridge Scholars Publishing, Cambridge.

Shrestha, B. K. and Parajuli, T. R. 2019. "Teaching practices of moral education in public and private schools of Nepal." *World Wide Journal of Multidisciplinary Research and Development* 5, no. 1, pp. 1–6.

Shweder, R. and Much, N. C. 1987. "Determinations of meaning: Discourse and moral socialization." In W. W. Kurtines and J. Gewirtz, eds., *Moral development through social interaction*, John Wiley, New York, pp. 197–242.

Shweder, R. A. and Bourne, E. J. 1984. "Does the concept of person vary cross-culturally?." In R. A. Shweder and R. A. LeVine, eds., *Culture theory: Essays on mind, self, and emotion*, Cambridge University Press, New York, pp. 97–137.

Singh, S. N., Upadhyay, U. and Chalise, H. N. 2021. "Living arrangement of older people: A study of community living elderly from Nepal." *Advances in Aging Research* 10, no. 6, pp. 133–42.

Skinner, D. G. 1990. "Nepalese children's understanding of self and the social world: A study of a Hindu mixed caste community." PhD book, The University of North Carolina at Chapel Hill.

Skinner, D. G., Pach III, A. and Holland, D. C., eds. 1998. *Selves in time and place: Identities, experience, and history in Nepal*, Rowman and Littlefield Publishers, Boston.

Skinner, D. G., Valsiner, J. and Holland, D. C. 2001. "Discerning the dialogical self: A theoretical and methodological examination of a Nepali adolescent's narrative." *Forum Qualitative Sozialforschung/Forum: Qualitative Social Research* 2, no. 3, pp. 1–17.

Slusser, M. S. 1982. *Nepal mandala: A cultural study of the Kathmandu Valley*, Princeton University Press, Princeton.

Snellinger, A. 2013. "Shaping a livable present and future: A review of youth studies in Nepal." *European Bulletin of Himalayan Research* 42, pp. 75–103.

Snellinger, A. T. 2018. *Making new Nepal*, University of Washington Press, Seattle.

Sointu, E. 2005. "The rise of an ideal: Tracing changing discourses of wellbeing." *The Sociological Review* 53, no. 2, pp. 255–74.

Sökefeld, M. 1999. "Debating self, identity, and culture in anthropology." *Current Anthropology* 40, no. 4, pp. 417–48.

Speck, S. 2017. "'They moved to city areas, abroad': Views of the elderly on the implications of outmigration for the middle hills of Western Nepal." *Mountain Research Development* 37, no. 4, pp. 425–35.

———. 2021. "Barriers to accessing social pensions in rural Nepal." *International Journal of Ageing in Developing Countries* 6, no. 1, pp. 76–97.

Speck, S. and Müller-Böker, U. 2020. "Population ageing and family change: Older people's perceptions of current changes in family composition in rural Nepal." *European Bulletin of Himalayan Research* 55, pp. 7–37.

Srinivas, M. N. 1976. *The remembered village*, Oxford University Press, New Delhi.

———. 1987[1952]. "A joint family dispute in a Mysore village." In M. N. Srinivas, ed., *The dominant caste and other essays*, Oxford University Press, Delhi, pp. 7–31.

Stone, L. 2018[1997]. *Kinship and gender: An introduction*, Westview Press, Boulder.

Subedi, B. P. 2003. "Customary images and contemporary realities: The activities of older people in Nepal." In G. W. Leeson and E. M. Schröder-Butterfill, eds., *Oxford Institute of Ageing Working Papers*, no. 403, Oxford Institute of Ageing, Oxford, pp. 1–43.

Suwal, J. 1997. "Sii Guthi: A Newar funeral organisation in Kathmandu." *Newah Vijñana, a Journal of Newar Studies* 1, no. 1, pp. 6–9.

Tamang, S. 2009. "The politics of conflict and difference or the difference of conflict in politics: The women's movement in Nepal." *Feminist Review*, no. 91, pp. 61–80.

Thapa, K. 2022. "A look at Valentine's Day celebration." *Kathmandu Post*, viewed 1 March 2022, https://kathmandupost.com/national/2019/02/14/a-look-at-valentines-day-celebration.

Thin, N. 2009. "Why anthropology can ill afford to ignore well-being." In G. Mathews and C. Izquierdo, eds., *Pursuits of happiness: Well-being in anthropological perspective*, Berghahn Books, New York, pp. 23–44.

Throop, C. J. 2012. "Moral Sentiments." In D. Fassin, ed., *A companion to moral anthropology*, John Wiley and Sons, New Jersey, pp. 150–68.

Tiné, P. 2020. "Parenting, food practices and health conceptions in Bhaktapur." *Dada Rivista di Antropologia Post-globale*, no. 2, pp. 107–24.

———. 2021a. "Painting the self in a study of modernity: Using art in anthropological research." *Re:think—a Journal of Creative Ethnography* 3, no. 1, pp. 1–14.

———. 2021b. "Maya's story: Spirit possession, gender, and the making of the self in a painted anthropological account." *Current Anthropology* 62, no. 4, pp. 498–504.

———. 2021c. "Seeking heartfelt help: The emergence of the friendship guthi as a middle-class practice in contemporary Nepal." *Studies in Nepali History and Society* 26, no. 2, pp. 313–45.

———. 2022a. "The anthropologist as artist: 'Voice' and 'positionality' when using art in anthropological research." In M. Carocci and S. Pratt, eds., *Ethnography as art/art as ethnography: Art, observation, and an anthropology of illustration*, Bloomsbury Academic, London, pp. 23–38.

———. 2022b. "Two kitchens and other modern stories: Rethinking the family in contemporary Nepal through household conflict and fission." *HIMALAYA: The Journal of the Association for Nepal and Himalayan Studies* 41, no. 2, pp. 127–43.

———. 2022c. "What makes a family? A visual approach to ontological and substantial dimensions of the domestic in Nepal." *HIMALAYA: The Journal of the Association for Nepal and Himalayan Studies* 41, no. 2, pp. 107–26.

———. 2023a. "Modern dharma: The moral worlds of Newar middle-class families in Bhaktapur, Nepal." *Asian Studies* 22, no. 3, 217–19.

———. 2023b. "Modern dharma: The moral worlds of Newar middle-class families in Bhaktapur, Nepal." *European Bulletin of Himalayan Research* 61, pp. 1–3.

———. 2024. *She fell and became a horse*, Dev Publishers and Distributors, New Delhi.

Toffin, G. 1975. "Jako: A Newar family ceremony." *Contributions to Nepalese Studies* 2, no. 1, pp. 47–56.

———. 1984. *Société et religion chez les Néwar du Népal*, Centre National de la Research Scientifique, Paris.

———. 2005. *From kin to caste: The role of guthis in Newar society and culture*, Social Science Baha, Lalitpur.

———. 2016. *Imagination and realities: Nepal between past and present*, Adroit Publishers, New Delhi.

Trawick, M. 1990. *Notes on love in a Tamil family*, University of California Press, Berkeley.

Turner, R. L. 2022[1931]. *A Comparative and etymological dictionary of the Nepali language*, viewed 25 June 2022, https://dsal.uchicago.edu/dictionaries/turner/.

Ungar, M. 2011. "The social ecology of resilience: Addressing contextual and cultural ambiguity of a nascent construct." *The American Journal of Orthopsychiatry* 81, no. 1, pp. 1–17.

United Nations Organisation. 2002. *Report of the Second World assembly on ageing*, United Nations Organisation, New York.

Vatuk, S. 1990. "'To be a burden on others': Dependency anxiety among the elderly in India." In O. M. Lynch, ed., *Divine passions: Dependency and anxiety among the elderly in India*, University of California Press, Berkeley, pp. 64–88.

Vergati, A. 1982. "Social consequences of marrying Visnu Nārāyana: Primary marriage among the Newars of Kathmandu valley." *Contributions to Indian Sociology* 16, no. 2, pp. 271–87.

———. 2002. *Gods, men, and territory: Society and culture in Kathmandu Valley*, Manohar Publishers, New Delhi.

Walter, A. 2021. *Intimate connections: Love and marriage in Pakistan's high mountains*, Rutgers University Press, New Brunswick.

Weber, M. 1947. *The theory of social and economic organisation*, Free Press, New York.

Weiss, H. 2022. "From desire to endurance: Hanging on in a Spanish village." *Cultural Anthropology* 37, no. 1, pp. 45–68.

White, S. 2010. "Analysing wellbeing: A framework for development practice." *Development in Practice* 20, no. 2, pp. 158–72.

Widdess, R. 2013. *Dāphā: Sacred singing in a South Asian city: Music, performance and meaning in Bhaktapur*, Nepal, Routledge. London.

Williams, M. 2002. "Generalization in interpretative research." In T. May, ed., *Qualitative research in action*, Sage, London, pp. 125–43.

Williams, R. 2010. "Cosmopolitan romance in Nepal: An investigation of emerging views on marriage and dating held by young Newari women." *Independent Study Project (ISP) Collection 1236*.

Wilmore, M. 2008. *Developing alternative media traditions in Nepal*, Rowman and Littlefield Publishers, Lanham.

Witzel, M. 1997. "Macrocosm, mesocosm, and microcosm: The persistent nature of 'Hindu' beliefs and symbolic forms." *International Journal of Hindu Studies* 1, no. 3, pp. 501–39.

———. 2018. "Moralities of wellbeing." *Bath Papers in International Development and Wellbeing*, no. 58, pp. 1–23.

Wolfgang, K. 1998[1976]. *The traditional architecture of the Kathmandu Valley*, Ratna Pustak Bhandar, Kathmandu.

Woolf, V. 2009[1929]. *A room of one's own*, Penguin Books, London.

World Bank. 2016. *Moving up the ladder: Poverty reduction and social mobility in Nepal*, World Bank Group, Kathmandu.

———. 2017. *Climbing higher: Toward a middle-income Nepal*, World Bank Group, Kathmandu.

World Health Organisation. 2017. *Monitoring health for the SDGs: Sustainable development goals*, World Health Organisation, Geneva.

Wright, D. 1877. *History of Nepal. Translated from the Parbatiya*, Cambridge University Press, Cambridge.

Zharkevich, I. 2019. "Money and blood: Remittances as a substance of relatedness in transnational families in Nepal." *American Anthropologist* 121, no. 4, pp. 884–96.

Zigon, J. 2007. "Moral breakdown and the ethical demand: A theoretical framework for an anthropology of moralities." *Anthropological Theory* 7, no. 2, pp. 131–50.

———. 2009. "Morality and personal experience: The moral conceptions of a Muscovite man." *Ethos* 37, no. 1, pp. 78–101.

———. 2010. "Moral and ethical assemblages: A response to Fassin and Stoczkowski." *Anthropological Theory* 10, no. 1–2, pp. 3–15

———. 2012. "Narratives." In D. Fassin, ed., *A companion to moral anthropology*, Wiley Blackwell, New Jersey, pp. 204–20.

———. 2013. "On love: Remaking moral subjectivity in post-rehabilitation Russia." *American Ethnologist* 40, no. 1, pp. 201–15.

———. 2014. "Attunement and fidelity: Two ontological conditions for morally being-in-the-world." *Ethos* 41, no. 1, pp. 16–30.

INDEX

Figures are indicated by page numbers followed by *fig.*

Newars (*continued*)
   practices, 84–85, 88–89, 90*fig.*, 98, 188n2;
   moral self-making, 2, 8, 170; mourning
   customs, 57–58, 70, 122, 186n1, 186n3;
   personal narratives, 1, 19–20; public
   morality, 115; quality of life, 150, 190n2;
   repression of language and literature, 40,
   185n13; social mobility and, 33, 186n25;
   traditional houses, 102–3; urban settlement, 5
Noonan, J. T., 162
nuclear families: adult children prioritization of, 3, 120, 151, 159; bedrooms and,
   102–3, 117–18; decrease in farming, 48;
   dining in restaurants, 188n16; domestic
   spaces and, 102–4, 106; emotional support and, 116; household fission and, 21,
   48, 100, 102, 106, 110–16, 119; increase
   in, 107; intimacy and, 102–3, 116–17, 119;
   modern housing and, 103, 108, 117–18;
   modernity and, 113–16; moral creativity
   and, 116, 120; mutual understanding and,
   117, 119–20; parent-child conflict, 59, 74,
   117; privacy and, 103, 116–19; relatedness
   and, 114, 117, 120; relationships in, 113–
   14; social order and, 114–15; spontaneous
   affection, 113–14; spousal conflict, 96–97;
   typology, 189n9; voluntary separation,
   107, 114–15; well-being and, 106, 113,
   117, 119; worship room (*pūjā kōthā*),
   188n4. *See also* family
NWPP. *See* Nepal Workers' and Peasants'
   Party (NWPP)

Oldenburg, R., 76
Ong, A., 171
Oosterhoff, P., 14
Orenstein, H., 112
Osella, C., 15, 190n19
Osella, F., 15, 190n19
Owens, B. M., 183n3, 189n4

Panchayat system, 41–42, 50, 186n26
Parajuli, T. R., 191n7
parent-child relationships: advanceness, 60,
   83; avoidance dynamics, 3, 58–59, 71,
   74–76, 81–83, 168; boundaries of acceptability, 59; care for elderly, 3, 152; concern
   with youth friendships, 78–80; conflict

in, 2–3, 57–59, 62–63, 68–69; controlling
   approach, 67–69, 76, 82; daughters and,
   59, 65, 159; dharma and, 154; domestic
   dharma, 74–75; education and, 63, 68,
   71–72, 81; emotional well-being, 60;
   empathy and, 82, 188n17; existential perspectives, 64; expectations and, 60, 62–63;
   father-son/mother-son, 59, 111, 114;
   food practices, 61–62, 187n7; friendship
   and, 57–60, 62, 64, 74; housing for sons,
   189n10; intergenerational reciprocity,
   154, 158–62; *jyāpu* (farmers), 62, 187n7;
   kinship preservation, 168; life plans, 81;
   marriage and, 154; middle-class and, 59,
   62; modernity and, 73; moral education,
   61, 158, 167–68; moral responsibilities
   and, 163; moral self-making, 60, 63–64,
   66–74, 81–82; mutual understanding
   and, 58, 64, 80, 82; negotiation in, 60, 64,
   68–69, 117; nuclearization and, 114–18;
   opacity of minds, 73–74, 117; open talks,
   68–69, 73–74, 82; permissiveness, 61–62,
   67; prioritization of nuclear families, 3,
   120, 151, 159; relatedness and, 2, 18, 117;
   rites of passage, 64–66, 68, 70, 187n13;
   samskāra rituals, 68; sense of balance, 68,
   71, 73; sense of duty, 72, 163; sexuality
   and, 73, 81; shame and, 60, 115; socialization and, 60, 68; unmarried roles, 66;
   vertical type, 59; well-being and, 2–3,
   59–60, 66, 68, 81; youth maturation and,
   64–66, 68, 71, 187n11. *See also* family
Parish, S. M., 2, 8, 19, 24, 36, 76, 82–83, 92,
   107–8, 173
Parry, J. P., 88, 95, 188n7
Paul, L., 72
People's Front, 51
People's Movement (Jana Āndolan), 50,
   186n27
personal identity, 2, 19, 97, 165–66
Pickett, M., 189n4
Pigg, S. L., 27
Pignède, B, 190n14
Piri, 187n8
Poletti, S., 188n17
poverty, 9–11, 183n5
Prajapati, Beena, 32–33, 52–53
Prajapati, Binod, 32–33, 47, 52–53
Prajapati, Devi, 30, 32–33, 45–46, 52

ACKNOWLEDGMENTS

The research on which this book is based was supported by a PhD bursary from the University of Adelaide and by a generous grant from the Sight and Life Foundation. The University of Adelaide provided additional support in the form of small grants awarded by the Department of Anthropology and the Graduate Centre. I wish to thank all of these institutions and the Australian government and the Nepali government for granting me a study and research visa. I also wish to acknowledge the British Nepal Academic Council for awarding me the BNAC PhD Dissertation Prize 2024. A version of Chapter 5 was the winner of the 2021 Bista Award from the Association for Nepal and Himalayan Studies and was published in the journal *Himalaya* (Tiné 2022b). A case study in Chapter 5 was published in *Current Anthropology* (Tiné 2021b). Chapter 6 was published in *Studies in Nepali History and Society* (Tiné 2021c). Brief summaries of my original dissertation have been published in *Asian Studies* (Tiné 2023a) and the *European Bulletin of Himalayan Research* (Tiné 2023b).

This book would not have been possible were it not for the support I received from a number of people throughout the last seven years. To them I express my deepest gratitude. I am particularly thankful to my doctoral supervisor John Gray for his guidance into the intricacies of anthropological thinking; to my co-supervisor Dianne Rodger for her insightful comments and continued encouragement throughout my studies; to my external supervisor at Tribhuvan University, Kapil Babu Dahal, for reading and commenting on my writings; and to my art mentor, Greg Donovan, for providing me with his support "in the making." Very special thanks go to my doctoral examiners Bruce McCoy Owens and Mark Liechty for their feedback. I am particularly indebted to Mark Liechty for his help in conceptualizing my take on social change in terms of "the imagined" and "the possible" and in situating people's experiences and understandings of well-being within these cultural bounds. Among scholars of Bhaktapur, I am grateful to Niels Gut-schow for providing me with guidance and reading material; I am glad that the "Two Kids" are now safe in his home and reminding him of "his Bhakta-pur." Thanks to my longtime friend and teacher, Massimo Squillacciotti, for following the progress of my research after my graduation from the University of Siena, and to many others who provided support and reading mate-rials, particularly Todd Lewis, Don Messerschmidt, Michael Hutt, Gerard Toffin, Ram Chhetri, Nirmal Thuladhar, Ludmilla and Gotz Hagmuller, my colleagues in the HDR writing retreat group, my colleagues in the Anthro-pology Department at Victoria University of Wellington, and Ramesh Sunam, Jacki Gray, Piergiorgio Solinas, Dipak Dhamala, Djordje Stefanovic, Graeme MacRae, Thomas Reuter, and Gyanendra Dhar Pradhananga and Geeta Devi Pradhananga. I am very indebted to Gyanendra for reading this book's draft and for his generous assistance in helping me to revise the local terms used here. My PhD also involved a visiting period at the University of Edinburgh, where I am grateful to Jeevan Sharma for providing invaluable insights in the early stages of my data analysis and dissertation writing. I also would like to thank Ian Harper for his advice at various stages of my research; Sumeet Jain and Ayaz Qureshi for providing useful feedback and welcoming me to their classes; and Lynn Jamieson for giving me the oppor-tunity to present some of my findings at the Centre for Research on Fam-ily and Relationships. I also would like to kindly acknowledge senior editor at The University of Pennsylvania Press Elisabeth Maselli, the copyediting team, and the anonymous reviewers for their invaluable assistance in devel-oping this book.

Within Nepal, a large number of people supported this research in many ways. Among them, I wish to thank my informants for their time, their friendship, and for having shared their thoughts and opened their hearts to me. I particularly wish to thank Keshab and Madhab Malla and their fam-ilies for welcoming us in their houses and taking care of us, and our dear friends Suresh Kayastha and Ileet Malla for their sincere friendship. Keshab's daily help in my interview process, from recruiting participants to clarify-ing my understanding, was vital for my research. The image I realized for this book's cover ("The Art Lesson") is inspired by a beautiful photograph taken by Suresh portraying his son doing his homework. Special thanks to my principal research assistant, Binod Manandhar; to my secondary assis-tants, Shandhya Shakya, Jeevan Vanyabari, and Sudil Sharma; and to our dear friends Kiran, Shuvam, Ashoke, and Pushpa Shrestha. Warm thanks also go to our families and friends in Italy and Australia for their continued support. But above all, this project would not have been possible without the love of my dear husband Josh, the best research ally I could have dreamed of throughout all the phases of this research, from its inception to its completion. Thank you for believing in me throughout the most difficult times: I look forward to new adventures with you.

www.ingramcontent.com/pod-product-compliance
Lightning Source LLC
Chambersburg PA
CBHW030405270326
41926CB00009B/1270